International Economic
Policy in the 1990s

International Economic Policy in the 1990s

William R. Cline

The MIT Press
Cambridge, Massachusetts
London, England

This book was set in Palatino by the Maple-Vail Book Manufacturing Group and was
printed in the United States of America.

Library of Congress Cataloging-in-Publication Data
Cline, William R.
  International economic policy in the 1990s / William R. Cline.
  p.   cm.
  "November 1993."
  Includes bibliographical references and index.
  ISBN 0-262-03221-X
  1. International economic relations. I. Title.
HF1411.C435   1994
337—dc20   94-19785
                                                                 CIP

Contents

Acknowledgments

I am grateful to the School of International Politics, Economics, and Business of Aoyama Gakuin University, Tokyo, for the opportunity to teach the course that gave rise to this book. In particular, my appreciation goes to Fumio Itoh, Dean of the School, and Professor Ryutaro Komiya. My gratitude also goes to Alexandre Kafka, Richard Portes, Alexis Rieffel, John Williamson, and anonymous readers for comments on portions or all of the manuscript; and to the Institute for International Economics for permission to reprint selected charts.

The lectures in this book derive primarily from my own research, which in turn has been heavily influenced over the past dozen years by the constant exchange of ideas with my colleagues at the Institute for International Economics. I take this opportunity to express my gratitude for their inspiration, especially that of C. Fred Bergsten, director of the Institute.

Prologue

Purpose

The objective of this book is to convey a way of thinking about international economic policy issues. The importance of these issues has been apparent for at least two decades. Through the 1960s it was perhaps possible for citizens of the United States, although few other countries, to consider their economic destinies strictly a matter of domestic determination. The first oil price shock of 1973–74, when the Organization of Petroleum Exporting Countries quadrupled oil prices, shattered the illusion of self-containment of the U.S. economy. The second oil shock of 1979–80 contributed to inflation that reached 14%, the highest level since 1917; and by 1982 to the worst recession since the 1930s. Immediately thereafter the Latin American debt crisis threatened to cause the bankruptcy of the large banks in the United States and other industrial countries. By 1985–87, overvaluation of the U.S. dollar was causing industrial dislocation as U.S. products were priced out of the international market, manufacturing imports soared, and exports stagnated. Then, in 1989–91, the Soviet empire collapsed, and there arose the potential for the most important event of political economy in the twentieth century: the transformation of communist regimes in Europe to mixed capitalist economies. The early 1990s also saw the emergence of global environmental issues, with their implications for economic impact, as well as the need for international cooperation.

This book seeks to convey an approach of rigorous economic analysis, informed by judgmental evaluation of political feasibility, as the proper framework for the consideration of these international economic issues. Often a simple supply-demand diagram suffices to demonstrate the direction policy should take. More generally, the policy problem can usually be thought of in terms of a few simple but fundamental equations. For example, the external current account deficit must equal the difference between domestic saving and domestic investment (see chapter 2). The policy targets may be seen as dependent variables (e.g., inflation) affected by independent variables (e.g., the money supply). The strength of the influence, or leverage, of a particular policy tool may be thought of as the size of the coefficient on the relevant independent (policy instrument) variable in the equation determining the dependent (policy target) variable.

Empirical evidence is the acid test of the theories used to examine international economic problems. The reader who would apply the methods here should constantly ask whether the data support the theory. The simplest means for this purpose is to compile tables of data demonstrating that the expected economic relationship did or did not materialize. A somewhat more formal method is the use of simple graphs to show the relationship between two variables. One trick that is effective in this regard is to plot the dependent variable on one of the vertical axes and the independent variable on the other vertical axis, with the year of each observation on the horizontal axis. If the two series demonstrably move together, the theory secures support. Even better, if the independent variable is lagged, then the joint movement of the two series provides considerable evidence that the one is causing the other (see for example the figure on U.S. trade performance and the real strength of the dollar two years earlier in chapter 2). Even more formal analysis applies statistical regression analysis. Students trained in this analysis will find ample hypotheses here for formal statistical tests.

The underlying objective of such analysis, whether formal or informal, is the maximization of both domestic and global economic well-being through the identification of appropriate economic policies. Economic welfare will generally be associated with increased production for consumption or saving, price stability, equitable income distribution, and environmental sustainability, all of which are dealt with in this book. This normative aspect of the analysis is of particular relevance to policymakers and scholars.

In addition, the approach here should serve as a sound basis for positive analysis: the diagnosis of why economic events transpire and what their path is likely to be in the future as opposed to what course they *should* take under ideal policies. Positive analysis of these issues is of special relevance for the business community. For example, important parts of the analysis emphasize the presence of time lags in the impact of economic variables, such as the effect of exchange rate changes on trade performance. Awareness of time lags and of such concepts as equilibrium positions provides the businessperson with a more informed view of the direction of markets than that which may be obtained solely from extrapolation of recent trends. Thus, with the analytical framework here, it would have been dubious in 1984 to expect that the dollar would stay indefinitely at its high level.[1]

There are three central reasons why economic results fall short of those suggested by normative analysis. The first is that the economic analytical framework is flawed. For example, the Reagan administration justified its fiscal strategy on the Laffer curve, which postulated that reducing tax rates would raise tax revenue because of incentive effects. Large U.S. fiscal deficits in the 1980s demonstrated that this analytical framework was in error. The second reason for economic performance below the potential suggested by normative analysis is that political obstacles preclude optimal policies. The presence of high import barriers that enrich special, well-organized interest groups at the expense of the general consumer is one example; the pursuit of populist policies seeking votes in the short term at the expense of long-term distortions is another, as is illustrated by artificially low utility prices or by the financing of patronage politics through the "inflation tax" in Latin America. The third reason is that economics is not mechanistically determined, largely because it deals with human behavior and psychology. If, as suggested by chaos theory, unpredictable shocks exist in the physical sciences, then their presence in the human ones should come as no surpise.

Proper economic analysis is thus a necessary but not sufficient condition for implementation of proper international economic policy. As defined here, this policy includes both domestic actions with external consequences and measures and regimes that explicitly concern economic interaction among countries. The impact of the U.S. budget deficit in the 1980s on the U.S. external account deficit illustrates the former. Multilateral trade negotiations are an example of the latter.

The Lectures

In 1992 and 1993, the School of International Politics, Economics, and Business of Aoyama Gakuin University in Tokyo invited me to present a series of lectures on international economic policy. This book is a compilation and development of those lectures. It is addressed in the

first instance to audiences similar to those in the Aoyama Gakuin
course, a mixture of young business executives and graduate students.
For their economic analytical techniques, the chapters in this book
should also be of relevance to students in schools of business and public affairs, as well as upperlevel economics undergraduates. They
should further provide a convenient collection of leading policy issues
for economics graduate students who seek to apply their analytical
skills to the real world.

Students of international politics may also find the lectures of use, if
only as a guide to the way economists think about these issues. There
is no doubt some truth to the now fashionable proposition that, with
the end of the cold war, the glue that has held the Western countries'
external policies together has been weakened—the implication being
that increased conflict among these nations may result. There is similarly some truth to the notion that international politics is now primarily about economic issues. Economic conflict in the late twentieth
century differs from that in the late nineteenth. This time the territories
in question are not geographic but sectoral and functional.

A sort of Parkinson's Law may require that, if the industrial Group
of Seven countries have no common enemy to occupy their confrontational energies, they may divert a greater part of these energies to
squabbling over such matters as agricultural protection, high technology market shares, a high German interest rate, or a large U.S. budget
deficit. Unlike the colonial disputes of the past, these matters can
hardly lead to military conflict. However, they can sour the atmosphere for international economic cooperation. The result can be a reduction in standards of living all around, as illustrated graphically by
the depression-widening impact of the wave of protection in the 1930s.
Dealing with global environmental issues that inherently require joint
action seems likely to be a functional area in which decreased international economic cooperation could carry a high price.

This book also seeks to state its arguments in terms accessible to the
broadest public possible, as ultimately it is the informed public and its
representatives that set international economic policy. Technical ap-
pendixes serve to harmonize this objective with the goal of challenging
those readers who have formal training in economics.

The purpose of this book extends to the substance of the specific
policy issues, as well as to the methodological approach for their analysis. The topics selected encompass the salient international economic
policy issues of recent years. For the most part, they are subjects on

which I have previously published empirical research. Cline (1989b) addresses the problem of adjustment of external deficits, the theme of chapter 2; Cline (1983b) surveys international trade policy (see chapter 3); Bergsten and Cline (1985) treats U.S.-Japan trade conflict (chapter 4); Cline (1984 and 1994) provide early and retrospective analyses of the debt crisis (chapter 5); and Cline (1992a) investigates the economics of global warming and thus the issues raised by global environmental concerns (chapter 8). The two exceptions—economic transition in the former Soviet Union and Eastern Europe (chapter 6) and the economic future of Europe (chapter 7)—are subjects too important to omit in a compilation such as this book.

Thus, the book's themes include most of the key issues of the 1980s and early 1990s. Moreover, there are important linkages among the issues. The weak outlook for growth in the industrial economies in the near term (chapter 1) has implications for the problems of international imbalance (chapter 2), trade negotiations and trade conflict (chapters 3 and 4), and to a greater or lesser degree, to all of the other issues examined. The experience of Latin American adjustment to the debt crisis (chapter 5) has relevance for strategies adopted in the economies in transition (chapter 6). International trade institutions (chapter 3) and regional free trade areas (chapter 4) affect international environmental policy (chapter 8) and vice versa. The analytics of exchange rate adjustment (chapter 2) have implications for the European goal of a single currency (chapter 7), and fixed exchange rates in Europe in turn have played a role in the region's recent economic stagnation (chapter 1).

The subjects covered here are not the only important issues in international economic policy in recent years. Other candidates include the oil market, as well as commodity markets in general; alternative strategies of economic development and the contrast between successful, mainly outward-oriented growth in eastern Asia at one extreme and economic retrogression in sub-Saharan Africa at the other; the relationship between international trade and income distribution (considered only briefly in chapter 3); the international monetary regime (discussed summarily in chapter 2); and the question of competing models of capitalism in a post-communist world. However, the analysis of the issues included in this book should provide important background and methodological approaches of relevance for these and other policy issues not directly examined in the following chapters.

Although proper economic analysis is a prerequisite for proper policy, analytical disagreement among competing schools of thought often exists and makes the setting of policy difficult. For example, one group of economists may consider exchange rate depreciation to be a useful tool of external adjustment, while another group may insist that depreciation will simply generate offsetting inflation. One group may cite one set of data to prove that Japan's trade policies are unfair, whereas another group cites different (or even the same) data to argue the contrary. One group may insist that shock therapy is the only way to accomplish transition from socialist to capitalist economies, while another may suggest that orthodox remedies may be inappropriate where the normal capitalist institutions and their response mechanisms are missing.

The chapters presented here tend to emphasize my own views, based on research on most of the above issues. However, an attempt is made to give the flavor of the professional debate on each subject. It is my hope that the resulting survey will prove useful to students, scholars, and policymakers.

1   The Risk of Global Economic Stagnation

Economic growth is the rising tide that can lift all boats. Growth in the industrial countries not only provides a basis for creating jobs and alleviating poverty at home, but it also expands the market for exports from developing countries, improving the prospects for their much poorer populations. In the first quarter century of the postwar period, the industrial country growth machine functioned smoothly. It has, however, been slowing down since the early 1970s. Policymakers face a major challenge if they are to assure the realization of potential growth rates—somewhere on the order of 2.5 to 3% annually for industrial countries, somewhat higher in the case of Japan. There are policy and structural distortions in each of the major industrial country areas that will require thoughtful and politically courageous action to achieve this potential growth.

Declining Growth in the Industrial Countries

In the early 1990s, the industrial countries experienced a rolling recession that began in the Anglo-Saxon countries and spread to Germany, the rest of Europe, and Japan. At first the recession was more subtle than those of 1974–75 and 1982. Figure 1.1 shows that, in each of those earlier cases, there was a severe world recession concurrent in the industrial countries that followed an oil price shock and, in the case of 1982, a surge in international interest rates to unprecedented levels.

It is less well known that there was a recession of nearly comparable severity in 1991 (figure 1.1). In that year, global production did not grow at all. Output collapsed by 14% in Eastern Europe and 9% in the former Soviet Union. The industrial countries eked out a feeble average growth of 0.6% But of the twenty-four industrial country members of the Organization for Economic Cooperation and Development,

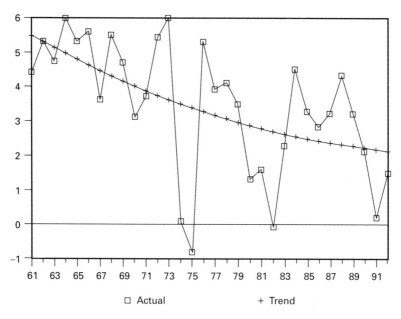

Figure 1.1
Industrial country growth (percent per year)

OECD, there was negative growth in eight: the United States, Canada, the United Kingdom, Australia, New Zealand, Finland, Sweden, and Switzerland. These countries in outright recession account for half of the aggregate gross domestic product, GDP, of the OECD. Output fell by 1.2% in the United States and by about 2% in Canada and the United Kingdom. Growth also fell sharply in Germany (from 4½% to less than 1%), decelerated to unusually low levels in France and Italy (1⅓%), and began a downward trend in Japan from 5¼% to 4½%. In short, 1991 was a dismal year for economies just about everywhere except in Asia and, ironically, Latin America, where countries were finally emerging from the debt crisis.

By 1992–93, the recession worsened in Germany and Japan, and the U.S. recovery was relatively weak. Germany's growth fell to 1.9% in 1992 and an expected −1.6% in 1993 (IMF 1993b). For Europe as a whole, growth was only 1.1% in 1992 and an expected −0.3% in 1993. Recovery in the U.K. was about the only bright spot in Europe, whereas France entered into recession and Italy had practically zero growth. Japan's growth fell to 1.3% in 1992 and an expected −0.1% for 1993. Although the U.S. economy staged a recovery, its growth of 2.6%

in both 1992 and 1993 was low for years immediately following recession.

The poor performance for 1991–93 came on the heels of a long-term decline in the growth rate for industrial countries. As shown in figure 1.1, average GDP growth for these countries fell from 5% in the 1960s to about 3½% in the 1970s, 2½% in the 1980s, and 1¾% annually in 1990–92. Although these averages incorporated violent swings, especially the recessions of 1974–75 and 1982, there was no mistaking the long-term downward trend. The 1990s were thus not only off to a bad start but one that seemed to continue a long-term decline, as indicated by the trend line in figure 1.1.

Economic growth was high in the 1960s, in part because of temporary phenomena, especially the catch-up growth in Japan, with an average growth of a remarkable 12%, and in Europe. However, further declines after the 1970s were more serious and difficult to explain. Although population growth did slow down, from 1% annually in Europe and Japan in the early 1960s to ½% in the 1980s and from 1½% to 1% in the United States, this decline accounts for very little of the reduction in growth.

Robert Solow (1956) provided the classic framework for analyzing the sources of economic growth. In his model, the growth rate equals a weighted average of the growth rates of factor inputs plus a term for technological change, the residual. The weights reflect the responsiveness, or elasticity, of output with respect to each factor (labor or capital). From economic theory, these elasticities equal the fraction of GDP paid to each respective factor. Intuitively this result simply means that proportionate changes in the more important factor have a greater influence on production.[1]

In the case of the United States, productivity growth per worker slowed down from a trend of 1.6% per year in 1956–73 to 0.8% in 1974–92 (calculated from CEA 1993). From Solow's theory, part of this slowdown can be explained by a reduction in the growth rate of the capital stock. Under alternative measures, the growth rate of U.S. real capital stock slowed down from about 4% per year in 1956–73 to about 3% per year in 1974–92 (Cline 1993e). With capital's share in the economy at 30%, this reduction should have caused a decline of about 0.3% in the growth rate ($= 0.3 \times 1\%$).

Similarly, there is some indication that the rate of constant-quality labor growth decelerated. If educational levels are weighted by relative wage rates to construct an index of constant-quality labor, this index grew at 0.8% annually in 1956–73 and only 0.65% annually in 1974–92 (Cline 1993e). The problem was not that educational upgrading had ended but rather that it was not progressing as rapidly as before, in part because in the earlier period education had started from a lower base. Applying the factor share weight for labor (70% of GDP), this deceleration should have caused a decline of 0.1% in the annual growth rate of labor productivity ($= 0.7 \times 0.15\%$).

Slower growth in capital and labor thus account for only about half of the slowdown in U.S. labor productivity, 0.4% out of a total slowdown of 0.8%. Although the rest of the decline in productivity growth remains a mystery, there is good reason to believe that macroeconomic shocks in the 1970s and 1980s meant that the U.S. economy spent a great deal of time growing below its potential rate. In contrast, the sources of growth approach assumes that full potential growth is achieved. Similar slowdowns in productivity growth occurred in Europe, where however the growth of employment was far lower than in the United States.

Whatever the full explanation for declining productivity growth, by the beginning of the 1990s, the trendline for industrial country growth stood at an anemic 2¼% annually (see figure 1.1). There is good reason to believe that the downward trend should not continue. A prime reason is that inflation, the plague of the 1970s and 1980s, has been brought to much more tolerable levels. Nonetheless, the fact remains that the decade opened with a lackluster trend growth rate, one that allows only minimal scope for rising per capita consumption even if there is no further decline.

Unfortunately, it seems more likely that, in the period 1992–95, economic growth in the industrial countries will be below average rather than above because of major special factors in each region. In the United States, the necessary process of fiscal adjustment is likely to exert a contractionary effect. In the European Union (EU), the spillover from Germany's high interest rates and the fiscal contraction to meet the conditions for convergence to European Monetary Union are likely to keep growth low. In Japan, the economy must adjust to the aftermath of the bubble economy after the puncturing of the bubble. When these forces for abnormally low growth are set against an already low trendline plateau of perhaps only slightly above 2% for normal growth, the prospects for the first half of the 1990s are sobering. Ironically, just as the communist world has discarded its economic system in favor of Western capitalism, the economies of the West seem to have lost their way.

Disinflation, Deflation, and Latent Inflation

A second long-term trend is evident in the international economy: there has been a return to relatively stable, or even falling, prices after two decades of inflation. Figure 1.2 shows the absolute level of the U.S. wholesale price index over the past thirty years, as well as a broad index of world commodity prices. Both series show that prices were stable in the 1960s. Then, from the late 1960s up until about 1985, the U.S. wholesale price level tripled. World inflation measured by commodity prices was even higher, spurred by the oil price shocks in 1974 and again in 1980. After a dip in 1986 (when oil prices collapsed) and renewed but slower increases in the late 1980s, U.S. producer prices stopped rising in 1991 and again in 1992. The rate of inflation had already slowed substantially in the 1980s. The trends seemed to be signalling a new period of price stability.

The pattern of stability in the 1960s, high inflation in the 1970s, and declining inflation thereafter was evident in international trade prices as well. The unit value of exports of industrial countries, expressed in dollars, rose at only 1½% annually in the 1960s, surged to 11% annually in the 1970s, and then slowed to 3% annual increases in the 1980s and early 1990s.

There were other important prices that showed a more dramatic reversal. By 1992, the United States, the United Kingdom, and Japan were embarked on a large asset price deflation. Prices of real estate and land were falling, not just flat. In Japan, stock market prices were down by 60% from their peak, and land prices in the major cities were down by 40%—after a large runup in both.

Absolute deflation turns out to have been present for more than a decade in another key area, commodity prices. The collapse of oil prices from $35 per barrel in 1980 to about $20 by 1992–93 is well known. However, other commodity prices have fallen as well, such as those for coffee, which peaked in the late 1970s, and during most of the 1980s, those for grains. If all commodities are aggregated by trade shares, with a weight of about 40% for oil, the overall commodity price index has been falling since 1980 and by 1992 stood about 25% below the 1980 level (figure 1.2). Of course, commodity deflation followed a decade of commodity price explosion in the 1970s. It is nonetheless striking that commodity prices have now been falling for more than a decade in absolute dollar terms. Commodity prices have fallen even more when stated as terms of trade against prices of manufactured goods.

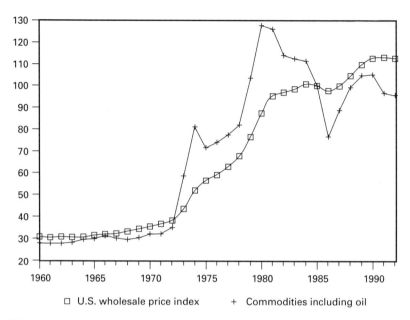

□ U.S. wholesale price index   + Commodities including oil

Figure 1.2
Commodity prices including oil (1985 = 100)

The pattern shown in figure 1.2 is suggestive of another phenomenon: the possibility that commodity prices led world inflation in the 1970s and have led world disinflation since the early 1980s. There is some logic in economic theory to this interpretation. Some economists have divided goods and services into auction markets, where products are relatively standardized and competitively traded, and customer markets, where products are differentiated and firms exert more oligopoly power. Prices tend to respond sensitively to supply and demand in auction markets but are sluggish and tend to be administered in customer markets. Commodities are the quintessential auction market products, whereas manufactured goods include many customer market goods. It is plausible that the price trends shown in figure 1.2 are telling us that the leading indicator for broad price trends is given by the auction market prices, those for commodities, and that the administered prices are slowly but surely responding to the deflationary trend begun by commodity prices in the early 1980s.

This same distinction helps explain the divergence between stable wholesale prices and ongoing inflation in consumer prices, which have continued to rise at 3 to 4%. Consumer prices include services, which are dominated by wage costs. Wages are one of the most administered price categories of all. If we extend the concept that auction prices are a leading indicator for administered prices, then we should expect that, just as wholesale price inflation has slowed down after falling commodity prices, consumer price inflation is likely to slow down in response to stable wholesale prices.

Low interest rates are another indicator of disinflation. Typically the interest rate contains an inflationary premium. For example, after U.S. consumer price inflation reached nearly 14% in 1980, the international dollar interest rate, LIBOR, (London Interbank Offer Rate) reached 17% in 1981. By 1993, the U.S. treasury bill rate and LIBOR were down to 3%, the lowest level in thirty years. Long-term U.S. treasury bond rates had fallen to around 6%. In a period of falling inflation, longer-term rates typically lag behind in their descent.

Overall, the trends for international prices and interest rates were pointing toward disinflation, stable prices, and even outright deflation as the decade of the 1990s opened. On the surface, it seemed likely that the decade, like the 1960s, would be one of stable prices and that, for some tradable goods, there could be further absolute price declines. If so, then many of the economic reflexes learned by households and businesses over the past two decades would no longer be relevant. In the 1970s, families that bought houses as a hedge against inflation were astute and reaped the benefit of large capital gains. Debtors who took on fixed interest obligations were able to repay later in softer dollars eroded by inflation. In contrast, in the 1990s, homes and real estate have been a source of capital losses, and repaying a given nominal dollar amount could prove considerably more burdensome than expected because of lower inflation.

If inflation were dead, economic authorities in industrial countries could comfortably lean harder in the direction of stimulus to help revive growth. Monetary authorities could increase the growth of money supply to seek even lower interest rates, and governments could ease efforts to reduce budget deficits with little fear of reigniting inflation. Unfortunately, it is by no means clear that inflation is dead.

Figure 1.3 shows the GDP-weighted average of consumer price inflation in four major industrial countries (the United States, Germany, France, and Japan) over the past three decades. The figure also reports the average inflation predicted for the same period in a backcast of a simple model that relates inflation to the rise in oil prices, the rise in commodity prices, the GDP gap from trendline, and the real interest

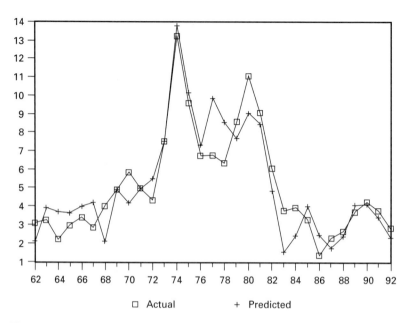

Figure 1.3
G-4 inflation, constrained model (percent per year)

rate (LIBOR minus U.S. inflation).[2] A backcast applies an estimated model to actual past values of the independent variables in order to calculate what the model would have predicted with perfect foresight about those variables.

In this model, the excess of actual over trendline GDP growth represents demand pressure. The real level of LIBOR represents whether monetary policy is tight (high real interest rate) or loose (low). Both variables are specified with a lag, that is, for the year prior to the year of the inflation observation.[3]

Comparing figures 1.1 and 1.3, it may be seen that a high positive GDP gap in 1973 contributed to inflation in 1974 and that high real interest rates in the early 1980s (not shown) contributed to the rapid reduction of inflation. For its part, the oil price has an obvious influence. In figure 1.3, inflation surges in 1974 and 1980, the two years of oil price shock. The level of inflation is also strongly influenced by the inflation rate in the previous year, indicating strong inertia from such mechanisms as cost-of-living clauses in wage contracts. Thus, 1% extra inflation in a given year causes the inflation rate in the subsequent year to rise by 0.77%, other things being equal.

Projections for 1994–2000 using this simple model suggest that in the base case (that is, under the most likely set of assumptions about independent variables), industrial country inflation could rise to about 4% in 1994 and 5% by 1995 and could drift upward to about 6% by the late 1990s. This increase from the low level of 3% in 1993 is primarily attributable to a recovery in growth, from about 1½% in 1993 for the four large industrial countries (G-4) to 2.7%, as well as to the lagged effect of the extremely low real interest rates of 1993. However, in an alternative formulation that allows greater influence for oil prices and as a result estimates less impact of the growth gap and real interest rate, the rise in inflation is more moderate, and the rate only reaches 4% by 1997.[4]

It is of course possible that features unique to the early 1990s make estimation of future inflation based on experience in the past three decades unreliable. For example, the new feature of asset deflation, as well as white collar job displacement, discussed below could make inflationary pressures less severe than in the past for given levels of growth, real interest rates, and inflation for oil and commodity prices. Nonetheless, these results suggest that the low inflation of 3% in 1992–93 may have been only a temporary victory.

The United States

The U.S. economy is the largest, as well as one of the most open, in the world, and it tends to set the pace for the world economy. It is thus of worldwide concern that U.S. economic growth was near the vanishing point in the period 1990–91 and that recovery was meager in 1992–93. U.S. output rose 1.2% in 1990, fell 0.7% in 1991, and rose by 2.6% in 1992. By late 1993, the International Monetary Fund (IMF) placed the expected U.S. growth rate for 1993 at 2.7%. Cumulative growth for the first two years after the recession would thus have amounted to 5.4%, far less than the two-year totals of 13.4% after the 1982 recession and the 11.3% after the 1974–75 recession (CEA 1993, p. 351). Even though the 1991 recession was milder than its two predecessors, the recovery looked anemic.[5]

An anatomy of the 1990–91 U.S. recession reveals weak investment and weak consumption as the main problems. From 1989 to 1991, real investment fell by 15%, and consumption stagnated with a meager 1% total increase over the period. The only bright spot in the economy was in international trade, as exports rose by 15% in real terms. By 1992–93, the rise in the trade balance had stalled.

Causes of the 1990–91 U.S. Recession

Excess Debt
In the 1980s, U.S. households and businesses built up debt at a rate twice as fast as their income grew. For a time, debt was offset by rising asset prices, especially for housing values. However, by the late 1980s and the initial years of the 1990s, housing prices turned flat and actually fell in many regions.

Total domestic debt, including governmental, had long stood at a level of about 130% of GDP in the U.S. economy. This ratio had risen to 200% by 1990. Business debt had risen, associated with such phenomena as the mid-1980s boom in commercial real estate and the wave of leveraged corporate buyouts. At some point, it was inevitable that there would be a pause in the growth of consumer and business spending so as to permit consolidation and adjustment to excess debt. Stagnant consumption and falling investment were the result.

Asset Deflation
Alan Greenspan, chairman of the U.S. Federal Reserve Board, stressed that in the United States and also in Japan, the 1990s recession was marked by a phenomenon not seen since the 1930s: falling asset prices. Greenspan argued that this new feature was responsible for the fact that the U.S. economy had been far weaker than the standard econometric models had predicted. Those models were based upon estimates from decades when asset prices were rising. If the value of a household's asset portfolio is falling, the household is likely to curb consumption in an effort to rebuild assets, so the omission of this influence will tend to overpredict consumption based upon the more usual forces, such as income and interest rates.

Ironically, the problem of asset deflation only seems to have affected the countries with the most advanced capital markets. The Anglo-Saxon financial systems outdid themselves in innovation in the 1980s, for example with the introduction of home equity loans and variable rate mortgages. Even Japan experienced a round of financial market liberalization, in part in response to pressure from the U.S. Treasury.

Continental Europe was much more old-fashioned in its ways, with more institutional rigidities. The more efficient markets seem to have provided the public and businesses enough rope with which to hang themselves, and it has been in the United States, the United Kingdom, and Japan where markets experienced a boom-bust sequence and hence the new problem of asset deflation.

What remains unclear is just how important asset deflation is in contributing to recent and future economic stagnation. Traditional, Keynesian demand analysis does allow for a propensity to consume out of assets. This propensity has typically been placed at about 5%, so that a loss of $20,000 in the value of a family's home would reduce annual consumption by about $1,000. However, it is primarily the permanent asset value that matters. A key reason why the world economy was not severely affected by the stock market collapse of about 25% in October of 1987 is that the decline followed a speculative runup so that households did not yet consider the higher stock prices to be permanent and reliable. Accordingly, they did not reduce their consumption much when the paper profits disappeared.

Increasingly, however, the asset deflation of the early 1990s has an appearance of permanence. Even so, there is a limit to its contractionary effect on the economy. Suppose that the value of U.S. residential housing and commercial real estate has declined by 15%. That loss would amount to somewhere on the order of $1 trillion.[6] Applying the traditional propensity to consume out of assets, the impact on annual consumption would be a contractionary shock of about $50 billion or 1% of GDP. Once at a lower level, consumption would resume its growth along a parallel but lower path. This estimate thus suggests that the problem of asset deflation may well have been important in the 1990–91 recession but that it is unlikely to exert strong ongoing recessionary pressure in the 1990s unless there is further asset deflation.

Financial Market Fragility
The problem of savings and loan bankruptcies, requiring a taxpayer bailout eventually reaching some $500 billion, as well as emerging problems of troubled commercial banks burdened in particular with real estate loans gone sour, added another unusual feature to the U.S. recession at the beginning of the 1990s. Bank problems brought an atmosphere of caution on the part of commercial banks and, to at least

some degree, a resulting credit crunch that made loans hard to get for even sound enterprises, especially small businesses.

The shift toward caution has been heightened by the transition toward new international (BIS, Bank for International Settlements) standards for capital adequacy. In the United States, regulators moved to a risk-adjusted capital requirement system, in which higher capital reserves were required for riskier loans. Because this system considers U.S. government obligations risk free, banks had a new incentive to place their assets passively in government paper rather than lend to business. It is difficult to gauge the overall effect of a credit crunch on the U.S. economy, but it was surely a hindrance to recovery.

Consumer Confidence
In the 1980s, U.S. consumers were confident that rising wages and falling taxes that followed the Reagan revolution would provide them with the purchasing power to make good on their rising consumer debt. The 1990s, however, began with an event that seemed to perforate consumer confidence, the Gulf War. After the war, confidence did not recover as expected, and by mid-1992, the various indexes of consumer confidence stood at about half of the normal levels. Public opinion polls showed that, for the first time, many parents were worried that their children would be worse off than they. All of the factors just outlined—excessive debt, asset deflation, even a possibly insecure banking system—contributed to weak consumer confidence. Probably of even more importance, the 1991 recession hit many white-collar, service sector workers, whereas previous recessions had been focused on blue-collar manufacturing jobs. Widely announced mass employment cutbacks in such trusted corporate names as Sears, IBM, and General Motors were hardly conducive to consumer confidence.

Defense Spending
From 1980 to 1987, during the Reagan military buildup, government spending on defense rose at a brisk rate of 6% annually. In the period 1988 through 1991, in contrast, defense spending was flat and made no contribution to GDP growth. And from the first half of 1991 to the first half of 1992, real defense spending declined by nearly 10%. Defense has accounted for about 6% of the U.S. economy, and for this enormous sector, demand turned from rapid positive growth to stagnation and then retrenchment.

State and Local Governments
Unlike the federal government, most state governments in the United States cannot run fiscal deficits. As a result, when the economy goes into recession and tax revenues decline, state and local governments begin cutting back their spending, aggravating the recession further.

The Price of the Party
Most of these individual causes of the recession may be summed up in the diagnosis that, during the 1980s, the U.S. economy enjoyed a boom that was fed by current consumption at the expense of a future day of reckoning. At the beginning of that decade, the Reagan administration cut income taxes by one-third. The much heralded Laffer curve (named for U.S. economist Arthur B. Laffer) had promised that lower tax rates would so stimulate the economy that revenue would rise and avoid any fiscal problem. As predicted by mainstream economists, the outcome was just the opposite, and the U.S. government entered a period of large persistent deficits. U.S. government debt held by the public rose from $1.1 trillion in 1980 to $2.8 trillion by 1992, at constant prices of 1990, or from 27% of GDP to 51% (CEA 1993, p. 435). Simultaneously, households trimmed their savings rates lower and lower.

Rising government deficits and falling private saving meant that a bill was being added up to pay for the party and sooner or later that bill would come due. The physical counterpart of high public and private spending was that the 1980s were characterized by unsustainable booms, such as the massive overbuilding of commercial real estate. The slowdown and recession of 1990–91 and the mediocre recovery by 1992–93 were equivalent to the hangover of the morning after. What was unclear was just how severe that hangover would be and for how long it would last.

Policy Constraints

By late 1990, as the weakness of the economy became clear, the Federal Reserve began to cut interest rates. The treasury bill rate fell from 8% in 1989–90 to 5½% in mid-1991 and 3% by late 1992. Monetary policy was the only game in town. Traditionally, both fiscal and monetary stimulus are available to counter recession. However, with the federal deficit already up to $300 billion, or 5% of GDP, the federal government was in no position to add further deficit spending for purposes of fighting the recession.

For its part, monetary policy seemed less effective than usual, whether because of a credit crunch, the novel feature of asset deflation, or otherwise. Moreover, long-term interest rates remained as high as 7½% in early 1992 before falling to 6% in 1993. With inflation at 3% and possibly falling, these long-term rates were high in real terms. The most powerful impact of monetary expansion occurs when it brings down long-term interest rates because these rates influence capital investment decisions by firms and home purchases. The resistance of the long-term rate indicated that the public remained skeptical that inflation had been definitively controlled. There was a risk that further monetary easing would simply stir up inflationary expectations and leave long-term rates unchanged or even conceivably raise them. That risk was doubly present for any major course of fiscal stimulus.

Structural Problems

Results from the 1990 U.S. census confirmed concern that over the decade there had been growing inequality in income and wealth, as well as inadequate expansion of job opportunities for unskilled workers. The average real wage was no higher at the beginning of the 1990s than in the mid-1970s, and the wage gap between skilled and unskilled workers had widened substantially. This structural problem was in addition to the problem of weak overall job creation. In the four years of the Bush administration, private sector jobs had not expanded at all, whereas they had risen by 19% in the eight years of the Reagan administration and 14% in the four years under Jimmy Carter.

Table 1.1 shows real wage rates over time grouped by level of education.[7] It is striking that, for each individual educational class, real wages have actually fallen in the past eighteen years. The decline has been the greatest for high school dropouts, with a fall of 22.8%. Even for workers with college and higher degrees, however, the average real wage has declined by 5 to 10%. The only saving factor was that the educational composition of the labor force improved as high school dropouts fell from one-fourth to one-eighth of total workers, while those with college and higher education increased from one-seventh to more than one-fifth. Nonetheless, workers with a high school education or less continued to account for more than half of the work force, and for this group, the real wage fell by about 16% even after taking account of the rising share of those who finished high school.

Table 1.1
The change in real hourly wage by education, 1973–1991 (1991 dollars)

Year	High school dropout	High school graduate	Some college	College	College 2+ years
Real hourly wage					
1973	$9.87	$11.28	$12.41	$16.45	$20.13
1979	9.59	10.69	11.85	14.72	17.85
1987	8.24	9.92	11.32	15.24	19.04
1989	7.95	9.63	11.14	14.99	19.20
1991	7.62	9.43	11.03	14.77	19.24
Percent decline					
1973–79	2.8%	5.2%	4.5%	10.5%	12.1%
1979–89	17.1	9.9	6.0	−1.8	−7.6
1989–91	4.2	2.1	1.0	1.5	0.2
1973–91	22.8	16.4	11.1	10.2	5.3
Share of work force					
1973	24.8%	40.8%	18.0%	9.1%	4.5%
1979	21.9	41.8	18.0	10.9	4.9
1987	14.2	41.3	21.9	13.7	6.3
1989	13.7	40.5	22.3	14.0	6.9
1991	12.6	40.0	23.1	14.7	7.0

Source: *State of Working America*, 1992–93 edition, Table 3.19; *International Economic Insights*, Sept.–Oct. 1992.
Note: This table excludes those with one year of schooling beyond college.

Over the same period, the wage gap widened. Thus, in 1973, the average wage of workers with college and higher education was 64% above that for workers with high school and lesser education; by 1991, the difference was 80%. Some economists (Bound and Johnson 1992) have argued that the widening gap stemmed primarily from technological change that was skewed in favor of high-skill jobs. They cited computerization of the economy in particular. It is noteworthy, however, that the erosion of real wages even for the higher educational levels meant that it was a sharper decline in low-skill wages rather than a boom in high-skill wages that drove the widening wedge. This pattern was consistent with the disappearance of low-skilled jobs in manufacturing, a sector that experienced major cutbacks in employment in the 1980s, in considerable part because of the overvaluation of the dollar and the loss of U.S. competitiveness internationally (see chapter 2).

U.S. Outlook and Policy Options

Most economists have tended to place the sustainable potential growth rate for the U.S. economy in the 1990s at about 2½% per year. Usually growth is well above the long-term potential rate during the initial year of a recovery. However, following the 1991 recession, U.S. growth in 1992–93 was approximately equal to this long-term potential growth rate rather than above it.

For the period 1994–96, it seems likely that U.S. growth could average no more than 2 to 2½% annually. The principal reason is that there will have to be a major fiscal adjustment. In 1992, the federal deficit stood at 4.9% of GDP or 3.3% of GDP even after removing the influence of recession, which reduces tax revenue and increases unemployment insurance outlays (CBO, 1994). The latter standardized employment deficit should be no higher than about 2% of GDP if federal debt is not to spiral out of control.[8] Many would argue this deficit should be cut to zero.

In 1993, the new Clinton administration finally enacted deficit-reducing legislation. Congressional Democrats knew that the public was tired of fiscal gridlock and expected action. The campaign of independent Ross Perot had removed from the fiscal debate the absolute taboo about mentioning taxes and placed the emphasis on the irresponsibility of passing along large debt to the next generation. The Clinton budget package promised to achieve correction without raising taxes except for the rich.

The package provided for a cumulative cut in the budget deficit from baseline by about $500 billion over five years. The result was that the actual deficit was scheduled to fall from 4.9% of GDP in 1992 and 4.0% in 1993 to 2.2% by 1996–98, instead of remaining as high as 3.7% by the latter period (CBO 1994, pp. xvi–xvii). However, the 1992 deficit was exaggerated by unemployment. The standardized employment deficit, which is more meaningful for economic analysis, was scheduled to fall from 3.3% of GDP in 1992–93 to 2.0% in 1996–98. This meant a corresponding decline in real government demand.

The Keynesian demand multiplier tells the percentage change in GDP for a 1% of GDP change in the fiscal balance. Lower government spending means in the first instance fewer real purchases from the private sector. There is a chain reaction as private suppliers buy less from others in turn. After taking account of offsetting factors, especially the crowding out of private investment when government deficit spending rises and claims a larger share of funds in the capital market, the multiplier is probably still at least 1.0 and perhaps 1.5 or so.

The Clinton package reducing the U.S. fiscal deficit (normalized for standardized employment) by about 1½% of GDP thus means that there will be a total demand contraction equal to perhaps 2% of GDP over four years. This contraction would amount to about ½ percentage point of GDP per year. On this basis, and with potential GDP growth at 2½% annually, we should expect U.S. growth to be only about 2% annually over the next four years or so. Eventually the U.S. economy can harvest the benefits of restraining the deficit as the consequence of lower long-term interest rates and a resulting rise in private investment. But the main effect of fiscal adjustment for the first few years is likely to be contractionary.

In addition to macroeconomic adjustment, the U.S. economy will need to undergo structural reform. There is a need for job training and other programs for low-skill workers. In addition, soaring costs for health care will have to be addressed, as will an eroding physical infrastructure, such as roads and bridges. The net effect of structural reform is unlikely to be an increase in the growth rate in the first few years, although these reforms should not necessarily impose a substantial decrease either. Overall, then, the outlook for the U.S. economy in 1994–97 would appear to be growth closer to about 2% rather than the 2½% long-term potential rate. Below-par growth is the likely price that must be paid for adjustment after the fiscal mismanagement of the 1980s.[*]

Europe

As of 1992–93, there were two principal forces that seemed likely to keep European economic growth at below-normal levels for a period of three to four years: the German problem and the process of convergence toward monetary union.

Germany's Policy Mismatch

The costs of incorporating East Germany in the historic reunification that began in 1989 were much higher than West Germans had anticipated and amounted to approximately 4% of GDP, about $70 billion,

---

[*] Author's note: By early 1994 this evaluation appeared to be too pessimistic, as discussed in the epilogue.

annually (IMF 1993b). Germany's politicians were no more perfect than those in most countries and chose to avoid inflicting the pain of reunification costs on the public directly through higher taxes. As a result, Germany shifted abruptly from a balanced budget in 1989 to a fiscal deficit of 3% of GDP in 1991–92. The German central bank, or Bundesbank, felt compelled to defend the country's traditional price stability by stepping in with an extremely tight monetary policy. Germany's treasury bill rate soared from 3.6% in 1988 to 8½% in 1990–92 (IMF 1993a). Essentially, Germany was repeating the policy mismatch of loose fiscal policy and tight money that U.S. President Ronald Reagan had adopted in the mid-1980s. The boom in demand for reconstruction in East Germany kept Germany's growth high at about 4% in 1989–90, but for consolidated Germany, growth was down to 0.9% in 1991 and was only 1% in 1992 as the high interest rates took their toll.

For the rest of Europe, German reunification was initially a stimulus as exports to the German market enjoyed a boom. However, by 1991, with no further trade gains, the rest of Europe began to face economic contraction from the spillover of high German interest rates. Most European countries held nearly fixed exchange rates against the deutschemark (DM) within the exchange rate mechanism (ERM) of the European Monetary System. Fixed rates could not be held without matching the German interest rate because otherwise there would be enormous capital flows from, for example, France to Germany. As a result, there was a generalized rise in interest rates in Europe in 1990–91. Higher interest rates choked off growth, leading to the recessions and slowdowns reviewed above.

By the third quarter of 1992, the strain of high German interest rates had caused a crisis in the ERM exchange rate regime. As discussed in chapter 7, such countries as Italy, Spain, Portugal, and the United Kingdom, perceived as being in a weaker position, were forced to devalue by about 15% against the deutschemark, and Italy and the United Kingdom temporarily left the ERM and its fixed exchange rates altogether. Even so, the Bundesbank refused to reduce interest rates by more than a symbolic ¼%. Despite small reductions in German interest rates in the first half of 1993, by August of that year, there was another round of currency crisis, this time with the result that countries still in the ERM were forced to set extremely wide bands (15%) around their central rates against the DM.

Exchange rate realignments, especially the float of the British pound sterling, meant some possible additional scope to pursue lower interest rate strategies and revive growth. Moreover, by mid-1993, Germany had eased interest rates moderately, as the treasury bill rate fell to 6½%. Nonetheless, it seemed likely that the contractionary pressure on European growth from the still relatively high German interest rates would persist for some time.

Maastricht Convergence

In late 1991, the members of the European Community agreed in Maastricht, the Netherlands, that they would form an economic and political union by the end of the decade. The European Monetary Union (EMU) would establish a single currency, and monetary policy would be run by a single European central bank (see chapter 7). The Maastricht Agreement provided that, by 1997, there would be a decision as to which countries qualified for inclusion in the EMU. Using five criteria, eligibility would be determined on performance during the two preceding years. First, a country's fiscal deficit would have to be held to 3% of GDP or less. Second, its government debt could be no more than 60% of GDP. Third, its inflation rate could be no higher than 1½% above the average for the three lowest-inflation members of the EC. Fourth, its long-term interest rates could similarly be no more than 2% above the average for the three low-inflation members. Fifth, it could not have carried out a major exchange realignment within the preceding two years.

During 1992–93, most of the countries in the European Community would have been unable to qualify for EMU membership. Only France and Luxembourg met all criteria. Italy had a fiscal deficit of about 10% of GDP, which in theory had to be cut to 3%. More generally, it seemed highly likely that, as European countries sought to meet these convergence criteria set forth by the Maastricht Agreement, there would be a period of three years or more of contractionary economic policies. Sharp reductions in fiscal deficits were likely to reduce demand, although with later beneficial effects from the lowering of interest rates.

Most economists interpreted the convergence criteria as contractionary. Researchers at the International Monetary Fund reportedly estimated that efforts to meet the criteria would cut 0.4 to 0.8% off of annual growth rates over the next four years, although this conclusion was so unpleasant (and, arguably, controversial) that it remained un-published.

Moreover, by 1992–93, Europe was facing intense problems of un-employment. The unemployment rate for the EC as a whole rose from under 9% in 1990 to 11% by 1993. Whereas the U.S. economy had cre-ated nearly twenty million jobs in the 1980s, the EC had created almost none. Even the meager increase in jobs in this period was heavily con-centrated in public sector employment. In the early 1990s, there was a convergence of cyclical downturn and new migration pressures from Eastern Europe. By 1993, some governments and firms in Europe were considering shorter work weeks to spread the available jobs among more workers. The environment of high unemployment was condu-cive to pressures for trade protection.

In sum, by 1993, there were two major reasons to expect European growth to be below average for the next three to four years: high Ger-man interest rates and the contractionary influence of meeting the Maastricht criteria for convergence to monetary union. It thus seemed likely that European growth would be in the range of $1\frac{1}{2}$ to 2% annu-ally rather than $2\frac{1}{2}$ to 3% or more during this period. If this scenario of lackluster growth materialized, there were likely to be intensifying political pressures associated with high unemployment.

Japan

Economic growth in Japan fell from an overheated 5% annual average in 1988–91 to less than 2% in 1992 and an expected 0% for 1993. This decline followed the puncturing of the bubble economy. The question was how deep and how long the slowdown in the 1990s would be.

Many analysts trace the bubble to the Louvre Accord in February of 1987. In that agreement, the Group of Seven (G-7) large industrial na-tions pledged to support the dollar, even as they had pledged to bring it down from its overvalued level at the Plaza Agreement in New York's Plaza Hotel in September of 1985. Finance ministers believed that the dollar had fallen too far too fast by early 1987 so that now it was time to support the U.S. currency. In its efforts to do so, the Bank of Japan lowered interest rates and pursued an expansionary monetary policy. It cut the discount rate on its loans to the banking system from its traditional level of 5% to only $2\frac{1}{2}$%. A low interest rate was neces-sary if investors were to be encouraged to place assets in the U.S. mar-ket and to buy dollars for that purpose. Moreover, exchange market intervention in support of the dollar, namely the buying up of dollars by the central bank, meant placing yen in the public's hands and thereby expanding the money supply.

The side effect on the Japanese economy was dramatic. Easy money and low interest rates encouraged a speculative boom. Prices on the stock market multiplied by about threefold, and land prices rose by about 40%. There was an investment boom as investment rose from 27% of GDP in 1987 to 31% by 1989–90.

There is an important aspect of the Japanese bubble that is difficult to explain. Why did monetary ease cause asset prices to skyrocket but not goods prices? The normal quantity theory of money states that, with unchanged volume of goods, prices of goods will rise proportionately with the supply of money.[9] Asset prices in turn will usually accompany general inflation. In Japan, from 1986 to 1989, the money supply rose by 17%, while consumer prices went up by only 3% (cumulative total). Yet, average stock prices rose by 94%. It seems likely that institutional changes liberalizing capital markets (e.g., stock market margin rules) played a pivotal role in permitting moderately expansionary monetary policy to unleash a massive boom in land and stock prices. Another factor may have been the bandwagon effect. Japanese stocks had been in a rising trend before the monetary ease of 1987 and had already more than doubled between 1982 and 1986.

By the middle of 1989, the Bank of Japan decided that matters had gotten out of hand in rampant asset inflation, and it began tightening money. It consecutively increased the discount rate up to 6% by mid-1990. The result was to puncture the financial bubble. Stock prices began a slide that eventually reduced the Nikkei index from its early-1990 peak of 40,000 to a low of about 14,000 by mid-1992. Land prices fell by 10 to 25% in the major cities over the same period. An atmosphere of gloom replaced euphoria as indexes of business confidence reached their lowest levels since 1975 and as real investment declined. By mid-1992, industrial production was about 6% below its level in mid-1991.

At the same time, there were concerns about vulnerability of the Japanese banking system. The banks were permitted to count the market value of stock and land holdings in their capital. When these values were high, Japanese banks seemed to be the Goliaths of world finance. As these values declined, there were concerns that the banks might not be able to meet their international (BIS, Bank of International Settlements) capital adequacy standards of 8% of loan assets in capital. Some estimates placed bad loans as high as $170 billion (*Wall Street Journal*, 16 October 1992). Suddenly, the Japanese banks entered a mode similar to that in the United States: with weak portfolios, it was feared that they would become cautious in lending and that a credit crunch could ensue that would affect the economy.

The Bank of Japan began to relax monetary policy by late 1991 when it realized that the economy was sliding into a serious slowdown. Monetary policy proved insufficient, however, and in August 1992, the government responded with a new program of economic stimulus— an important reversal of a tough balanced-budget policy. The package amounted to 10.7 trillion yen or 2.3% of GDP. Its spending component focused on public infrastructure. In addition, it included proposed lending to small businesses and a special program whereby a new entity would be established to purchase land from the banks in order to avoid a situation in which forced sales drove the market down further.

At the time, Japanese experts anticipated that the fiscal stimulus would increase GDP by about 2% from levels that it would otherwise reach. It thus seemed possible that growth by 1993 would be in the vicinity of 3%. Instead, the economy fell into even deeper recession. One reason was a delay in implementation of the stimulus package. The fundamental problem, however, was that investment remained depressed after excessive investment in the bubble economy and that consumers were too cautious to pick up the slack.

The Japanese government added further fiscal stimulus packages of 13.2 trillion yen in April of 1993 and 6.2 trillion yen in September of 1993, bringing the total to nearly 7% of GDP. Even though perhaps half of the total was window dressing, the potential stimulus was still large. Monetary policy also eased further.

By late 1993, it remained to be seen whether these measures would suffice to return the postbubble economy to sustained health. Despite the stimulus packages, it seemed likely that, at best, growth would be only in the 2½ to 3½% range in 1994 and the following few years rather than the average of 4½% experienced through most of the 1980s. One reason was that Japan's trade surplus had once again returned to high levels, reaching well over $100 billion (see chapter 2), and it was unlikely that the rest of the world would be content to see still higher Japanese trade surpluses. Export growth was thus unlikely to remain a major source of economic expansion.

Overview

In sum it is more likely that, for special reasons in each case, economic growth in the United States, Europe, and Japan will be below average in the next three to four years than that growth will be above average. Indeed, the trendline for the average was already a disappointing 2¼% or so for the industrial countries by the opening of the decade. However, there are three qualifications that suggest a limit to the downside.

First, the industrial countries have brought down inflation to a range of 3 to 4% annually and thus face much less need to apply austerity measures to fight inflation than they had in the 1980s. Second, there are few indications that a severe depression is ahead, despite the signs of disinflation and the special problems of asset deflation. The malady for the early 1990s is more likely to be sluggish growth than global depression. That outlook provides cold comfort, however, as slow growth means serious limits to how fast jobs can be created, social problems addressed, and markets expanded for developing country exports.

Third, governments are finally beginning to take necessary action. The Clinton budget package in the United States is a crucial reform that means that fiscal problem should no longer spiral out of control. Modest budget correction also began in Germany, providing a basis for initial, albeit timid, reduction in interest rates. In Japan, by 1993, a new government was moving to widen the fiscal stimulus to end the severe recession. The challenge is to consolidate and extend these corrective policies, to improve the chances that the 1990s will be a decade of growth rather than stagnation.

Suggested Readings

IMF (1993b) and subsequent semi-annual issues.

2   Adjustment of External Imbalances

The Problem

In the mid- and late-1980s, the large U.S. external deficit and the correspondingly large trade surpluses of Japan and Germany posed a serious threat to the international economy, and measures to reduce these imbalances were high on the agenda of policy cooperation among the major industrial countries. In 1987, the U.S. current account deficit, which includes trade in both goods and services, reached a peak of $167 billion, or 3.7% of GDP. Japan's current account surplus reached $87 billion and had peaked at 4.3% of GDP. Germany's current account surplus reached $40 billion in 1986, or 4½% of GDP (IMF 1993b, p. 164). Although external accounts need not be in exact balance, deficits and surpluses of this size were dangerous for several reasons.

First, there was a risk of a hard landing for the U.S. dollar and the U.S. economy (Marris 1984). Foreigners who continued to lend larger amounts to the United States to cover its external deficit were likely to conclude at some point that the situation could not continue, and they would begin to reduce their exchange rate risk by cutting back their lending. At that point, there would be a risk of a bandwagon effect, with all foreign lenders trying to withdraw their money at the same time. As foreign capital dried up, there would be a rise in the U.S. interest rate because of lesser capital availability and because of the likely efforts of the Federal Reserve to limit a plunge in the dollar. A sharp rise in interest rates would in turn be likely to precipitate a recession. As it turned out, no abrupt rout of the dollar occurred but rather a gradual, though deep, decline over 1985-87.[1] Nonetheless, through the late 1980s, there was a constant risk that the hard-landing scenario would materialize. That risk was a major reason that it was important to reduce the external deficit.

Second, the collapse of the U.S. external accounts in the mid-1980s caused stagnation in the manufacturing sector. Rising imports and falling export sales cut into production volumes and employment. Some estimates place U.S. manufacturing employment losses from the growing trade deficit in the mid-1980s at one million jobs (Branson and Love 1987). Although there were employment gains in other sectors associated with defense spending and a real estate boom, the dislocation for manufacturing was painful.

Third, the adverse impact on U.S. manufacturing triggered rising protectionist pressure. Thus the Trade Act of 1988 incorporated provisions for an aggressive policy of threatening retaliation against countries practicing a pattern of exclusion of imports, through its Super 301, referring to a stronger version of U.S. unfair trade provisions in section 301 of the previous trade laws. U.S. protectionism was especially directed at Japan, which had the largest bilateral surplus against the United States ($56 billion in 1987), as well as the largest overall trade surplus of any country. To many, the Japanese surplus seemed to confirm the view that the Japanese market effectively screened out imports by use of invisible protective barriers.

Fourth, the large U.S. external deficit was fundamentally unsustainable. It meant that each year the net U.S. external asset position was falling by well over $100 billion. Eventually, there would be a major burden from interest and dividends payable on net external debt.

Fifth, it was perverse for large amounts of capital to be flowing from other countries to the richest country in the world. Traditionally, economists have expected the rate of return on capital to be high in developing countries where capital is scarce, and accordingly, they expect net capital flows to be from the rich to the poor countries. However, just the opposite was happening, and not because of fundamentally more productive capital in the United States but because of unsustainable policy distortions.

Causes

The underlying cause of the U.S. external deficit was that the domestic use of resources exceeded the domestic availability of resources. The external deficit represented a resource gap being filled by goods and services from abroad. The resource gap developed in the early 1980s from a rising fiscal deficit and falling private saving. The great Reagan experiment in cutting taxes led to large fiscal deficits. The Laffer-curve proposition that lower tax rates would actually raise revenue because of incentive effects on the volume of activity failed the reality test.[2] At the same time, government spending rose as the result of a major defense buildup. For its part, the household savings rate fell from a typical level of some 8 or 9% of disposable income to as low as 4% for reasons not fully understood but which probably included the perception that rising home valuations satisfied savings needs.

A fiscal deficit amounts to government dissaving. With a rise in government dissaving and a decline in private saving, domestic saving was inadequate to cover domestic investment, which had remained constant at about 17% of GDP. Foreign goods and services were required to cover the difference.

The resource-imbalance origins of the external deficit may be seen by considering national income accounts identities. Gross national product (GNP) may be considered from either the product side (demand) or the factor payments side (supply). On the product side, we have:

$$Y = C + I + G + X - M, \tag{2.1}$$

where Y is GNP, C is consumption, I is investment, G is government purchases, X is exports, and M is imports. All elements on the right-hand side contribute to domestic demand except imports, which enter negatively because imports are an alternative to demand for domestic production.

On the factor payments side, we have:

$$Y = C + S_p + T, \tag{2.2}$$

where C is again consumption, S_p is private saving, and T is tax revenue. Here the right-hand side shows that payments received by factors of production are exhausted by their alternative uses, for consumption, for saving, or in tax payments to the government.

We may subtract equation 2.2 from equation 2.1 to obtain:

$$0 = [I - S_p] + [G - T] + [X - M]. \tag{2.3}$$

Rearranging, we may identify the resource gap as:

$$M - X = [I - S_p] + [G - T]. \tag{2.4}$$

Thus, the excess of imports over exports must equal the excess of investment over private saving plus the excess of government purchases over tax revenue. Considering that the government's fiscal balance is tax revenue minus government spending, or $[T - G]$, and that this balance may be thought of as government's saving, we may write the fiscal balance as: $T - G = S_g$. We may therefore rewrite the resource gap as:

$$M - X = I - S_p - S_g = I - S, \qquad (2.5)$$

where S is the total of all saving, government plus private. Thus, the need for external resources, and therefore the trade gap, equals the excess of domestic investment over total domestic saving, government plus private. For the United States in the 1980s, investment was a relatively constant share of GDP; total saving was falling because of rising government dissaving $(-S_g)$ and falling private saving (S_p), and as a consequence, the trade deficit, $M - X$, had to be rising.

National income accounts tell the relationships that must hold ex post, but they do not directly reveal the mechanisms and forces that lead to these results. In the case of the United States, the transmission mechanism involved a chain that led from fiscal deficits to higher interest rates to a stronger exchange rate and a resulting erosion in the trade balance. This mechanism worked in the following way.

The rise in the fiscal deficit and the decline in private saving put pressure on both the credit and goods markets. In the absence of other influences, both the real interest rate and the rate of inflation would have been expected to rise as a consequence. However, there was an important additional influence. The Federal Reserve, led by Paul Volcker, had already carried out a painful tight-money policy in the period 1979-82 to reduce historically high inflation. The Fed was unwilling to let the fiscal deficits of 1983-84 translate into a renewed outbreak of inflation. Thus, the central bank tightened money once again after having permitted monetary ease to deal with the 1982 recession. Monetary tightening put further upward pressure on the interest rate.

The result was that, in the mid-1980s, the United States experienced the unusual policy mix identified with Reaganomics: loose fiscal policy combined with tight monetary policy. This mix had the effect of causing high interest rates. The high interest rate, in turn, was the key link in the chain from high fiscal deficits to a large trade deficit.

In this chain, the high interest rate induced foreign investors to place funds in the U.S. capital market. As they sought to convert their deutschemarks and yen into dollars, these investors bid up the price of the dollar. The strong dollar made U.S. exports more expensive to foreigners and imports cheaper to Americans. After a time lag, exports stagnated and imports surged as a result.[3]

In analyzing the impact of the exchange rate on the trade balance, it is important to distinguish between the nominal exchange rate and the real exchange rate. It is the *real* rate, after deducting inflation in both the home and foreign country, that exerts an effective price signal that influences the trade response.

The real exchange rate of the dollar against, for example, the yen, is defined as:

$$ER^* = \{[\yen/\$]/[P_J/P_U]\},\qquad\qquad (2.6)$$

where ¥/$ is the nominal exchange rate (e.g., 200 yen per dollar), P_J is a price index for Japanese goods, and P_U is a price index for U.S. goods. Typically, the wholesale price index is the most relevant for traded goods, but other indexes, including consumer prices and comparative wage rates, are also used.

Essentially the real exchange rate removes the illusory influence of both U.S. and foreign inflation to determine what is happening to the real purchasing power of the dollar compared with that of the foreign currency. The real exchange rate appreciates when there are more real units of foreign exchange obtainable for a real unit of the domestic currency. That outcome can result from a rise in the nominal exchange rate (from the U.S. standpoint, an increase in the number of yen per dollar) or from a rise in domestic (U.S.) inflation relative to foreign (Japanese) inflation with an unchanged nominal exchange rate (yen per dollar).[4] Thus, in equation 2.6), for a given nominal yen/dollar rate, a higher price level in Japan (P_J) reduces the real value of the dollar (ER^*), but a higher price level in the United States (P_U) increases it.

So far, the transmission chain includes the following links: a rising resource gap places pressure on the domestic capital market, causing a rise in interest rates. A policy mismatch of loose fiscal policy and tight monetary policy further contributes to the rise in the interest rate. The higher interest rate attracts capital from abroad. The entry of foreign capital bids up the dollar. This causal chain was responsible for most of the rise in the real value of the dollar by about 40% from 1980 to the first quarter of 1985.

The final link in the chain concerns the impact of the dollar on the incentive to import or export. The real exchange rate for the dollar is essentially a price for imports and exports. When the dollar is strong, imports are cheap, and exports are costly to foreign purchasers. When the dollar rose in real terms by 40%, the result was analogous to imposing a 40% subsidy on imports and a 40% tax on exports. The predictable response to this sharp change in the price incentive was a decline in exports and a rise in imports.

The trade equation chain in the causal link is thus:

$$M - X = M(\overset{+}{ER^*}, \overset{+}{Y_D}) - X(\overline{ER^*}, \overset{+}{Y_F}], \tag{2.7}$$

where Y is GDP, and subscripts D and F refer to the domestic and foreign countries. Imports are a function of the real exchange rate and the level of domestic demand from economic activity, while exports are a function of the real exchange rate and the level of foreign demand stemming from foreign economic activity. The signs above the real exchange rate terms indicate that a stronger real exchange rate for the dollar increases U.S. imports (+) and decreases U.S. exports (−). Similarly, the positive signs above the GDP growth variables show that domestic growth increases imports and that foreign growth increases exports.

In sum, the transmission mechanism from the resource imbalance (e.g., potential or incipient resource imbalance) to the trade gap (that is, actual or realized) may be summarized as:

$$\uparrow[\text{Resource Use} - \text{Resource Availability}] \tag{2.8}$$
$$\rightarrow \uparrow i \rightarrow \uparrow ER^* \rightarrow \uparrow M, \downarrow X \rightarrow \uparrow[\text{ External Deficit}],$$

where the upward arrow indicates a rise, the downward arrow a decline, and the arrow from left to right a causal force.

From 1980 to the first quarter of 1985, the real value of the dollar rose by 40%. This increase reflected not only the direct effect shown in the transmission mechanism of equation 2.8, but it incorporated what scientists would call a positive feedback and economists, a bandwagon effect. In speculative markets of all types, strong trends in expectations tend to develop. Stock market pundits use the phrase, "the trend is your friend." Formally, this dynamic is one of extrapolative expectations, whereby investors extrapolate the recent past trend into the future.[5]

There are strong indications that this bandwagon effect accounted for at least the last 10% of the 40% rise in the dollar in the mid-1980s. The dollar rose by about this much at the tail end of the rising-dollar phase, the last quarter of 1984 and the first quarter of 1985, despite the fact that there was no further rise in the U.S. interest rate in that period to attract further capital. Extrapolative expectations thus added positive, or reinforcing, feedback to the rise of the dollar that was caused initially by the direct influence of the rising resource gap and rising interest rate.

The bandwagon effect meant there was a bubble of dollar strength unexplained by the fundamentals of the first quarter of 1985. Like all bubbles, this one burst. The puncturing event may have been strong intervention by Germany's central bank to raise the deutschemark against the dollar in February of 1985. In any event, the dollar then began to trend downward through the second and third quarters of 1985 but at a moderate pace rather than in a collapse as feared by those concerned with a hard landing.

Policy Response

In September of 1985, finance ministers from the major industrial countries (Group of Seven) met at the Plaza Hotel in New York and agreed to joint intervention in currency markets in order to reduce the dollar to levels more compatible with U.S. external adjustment. They had the trend in their favor, as the dollar had been declining since March, but there was little assurance that it would continue to do so on its own. The historic decision was prompted in part by intense protectionist pressure in the U.S. Congress. In part, it reflected a shift in the U.S. economic team. Donald Regan as treasury secretary and Beryl Sprinkel as undersecretary had favored a market knows best approach and extolled the strong dollar as a sign of U.S. economic strength. Their successors, James Baker as secretary and David Mulford as undersecretary, constituted a team with less ideological orientation and with more inclination toward fixing obvious problems.

Ideally intervention would have been only a complementary action to more fundamental adjustment through aggressive reduction of the U.S. fiscal deficit. A lower fiscal deficit would have reduced pressure on the U.S. capital market and enabled the Federal Reserve to relax monetary policy without fear of inflation; both effects would have reduced the interest rate. A lower interest rate would have lessened the attraction of the U.S. capital market to foreign capital, and with fewer bidders for the dollar, the price of U.S. currency would have fallen, adding more fundamental pressure for a lower dollar to the effect of central bank intervention.

The United States, however, did not adopt major fiscal adjustment. There was an important tax reform in 1986, but whereas it improved efficiency by reducing marginal rates and widening the base, it did not raise overall revenue.[6] Congress was aware of the fiscal problem. In 1985, it passed the Gramm-Rudman-Hollings bill mandating an elimination of the federal deficit (then about $220 billion) over a five-year period. The bill provided that the president could sequester spending if Congress did not directly reduce spending programs. However, these spending cutbacks imposed by the president had to be proportionate in both defense and domestic spending, and key items, including social security and interest on debt, were exempt. As the Reagan administration was unwilling to cut military spending, it was unprepared to invoke the witholding of spending permitted under the law, yet congressional Democrats were unwilling to reduce the deficit by cutting domestic spending alone.

Trade Response

U.S. Export Boom

From 1980 to 1987, U.S. exports remained almost unchanged in a range of $225 billion to $250 billion, while non-oil imports more than doubled from $180 billion to $380 billion. The trade and current account deficits peaked in 1987. There was great public frustration by then because, fully two years after the dollar had started to decline, the trade deficit was larger than ever. Some economists began developing theories of hysterisis: a fundamental change in the relationship of a dependent variable (trade) to the independent variable (the exchange rate). Then in 1988–89, there was a massive increase in exports, which rose by about 45% to approximately $360 billion. The current account deficit fell from over $160 billion to about $100 billion by 1989–90 or from over 3½% of GDP to under 2%.

The reason for this delayed response was simple: for the U.S. economy there is a lag of about two years from the exchange rate signal to trade response. There are at least three components to the lag: (a) perception, the market decides whether a new exchange rate is persistent or transitory; (b) decision, firms take new purchasing decisions based on the new prices; and (c) delivery, orders must be filled and shipped. Moreover, in the first year after a dollar depreciation, there is a J-curve worsening of the dollar size of the trade deficit. The physical volume of imports has not yet responded to the new price, yet some of the imports are invoiced in deutschemarks, yen, or francs so that the dollar cost when the bill comes due is higher because of the depreciation. With dollar import values temporarily rising and exports still in the lag phase of response, the dollar trade balance goes down before it turns up (hence J-curve).

Dollar Resurgent

Despite the improvement by 1989 and 1990 when the current account deficit fell to $90 billion, projection models indicated that there could be a renewed widening of the U.S. external deficit, with a return to the range of $150 billion by 1992–93 (Cline 1989b). The outlook was thus for a U-shaped curve for the current account deficit. The proximate reason was that the dollar had started to rise again. Whereas the dollar had fallen from its highs of 3.25 deutschemark (DM) per dollar and 258 yen per dollar in the first quarter of 1985 to lows of 1.58 DM and 123 yen per dollar at the end of 1987, the U.S. currency rebounded to 1.95 DM and 144 yen per dollar by the second quarter of 1989, and the dollar kept rising against the yen to 155 by the second quarter of 1990. Faster inflation in the United States than in Germany and Japan meant that the rebound of the dollar was even larger in real terms.

The related and more fundamental reason for this widening external deficit was that the United States was not sufficiently reducing its fiscal deficit and thus not addressing the problem of excess resource use. The trade and macroeconomic models tended to show as a rule of thumb that a $1 billion reduction in the fiscal deficit would result in a $500 million decline in the trade deficit, a 50-percent rule.[7] The fiscal deficit did fall from about $210 billion in 1986 to about $140 billion in 1989, but in view of the 50-percent rule, this $70 billion budget correction was far too small to generate the adjustment of over $100 billion needed to cut the U.S. current account deficit to a sustainable level of about $60 billion, or 1% of GDP.

Although the dollar turned back up after 1987, it had needed to go down still further by perhaps 10% to achieve a target current account deficit of 1% of GDP. A still lower dollar would have placed the currency well below its level in 1980 when the U.S. external accounts were balanced. By the beginning of the 1990s, there were at least two reasons why a lower dollar was needed to achieve the same balance as a decade earlier. First, the accumulation of U.S. external debt meant that the net asset position had fallen so that net capital earnings could not be expected to contribute as much to the current account balance as before and so that eventually net asset earnings were likely to turn negative because of net foreign debt. The current account depends on both the trade balance and the balance on services, including capital services (interest and dividends). Second, the price of oil had fallen sharply from 1980 to 1990, especially in real terms. Europe and Japan depend on imported oil, whereas the United States supplies half of its own oil so that lower oil prices benefit Europe and Japan proportionately more than the United States. Accordingly, the real exchange rates should be expected to appreciate for Japan and for European countries when the price of oil declines; by implication, that for the United States should depreciate. Third, although more questionably, the United States may have a structural tendency to need a declining real exchange rate over time because imports tend to grow faster than exports in response to economic growth, as discussed below.

Recessionary Adjustment

Despite the predicted U-curve, by 1990–91 the U.S. current account deficit had shown further improvement rather than beginning a rebound along the upward leg of the U, and the deficit fell to $66 billion in 1992. The principal reason was that the U.S. economy had gone into recession, with growth of only 1.2% in 1990 and −0.7% in 1991. The shortfall from potential growth of 2.5% amounted to a cumulative 4.5% points for the two years. Slower growth reduces imports (see equation 2.7 above), and for the United States, a one-percentage-point reduction in growth reduces the current account deficit by $15 billion (Cline 1989b). After taking account of somewhat slower than normal growth abroad as well, the net effect was probably to cut about $50 billion off the U.S. current account deficit.

Recession is a costly way to purchase external adjustment. Nonetheless, if the recovery is sluggish, the new GDP trendline never catches up with the old trendline, and the external adjustment purchased is largely permanent. However, in 1993, the U.S. current account deficit rebounded sharply to an expected $112 billion, and the International Monetary Fund predicted that the deficit would reach $130 billion by 1994 (IMF 1993b). A somewhat weaker U-curve was thus back on the agenda, despite the illusion of recessionary adjustment in 1990–91.

There were two reasons why the U.S. recession failed to lock in a lower external deficit. First, recession soon spread to Europe and Japan, depressing the demand for U.S. exports. Second, in 1993, the dollar rose substantially against the currencies of Europe and Canada, by more than enough to offset the decline of the dollar against the Japanese yen. The combined effects of feeble foreign activity and a more expensive dollar meant that a widening trade gap was in the pipeline through 1994. Even so, a current account deficit of $130 billion in 1994 would amount to about 2% of GDP, still only about half the size of the external gap reached in 1987.

Did the Adjustment Process Work?

Figure 2.1 shows that the massive current account imbalances of the three largest industrial countries in 1986–87 returned to much smaller levels by 1989–90.[8] So, at least temporarily, the external adjustment process worked. However, it is reasonable to ask whether adjustment worked as economists had expected or whether other forces were responsible for the sharp reduction in the external imbalances.

In late 1990, the Institute for International Economics held a conference to examine this question (Bergsten, ed., 1991). In a paper for that conference, I found that the U.S. current account had behaved approximately as the mainstream models had predicted (Cline 1991c). The im-

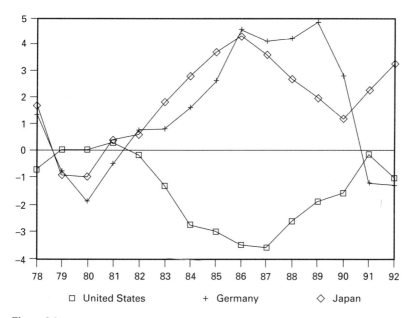

Figure 2.1
Current account, G-3 countries (percent of GDP)

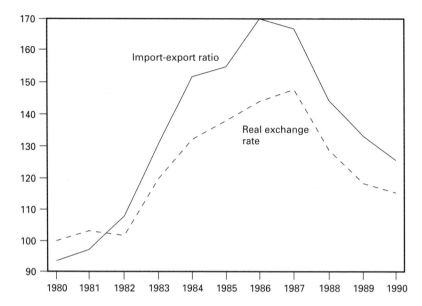

Note: The exchange rate measure is the International Monetary Fund's multilateral effective index for the United States deflated by unit value of exports; it is plotted with a two-year lead.

Figure 2.2
United States: Real effective exchange rate and its ratio of nonoil imports to nonagricultural exports, 1978–90

pact of the real exchange rate on the trade balance is graphically evident in figure 2.2. Here, the solid line shows the ratio of non-oil imports to exports (percentages). The dotted line shows an index of the real value of the dollar (trade-weighted, deflating by unit value of exports, with 1978 = 100). The exchange rate observations are plotted with a two-year lead so that the figure for 1987 refers to the import/export ratio for 1987 and the real exchange rate of 1985.

There is an unmistakable correlation between the strength of the dollar and the import/export ratio and thus the trade deficit. Moreover, the exchange rate signal comes first so that the causation runs from exchange rate to trade performance. This simple test confirms the standard view that the real exchange rate influences the trade balance. Of course, the full models include other variables as well, particularly economic growth in the United States and abroad. An important finding of tests run with these models is that if the dollar had stayed at its 1985 high, the U.S. current account deficit could have soared to the range of

$300 billion or even more by the early 1990s. Thus, the adjustment is much larger than it at first appears. Instead of narrowing the current account deficit from $160 billion to a range of $60–$100 billion, the decline of the dollar reduced the deficit by a much larger amount from a much higher baseline that otherwise would have been reached.

Do Exchange Rates Influence Trade?

There are perhaps two fundamental arguments that allege that exchange rates do not affect the trade balance. Economists Ronald McKinnon of Stanford University and Robert Mundell of Columbia University are leading exponents of this critical view. The first argument is that it is impossible to affect the real exchange rate by changing the nominal exchange rate. According to this argument, if the U.S. dollar depreciates by, say, 10%, there will subsequently be an induced domestic inflation of an extra 10% that offsets the depreciation and leaves the real exchange rate unchanged. Unfortunately for this contention, the historical record is to the contrary. Consider figure 2.2. In 1984–85, when the nominal dollar was high, so was the real dollar (shown in the graph for the years 1986–87 because of the two-year lead). The increase from 1978 was a massive 40%. If the argument is correct that nominal changes in the exchange rate have no effect on the real rate, then the exchange rate curve in figure 2.2 should be a horizontal line at a constant value. Instead, there are large swings in the real exchange rate.

The second argument against the mainstream view that exchange rates matter is an appeal to the national income accounts identity in equation 2.5 above. The identity states that the external deficit equals the excess of domestic investment over domestic saving. Some economists, therefore, argue that the exchange rate cannot change the trade balance because the trade balance is determined by the more fundamental influences of investment and saving. The flaw in this approach is that it ignores the fact that there is a system of equations that must hold, not just the I-S identity. The crucial other equation in the system is the behavioral equation relating imports and exports to the real exchange rate and to domestic and foreign growth, equation 2.7 above. It is a mistake to think that the income identity, equation 2.5, is strictly independent or exogenous and that the exchange rate-trade equation, equation 2.7, is strictly dependent or endogenous.

Instead, changes in the real exchange rate can change the levels of saving and investment so that causation runs in both directions between these two equations in the system. The discussion above recounted how causation had run from a large fiscal deficit (high potential I-S gap) to the exchange rate and thence to the trade balance in the mid-1980s. However, there is also scope for causation to run from a change in the exchange rate to a change in the I-S balance.

The simplest way to demonstrate this causal influence of the real exchange rate is to recall elementary Keynesian income determination. In that analysis, the level of saving is sensitive to the level of income. Higher income causes a more than proportionate rise in saving. In contrast, investment is relatively unresponsive to the current level of income in the Keynesian model. Consider the implications for the influence of the real exchange rate on the external balance. Suppose that a surplus country, such as Japan, experiences a real appreciation of the exchange rate. The consequence is an incipient reduction in exports and increase in imports as the country becomes less competitive internationally. The initial reduction in the trade balance causes a reduction in aggregate demand and thus national income. The lower income causes a substantial drop in saving but little reduction, if any, in investment. Therefore, the excess of saving over investment will decline and so will the external surplus. This conclusion is reinforced when government fiscal balance is considered because a falling GDP tends to widen the government deficit as a result of automatic stabilizers (unemployment insurance) and lower tax revenue. The real appreciation of the exchange rate and the initial reduction in the trade surplus and income thus cause a sensitive reduction in both private and government saving but little reduction in investment, causing the surplus of saving over investment to fall.

As a result, a real appreciation of the exchange rate in equation 2.7 will have altered the saving-investment gap in equation 2.5, through the vehicle of Keynesian income and saving determination. Although lower income in turn will cause a reduction in imports and thus some moderation of the initial reduction in a trade surplus, this offset will be small because most spending is on domestic goods, including nontradables. When income falls by the amount of the initial reduction in the trade balance, the reduction in spending will be primarily on domestic goods, while imports will fall only by the marginal propensity to import multiplied by the reduction in national income. For a large country, the average import ratio to GDP is usually about 10%, and even if imports are more sensitive at the margin, one would expect the offset from falling imports to be only about one-fifth of the initial reduction in the trade balance and national income level. Moreover, if the reduction in income level pushes the economy substantially below full employment, there may be an induced policy response that increases government spending. This induced stimulus will partially or fully eliminate the import-reducing side effect of the initial income decline.

This analysis reveals that, on the basis of theory, the saving-investment gap is not exogenous and therefore that changes in the real exchange rate can have an effect on the trade balance. What about actual experience? Consider figure 2.2 once again. If it were true that an exogenous investment-saving gap predetermines the trade balance and the exchange rate has no effect, then in the graph, there should be no relationship whatsoever between the real exchange rate curve and the curve for subsequent trade balance behavior. Instead, the import/export curve fits the real exchange rate curve like a glove. The facts thus confirm the theory that the exchange rate matters.

In an overview paper prepared for the 1990 Institute for International Economics conference, Krugman (1991) set forth a useful conceptual framework for the debate on the influence of the exchange rate on trade. He identified three alternative views of the external deficit. The first school was that of the mainstream Massachusetts Avenue model, so named because the National Bureau of Economic Research is located on Massachusetts Avenue in Cambridge, Massachusetts (near the economics departments at MIT and Harvard), while the Brookings Institution and the Institute for International Economics are located on Massachusetts Avenue in Washington, D.C. This centrist model consists of two core equations. First:

$$TB = f(\overline{ER}^*_{t-k}; \overset{-}{g_D}; \overset{+}{g_F}), \tag{2.9}$$

where TB is the trade balance, ER^* is the real exchange rate, g is the growth rate, subscript $t - k$ refers to k years prior to the present year t, and subscripts D and F are domestic and foreign, respectively. This equation is essentially the same as equation 2.7 above. Again, the sign above the variable shows the direction of its impact.

The second equation is for the exchange rate:

$$ER^* = h(i^*_D - i^*_F), \tag{2.10}$$

where i* is the real (inflation-adjusted) interest rate. Thus, the real dollar appreciates when the real interest differential between the U.S. and foreign capital markets rises.

Krugman's second school is that of the structuralists. This group sees technology and other structural factors as dominant and attributes little, if any, influence to the price signal from the real exchange rate in determining trade outcomes.

Krugman's third school is that of the advocates of "schmoo theory." In the U.S. cartoon strip "Little Abner," there was a loveable animal shaped like a snowman and called a schmoo. It could be infinitely divided up for use in whatever sizes were desired. In economic terms, it was strictly homogeneous and divisible. Krugman describes a third group of economists as treating output like schmoos because in this school of thought, output in the United States is considered identical to and easily interchangeable with output in the rest of the world.

This third approach judges that a trade deficit can be easily eliminated by reducing domestic absorption, or spending. More U.S. goods will be left over, and foreigners will buy them up readily because, like schmoos, the U.S. goods are perfectly interchangeable with, say, French goods. Schmoos have no nationality. Under these conditions, a fiscal cutback is sufficient to achieve adjustment with no change in the exchange rate and thus no price incentive. Fiscal adjustment achieves what John Williamson has called immaculate transfer of resources abroad and thus external adjustment as well.

Krugman rejects the schmoo school, associated today with U.S. economists Robert Mundell and Ronald McKinnon. His reason goes back to a debate held decades ago between John Maynard Keynes and Bertil Ohlin, a debate later described as between the elasticity and absorption approaches. The central issue in the debate is whether a real exchange rate depreciation is necessary or helpful to the adjustment process.

Krugman returns to the Keynesian diagnosis that simple reduction of absorption by country A with no exchange rate change is likely to cause unemployment. The alternative (Ohlin) view requires a strong, unrealistic assumption about spending patterns. The traditional debate was about the transfer problem: whether country A making a financial transfer to country B could carry out the corresponding increase in its (A's) net exports of goods and services without having to devalue the real exchange rate. Ohlin argued that, when country A raises taxes to finance the transfer payment, the public in A will reduce consumption and that, when the public in country B receives the transfer, it will increase consumption. The excess goods in A will just equal the new shortfall of goods in B, with no need for devaluation.

However, this felicitous (immaculate) transfer would require the extreme assumption that country B has a marginal propensity to import that is equal to country A's marginal propensity to consume domestically. Suppose the transfer is \$100 million. Then country A frees up \$100 $\times MPC_A$ goods at home, and country B purchases an additional \$100 $\times MPM_B$ goods, where MP is marginal propensity, C is domestic consumption, and M is imports. Clearly, the goods released in country A will only be matched by the new demand for imports in B if $MPC_A = MPM_B$. But this is highly unlikely. People in country A will tend to spend most of their income on goods produced in A so that MPC_A is high. People in country B will similarly tend to spend most of their income on home goods, whereas their marginal propensity to spend on imports will be considerably lower. Therefore, it is almost certain that $MPC_A > MPM_B$. It follows that it is almost certain that the attempt to make the transfer without the help of an exchange rate depreciation to make A's goods more attractive to customers in country B will be an excess of goods in country A because the new sales to country B will fall considerably short of the cutback in domestic consumption in A.

The attempt to correct an external deficit by reducing domestic spending without devaluation is analogous to this transfer problem, although without an initial financial transfer from A to B. When country A reduces its home use of its products and offers them to country B, there is a tendency for the price of A's exports to fall—a terms of trade decline. This price change gives country B a higher real income. At higher income, B consumes more. Only if B's marginal propensity to import is equal to A's marginal propensity to consume domestically will B readily buy up the exports offered by A. If so, the trade deficit of A will smoothly decline with just a minimal change in terms of trade.

When the goods are much less interchangeable, country B spends most of the increase in its real income on its home goods, importing relatively little from country A. Under these conditions, the cutback in domestic absorption in country A translates into a decline in production rather than an increase in exports. Hence, there is a need for real exchange rate depreciation to help out the adjustment process. Otherwise, external adjustment at a fixed real exchange rate will end up imposing unnecessary recession on the adjusting country.

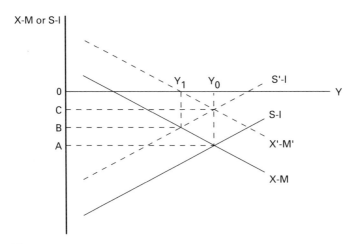

Figure 2.3
External adjustment with and without depreciation

Overall, Krugman finds that the evidence supports the Massachusetts Avenue, or mainstream, school rather than the schmooist school
whereby adjustment could occur smoothly with no change in real exchange rate. He also allows some element of validity for the structuralist school, however, because long-term trends suggest that a real
depreciation of about 1 to 2% per year is required in order to keep U.S.
trade in balance.

The importance of change in the real exchange rate in contributing
a price signal for adjustment, facilitating the demand level adjustment,
and avoiding unnecessary recession may be seen in figure 2.3. Here
the country's national income, Y, is on the horizontal axis. Resources
are fully employed at level Y_0. There is an upward sloping curve relating the excess of saving over investment (on the vertical axis) to national income because households tend to save more as their income
goes up, while the amount of investment firms plan to undertake is
relatively fixed (as discussed above). Conversely, the curve showing
the excess of exports over imports is downward sloping. At higher
income, the country has a larger demand for imports and a lower trade
surplus. At equilibrium income, the savings-investment gap (S-I) must
just equal the trade gap (X-M) by the accounting identity in equation
2.5) above.

The country begins with a trade deficit of OA at equilibrium income
Y_0. If the government relies on the absorption (schmoo) approach alone
and increases taxes so that total national saving rises to S', the saving

minus investment curve rises to S'-I, and the new equilibrium income occurs at the new intersection with the X-M curve, at Y_1. This income level is well below full employment, and recession occurs. However, if fiscal tightening can be accompanied by a real depreciation of the exchange rate, there will be a shift in the X-M curve to X'-M'. At any given level of income, exports will be higher and imports lower because the real exchange rate has depreciated and caused a price incentive to reduce imports and increase exports. The new equilibrium income occurs where the new S'-I curve intersects the new X'-M' curve. If the right amount of real depreciation is combined with the fiscal (absorption) adjustment, income can be restored to the full employment level Y_0. Moreover, the amount of external adjustment is increased as well because the remaining trade deficit OC is smaller than the trade deficit OB obtained with an absorption cutback unaccompanied by real exchange rate depreciation.

This analysis obviously has implications for the exchange rate regime. A regime of rigidly fixed exchange rates will tend to be recessionary because adjustment has no exchange rate price signal to assist demand restraint in the adjustment process and adjustments will tend to work as shown in the shift from equilibrium Y_0 to Y_1. If instead the real exchange rate can change, it will be easier to maintain full employment while accomplishing external adjustment.

Against this benefit of flexible exchange rates, a rigidly fixed exchange rate may have the advantage of providing an optimal currency area, especially for small countries whose home currency has a command over a small (home) market only. Moreover, there may be macroeconomic benefits from using a rigidly fixed exchange rate as an anchor against inflationary expectations. These are the central trade-offs for European countries considering the adoption of a single currency in European Monetary Union (EMU) (see chapter 7). They are also relevant for such countries as Mexico and Argentina, which are attempting to achieve price stabilization and external adjustment at the same time. The implications of figure 2.3 tend to reinforce the concern that the move to the EMU may be biased toward economic contraction because of the loss of the exchange rate instrument as a nonrecessionary means of adjustment.

There is an important caveat to the conclusion that real exchange rate depreciation effectively contributes to adjustment of an external deficit. The analysis here has assumed that one country is acting in isolation. If instead several major countries simultaneously attempt competitive devaluation, as occurred in the 1930s, none of them will experience the trade balance improvement otherwise expected. It is thus an implicit rule of the international adjustment game that deficit countries should be expected to employ real exchange rate depreciation, whereas surplus countries tolerate, or actively seek, real exchange rate appreciation instead of resorting to competitive depreciation. The same considerations mean that, if several countries are in unemployment, they will need to apply domestic fiscal and monetary stimulus to address their unemployment problem rather than relying on a beggar-thy-neighbor strategy of real depreciation to increase income and employment through exporting unemployment.

Overall, the conclusion is that, in the 1980s and early 1990s, external adjustment worked for the United States about as the models would have predicted. However, as noted above, the actual decline in the U.S. external deficit was larger than would have occurred without the 1990–91 recession, so although the models worked, policy did not work as successfully as it might have. Better policy would have sought to avoid the recession and would have carried out the same external adjustment with greater real depreciation and more fiscal correction.

Adjustment in Germany and Japan

Germany and Japan ran extremely large external surpluses in the mid-1980s, and the international adjustment process meant a need to reduce these surpluses just as it required lower U.S. external deficits. In principle, surpluses provide capital for the rest of the world, and in that sense, they can be desirable when the constraint on global growth is scarce capital. However, high trade surpluses can also cause trade friction that results in protection. Moreover, if the world economy is headed toward recession, the high-surplus countries are depriving other economies of demand that otherwise could keep these economies operating at full employment. By importing too little from other countries and exporting too many goods to them, high-surplus countries in effect cause other countries to curtail their own production.

Germany's external adjustment was long delayed. The nation's current account surplus was on the order of $50 billion annually for the whole period 1986–90 or about 4½% of GDP (the level for Japan's surplus at its peak). Ironically, this surplus was sharply higher than the level of about $15 billion annually in 1984–85 when the deutschemark had been much weaker against the dollar. Essentially what happened

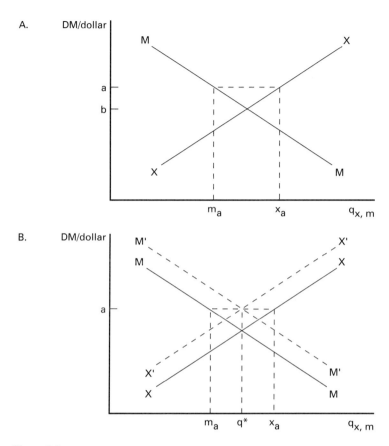

Figure 2.4
Impact of reunification on Germany's trade balance

was that there was relatively little response in German trade to the dollar devaluation, but the same broad magnitude of the trade surplus with Germany's main European partners suddenly looked much larger when converted from DM into dollars at the postdevaluation exchange rates of about 1.5 DM rather than 2.5 to 3 DM per dollar.

Then, in 1991, Germany's external surplus experienced a massive turnaround, to a deficit of $20 billion annually. However, it was a structural shock that precipitated this change rather than a smooth international adjustment process. Figure 2.4, panel A, shows that, in principle, the appreciation of the DM from level a to level b would eliminate the trade surplus, which initially stands at amount $x_a - m_a$. There is an upward-sloping export supply curve (XX) because, when there are more DM per dollar, German firms are more interested in exporting for a given world dollar price. The import curve, MM, is downward sloping because, at a larger number of DM per dollar (depreciated DM), imports are more expensive to German consumers.

Figure 2.4, panel B, shows what really caused German adjustment, however. The economic shock of reunification with East Germany suddenly shifted the import demand curve outward to $M'M'$ because there was increased need for imports to meet East German requirements. At the same time, the export supply curve shifted backward to the left to $X'X'$. At any given exchange rate, West German firms now had less available to export to the world market because they were diverting goods to the East German market. With no change in the real exchange rate from the 1986–89 period, the external surplus suddenly collapsed. Thus, in figure 2.4(B), exports fall from x_a to q^*, and imports rise from m_a to q^*, eliminating the trade surplus even though the exchange rate remains unchanged at "a."

In Japan, the adjustment process seemed to have worked by 1990, when the current account surplus had fallen from its 1987 peak of about $90 billion to only $35 billion. The surplus fell from a peak of 4.3% of GDP in 1986 to only 1.2% of GDP in 1990. Some Japanese economists noted by 1990 that the surplus that year was lower than could be explained by their models (Yoshitomi 1991). However, few expected the sharp rebound in the current account surplus that took place in 1991 (to about $75 billion) and 1992 (to about $115 billion).

My international trade model did capture the low Japanese surplus of 1990, and as early as April of 1991, it predicted the dramatic rebound of the Japanese surplus likely to occur in 1991–92 (Cline 1991a). The influences identified by the model included the following. First, the price of oil imports had been abnormally high in 1990 because of the Gulf War so that a decline of about $10 billion in import costs could be expected from normalization by 1991 and after. Second, the yen had been weak in 1989–90, as discussed above. Accordingly, applying the two-year lag, it could be expected that there would be a strong increase in the trade surplus as exports responded to the depreciated real exchange rate and imports were discouraged by it.[10]

One reason for the strong tendency toward external surplus in the Japanese economy is the gap factor, the large initial difference between imports and exports. Thus, in 1989, exports were about one-third higher than imports ($275 billion versus $210 billion). It was thus necessary for the growth rate of imports to be one-third greater than that of exports just to keep the absolute gap from widening. Moreover, Japan was building up larger and larger external financial assets as its current account surpluses accumulated over time, and the interest and dividend earnings on these assets were making a growing contribution to the current account surplus.

In view of the resurgence of the large Japanese surplus, it may be said that there was a policy failure in the 1988–90 period. There should have been an effort to avoid the depreciation of the yen against the dollar that occurred after 1987 and through mid-1990. That excursion of the yen in the wrong direction for purposes of correcting external imbalances meant an unnecessary return to megasurpluses. Indeed, correction of this policy failure would have had the important benefit of reducing the size of the Japanese bubble because monetary policy in the late 1980s would not have been as expansionary if there had not been an attempt to weaken the yen against the dollar after the Louvre.

By 1993, Japan's current account surplus rose to an estimated $135 billion or about 3% of GDP (IMF 1993b). In view of the fact that the German surplus had disappeared and that the U.S. current account deficit had moderated to the range of about 1½% of GDP by 1992–93, it appeared that the principal remaining case of external imbalance was that of Japan. Moreover, the argument that Japan's surplus was good for a capital-starved world looked increasingly doubtful in view of the slide of the world economy toward stagnation or recession. Again, when there is unemployment, a neighbor's surplus is a hindrance rather than a help because it is demand that is scarce rather than capital supply.

As discussed in chapter 4, the sharp rise of the yen in 1992 and especially 1993 set the stage for a correction of Japan's outsized surplus by 1994 and after. If this reversal occurs, it will be another confirmation of the role of the exchange rate in achieving external adjustment.

Exchange Rate Regime

The lesson of the 1980s was that, under the floating exchange rate regime, the exchange rate can become seriously misaligned and cause serious economic damage and risks. As noted, nearly one million American jobs in manufacturing may have been lost in the mid-1980s because of the overvalued dollar and not surprisingly protectionist pressures escalated as a result. The exchange rate is an important matter of concern for policy, and it is a mistake to be indifferent about the level of the exchange rate. Seemingly learned by the time of the Plaza Agreement, this lesson was partially forgotten later as the yen once again became undervalued in 1989–90. By 1989–90, authorities in the G-7 countries had lost their focus on equilibrium levels for exchange rates and were sitting idly by as the Japanese yen was weakening and the dollar strengthening.

The Plaza Agreement was a first step toward disciplining exchange rates and seeking greater adherence to long-term equilibrium values. Intervention in the exchange market was the Plaza mechanism. That policy raised the question of whether intervention really makes any difference.

The dominant view on this matter was established by the Jurgensen report to the major industrial countries at the beginning of the 1980s. That report concluded that intervention only has a lasting effect on the exchange rate if intervention alters the money supply. The basic idea is that the exchange rate is a price between two moneys (e.g., dollar and deutschemark). This price is unlikely to change unless there is an increase in the supply of one money or a decrease in the supply of the other.

However, typically, central banks are highly reluctant to allow intervention for exchange rate stabilization purposes to affect their underlying monetary policy, which has a more fundamental task, avoiding inflation and maintaining economic activity. So central banks usually sterilize intervention by taking offsetting monetary measures. Thus, suppose the Bundesbank intervenes to support the dollar. It pays deutschemarks to investors in exchange for dollars placed into the government's exchange reserves. With more deutschmarks in investors' hands, the German money supply increases. In the absence of offsetting action, there could be an inflationary result. The Bundesbank thus sterilizes the intervention by selling government bonds to the market. As investors pay deutschemarks for the bonds, the money supply returns to its original level. If two propositions are combined— sterilized intervention does not work, and central bankers do not like unsterilized intervention—the conclusion might seem to be that there is little if any role for intervention.

However, more recent studies using previously unavailable central bank data have demonstrated persuasively that the principal coordinated interventions of the central banks in the 1980s were usually successful in reversing an undesired trend of the exchange rate. Figure 2.5 is reproduced from one of these studies (Catte, Galli, and Rebecchini

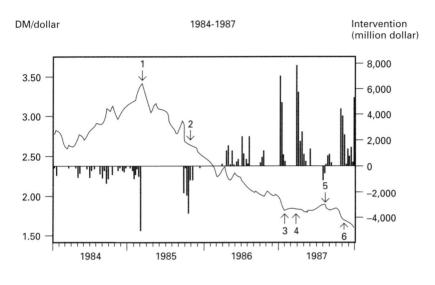

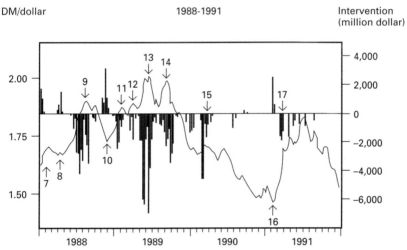

Note: Weekly data. Intervention is defined as ($ purchases – DM purchases)/2.
Source: Catte, Galli, and Rebecchini 1992.

Figure 2.5
DM/$ exchange rate and the intervention by G-3 central banks

1992). The figure shows that most of the seventeen interventions coincided with turning points at which the exchange rate reversed direction as desired. Thus, the Plaza Agreement intervention in late 1985 (number 2) reversed a temporary rebound in the dollar, and the interventions to support the dollar after the Louvre Accord of 1987 (numbers 6, 7, and 8) had the desired effect—indeed, too much success in view of the excessive strength of the dollar again by 1989.

Similarly, Dominguez and Frankel (1993) have shown that exchange market intervention does affect the exchange rate. Using data for Germany, the United States, and Switzerland, the authors find that intervention is particularly effective when it is publicly announced and coordinated among the monetary authorities of the principal countries. Indeed, the announcement effect alone can move the exchange rate by 1½ to 3% (p. 133). The additional contribution of actual change in the money supply from an unsterilized intervention is much smaller.

This finding shows that the key to the impact of intervention is its effect on private market expectations about the future exchange rate. This implication is consistent with the fact that the magnitudes of the interventions, typically on the order of $100 million to $200 million in a given day of a particular intervention effort, are dwarfed by the volume of normal transactions in the exchange market, which may be on the order of $1 trillion daily (Dominguez and Frankel 1993, p.89).

The critical role of expectations is also consistent with the experience that intervention does not work when authorities are attempting to defend an unsustainable rate. Thus, the efforts to defend the parities of the Italian lire and the pound sterling against the deutschemark in the currency crisis of September 1992 were futile because the cumulative excess of inflation in Italy and the United Kingdom above German inflation, as well as large current account deficits, meant that the market did not consider it credible that the exchange rate parities could be sustained indefinitely. In constrast, when the yen moved from 125 to 105 against the dollar in the first half of 1993, providing a large incentive to correction of the Japanese surplus, it was highly credible to the markets that the yen could be stopped from strengthening still further beyond the level of 100 to the dollar. Accordingly, joint U.S. and Japanese intervention in mid-1993 to halt the yen's rise when it reached that range was immediately successful.

The implication is that forceful intervention by central banks can send a strong signal to the market to break bandwagon expectations that have taken the exchange rate to an unrealistic and unsustainable level. If so, that is good news for the potential of exchange rate policy coordination to avoid the most extreme overvaluations and undervaluations.

Since the breakdown of the Bretton Woods system of fixed exchange rates in 1973, the principal currencies have been in a floating regime. This regime at first seemed to work well. For example, floating provided necessary flexibility for differential impacts of the oil-price shocks in 1974 and 1980. By the 1980s, however, the scope for serious distortions from floating rates became evident with the U.S. experience. The European countries had already sought to limit fluctuations among their own exchange rates by constructing the European Monetary System and its exchange rate mechanism of narrow bands among member currencies (see chapter 7). By the time of the Plaza Agreement, the pendulum was shifting back from purely floating exchange rates. There was no desire to return to the straitjacket of rigidly fixed exchange rates because the contribution of exchange rate realignment to external adjustment (as analyzed above) was recognized. But there was also a recognition of the need to avoid the extremes possible under pure floating.

Williamson (1983) has been at the forefront in advocating a new international monetary regime that incorporates the best of both fixed and floating exchange rates. His target zone system would first identify the long-term sustainable level of a country's current account surplus or deficit. This level would be the mirror image of the sustainable level of capital inflows or outflows for the country. The approach would then identify the real exchange rate consistent with the target current account. There would be a band of, for example, plus or minus 10% around this target real equilibrium exchange rate. If underlying policy distortions began to push the exchange rate toward one outer band or the other, the country would alter monetary and fiscal policy until they became consistent with the long-term equilibrium rate. If there were speculative runs in favor of the currency or against it unsupported by changes in the fundamental economic policies, there would be a coordinated, sterilized intervention to break the expectational trend.

The Plaza Agreement inaugurated a new period in the exchange rate system that gave it some of the attributes of a target zone system, although not all. Finance ministers did sit down and establish desired ranges of exchange rate parities. They did engage in intervention when the rates got too far away from these targets. However, their ad hoc procedures had several limitations. They did not specify exchange rate targets and bands in real terms but rather in nominal terms; yet, it is the real exchange rate that drives the current account performance, and adjustment for inflation is important. The ministers had a tendency to set the desired rate at its recent level rather than evaluating on a more fundamental basis the levels of rates that would be consistent with sustainable or equilibrium current account balances.

Indeed, their deliberations seemed to contain no notion of the equilibrium current account position. Moreover, the G-7 exchange rate discussions did not divulge target exchange rates to the public, largely from fear that, if the central banks could not make the limits stick, they would lose credibility with the markets. In contrast, Williamson calls for openly announced targets so as to provide a clearer signal to the market and to serve notice of the governments' commitments to appropriate exchange rates. Finally, over the course of seven years, beginning with the Plaza Agreement, the G-7 exchange rate consultation regime oscillated from being active to being inactive and there were periods of minimal coordination or even outright conflict.[11]

Economic Policy Mix and Trade Balance Outcome

Identification of a target real exchange rate and of equilibrium external balance calls for a set of policy instruments that can achieve the desired results. The underlying instruments are monetary and fiscal policy. It is important to recognize the linkages between these policies and the exchange rate and trade balance outcomes.

Figure 2.6 provides a framework for these linkages. In this framework, the basic objective is to choose appropriate combinations of fiscal and monetary policy to obtain both domestic full employment (internal balance) and external balance at the target sustainable level. The figure divides fiscal and monetary both into postures of ease and tightening. The four resulting possible combinations will have different effects on the exchange rate and trade balance.

In the southwest corner, fiscal policy is loose and monetary policy is tight. This is the combination of Reaganomics for the United States in the 1980s and the situation of Germany after reunification. In this combination, tight money pushes up the interest rate ($\uparrow i$). The rising interest rate causes exchange rate appreciation ($\uparrow ER$). The rising exchange rate causes a rise in the trade deficit or a decline in trade sur-

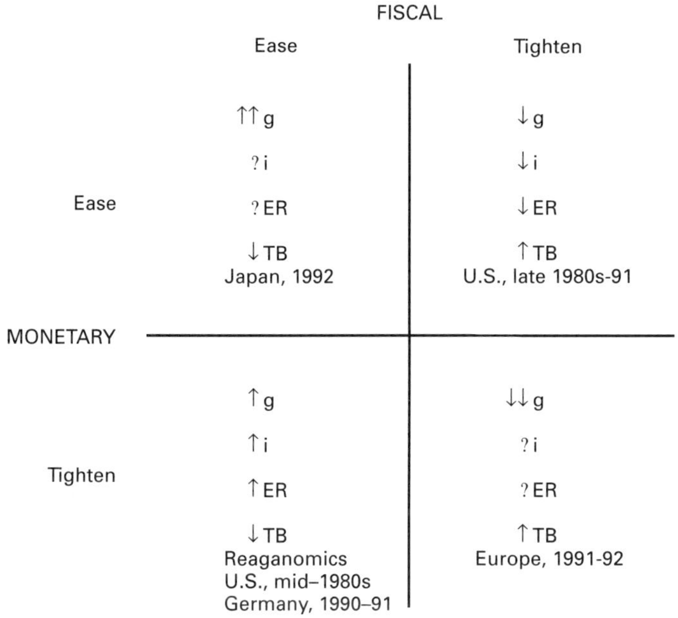

FISCAL

	Ease	Tighten
Ease	$\uparrow\uparrow$ g ? i ? ER $\downarrow$ TB Japan, 1992	$\downarrow$ g $\downarrow$ i $\downarrow$ ER $\uparrow$ TB U.S., late 1980s-91

MONETARY

	Ease	Tighten
Tighten	$\uparrow$ g $\uparrow$ i $\uparrow$ ER $\downarrow$ TB Reaganomics U.S., mid–1980s Germany, 1990–91	$\downarrow\downarrow$ g ? i ? ER $\uparrow$ TB Europe, 1991-92

Figure 2.6
Direction of policy change and trade balance outcome

plus ($\downarrow TB$). As fiscal policy probably dominates monetary policy for growth impact, there is some net expansionary effect on activity ($\uparrow g$).

The opposite extreme occurs in the northeast corner. Here fiscal policy is tight and monetary policy is loose. The monetary ease lowers the interest rate, which causes exchange rate depreciation that in turn leads to an increase in the trade surplus (decline in trade deficit). The United States was arguably moving in this direction by 1991 with extreme monetary ease and the 1990 budget summit timetable in place.

In the northwest corner, both monetary and fiscal policy are in a posture of ease. There is a strong stimulus to economic growth. The interest rate is bid up by rising investment activity but held down by easy availability of money so that its trend is ambiguous. So is the change in the exchange rate. There is likely to be some decline in the trade balance because of the upturn in domestic activity. Japan's policy package of August 1992 was moving in the direction of both monetary and fiscal ease, as reflected in the serious economic slowdown.

In the southeast corner, both monetary and fiscal policy are tight. Economic growth is substantially curtailed. Tight money tends to increase the interest rate, but low activity tends to reduce it for an ambiguous net effect. With the interest rate little changed, change in the exchange rate is small and ambiguous. Nonetheless, there is likely to be a moderate increase in the trade balance because of the impact of slower growth in reducing import demand. By 1992, the European economies were largely in this policy stance.

Incorporation of exchange rate and trade targets into policy determination will affect the mix of policy. The most extreme example is that of Reaganomics. If the early Reagan administration had been concerned about overvaluation of the dollar and the rising U.S. trade deficit, it would have tightened fiscal policy and enabled the Federal Reserve to loosen monetary policy. The result would have been a lower interest rate, lower dollar, and smaller trade deficit. Approximately the same level of domestic activity could have been achieved because the expansionary effect of easier money would have largely offset the contractionary effect of tighter fiscal policy. Thus, internal balance would have been maintained but with a different policy mix. However, there would have been external balance rather than severe external imbalance.

Similarly, after the Japanese bubble burst in 1989–90, it would have been more appropriate for the Japanese government to focus its expansion on fiscal policy while avoiding much ease of monetary policy. There would have been comparable or greater maintenance of economic activity without the aggravation of the trade surplus associated with monetary ease, falling interest rates, and depreciation or lesser appreciation of the yen.

Conclusion

Much has been learned about the importance of maintaining external balance and sustainable real exchange rates within the context of a floating exchange rate regime. The lessons came at a high cost for the U.S. economy in particular. It is important that policymakers remember these lessons in the future and not repeat the mistake of allowing the external account to become severely out of balance on grounds that exchange rates are a matter for markets alone to determine. As figure 2.6 shows, it is the policies that the authorities adopt that provide the underlying incentives to the foreign exchange markets in the first place.

The experience of the past quarter century has further shown that the international exchange rate system needs to have greater flexibility than under a regime of strictly fixed exchange rates but greater discipline than under a purely floating regime. One of the challenges of the 1990s is to build on the nascent and imperfect exchange rate regime begun by ad hoc cooperation among major countries in the Plaza Agreement and subsequent G-7 coordination. Improvement in this regime, as well as the avoidance of severe external imbalances, will be important if protectionist pressures are to be minimized in the 1990s and if the major economies are to come as close as possible to meeting their potential growth rates.

Suggested Readings

Krugman (1991), Cline (1991c).

3 International Trade and Protection

Review of Theory

Free trade is at the heart of economics as a science. In 1776, the founding father of the discipline, Adam Smith, analyzed the mutual gains to countries entering into trade in his book *The Wealth of Nations*. These gains arose from the opportunity for each country to specialize in what it could best produce. Smith emphasized the increased efficiency when production occurs at large scale, that is, economies of scale. His famous example was a pin factory. If one firm specialized in making pins, it would have the proper equipment, and its workers would master pin-making techniques so that the factory could produce far more pins per worker-hour than if each household in the region attempted to make its own pins.

Comparative Advantage

At the beginning of the nineteenth century, David Ricardo more explicitly set forth the theory of comparative advantage. This theory clarified the less obvious proposition that it was to a country's benefit to trade with other countries even if the other countries had lower absolute efficiency in all products than the home country. The reason was essentially the concept of opportunity cost.

Consider England's decision not to produce both wine and cloth at home but instead to specialize in cloth, export some of it to Portugal, and import wine in return. Workers in England might be absolutely more efficient in both products, with a worker in England perhaps producing both more bottles of wine and cloth in a day than his counterpart in Portugal. However, suppose that in England the worker was relatively more efficient in cloth production, and cloth output per worker was far higher than in Portugal, whereas wine production per worker was only slightly higher. For example, the advantage of weather in Portugal might well make up most of the difference between the two work forces in labor skills in the case of wine but not in the case of cloth.

Under these circumstances, the opportunity cost of producing wine domestically in England would be high because a large amount of cloth would have to be sacrificed by deploying the workers in question to wine production. In contrast, the opportunity cost of obtaining wine from Portugal would be low. The workers in England could be allocated to producing extra cloth for export to Portugal, where it would be exchanged for much more wine than could be produced with the same workers if they had been diverted to wine production at home. In sum, because of comparative advantage, England will have found that it can gain through trade with Portugal even though England has an absolute advantage of greater efficiency in all products. However, the reason is that there will still be products in which Portugal is relatively, or comparatively, more efficient, and thus the opportunity cost of obtaining these products will be lower through the indirect route of trade than through domestic production in England.

Appendix 3A presents a numerical illustration of the principle of comparative advantage. The appendix also uses a diagram of the production possibility curve to demonstrate the gains from trade. Essentially this demonstration shows that the home country can gain through trade because it can obtain the goods in which it is relatively less efficient at a lower price abroad than at home.

The notion of comparative advantage is the most intuitively apparent for trade in goods requiring unique natural resources. No one disputes that the opportunity cost of obtaining coffee for the American market is lower through the indirect route of exporting jet aircraft to Brazil and then importing coffee from Brazil than through an attempt to grow coffee in hothouses in Iowa. The essential contribution of the theory of comparative advantage is to show that this same source of gain arises even in much less obvious cases, even those instances in which one country has higher absolute efficiency in both goods.

Factor Endowments

In the 1930s and 1940s, Swedish economists E. F. Heckscher and Bertil Ohlin combined the theory of comparative advantage with neoclassical production theory to reach a more specific conclusion: countries would have comparative advantage in the product that intensively used their relatively abundant factor of production. Thus, industrial countries have built up large amounts of capital equipment but have relatively scarce unskilled labor, whereas developing countries have large unskilled labor forces and relatively little capital. The Heckscher-Ohlin theory predicts that capital-abundant industrial countries will have comparative advantage in capital-intensive products, such as steel and aircraft, while labor-abundant developing countries will have comparative advantage in labor-intensive products, such as footwear and clothing. The theory conforms well to the observed trade patterns between industrial and developing countries, especially if natural resources are incorporated into the definition of factor abundance. For example, the exporting of U.S. machinery to Costa Rica in return for footwear and coffee comfortably fits the Heckscher-Ohlin theory.

Appendix 3A illustrates the Heckscher-Ohlin approach by applying a specific production function. The discussion there describes a field of isoquants, alternative levels of production obtainable by differing combinations of labor and capital for the production function in question. As shown in the appendix, if the isoquant field for one product (say, aircraft) tends to combine large amounts of capital with small amounts of labor, while the field for another product (say, footwear) tends to do the opposite, then the country with relatively abundant capital will tend to produce and export the former good, and the country with relatively abundant labor will tend to concentrate on the latter good.

Intra-Industry Trade

Despite the logic and evident relevance of the Heckscher-Ohlin theory of trade, it became increasingly obvious in the postwar period that a large volume of trade was occurring that did not seem to be between countries with different factor endowments. In particular North-North trade among industrial countries with relatively similar capital and labor availabilities could not be readily explained by the Heckscher-Ohlin theory, while North-South trade between industrial and developing countries could. There was a growing volume of intra-industry trade, whereby a country might export some lines of steel products but import others rather than exclusively exporting steel and importing coffee.

In the 1960s, Staffan Burstein Linder suggested a theory of trade in differentiated products to explain North-North, intraindustry trade.

He observed that most industrial goods are not homogenous or identical, but are differentiated. He suggested that national producers will develop products for their home market first. Then, when they turned to the export market, they would be exporting industrial goods that were similar but not identical to the differentiated products of producers in other industrial countries. Germany would export Volkswagens to France, and France would export Peugeots to Germany. This trade would occur because a Volkswagen is differentiated from a Peugeot even though both are in the same product category and require similar factor inputs. Moreover, trade between two countries would tend to be greater the more similar their demand patterns; hence the importance of North-North trade.

The New Trade Theory

In the early 1980s, Krugman (1980) used a simple but elegant mathematical model to explain intra-industry trade as the consequence of economies of scale. One country will specialize in one variety of the good and produce at large scale to obtain low-cost production, while another country will do the same in an alternative variety. Other authors in the new trade theory similarly stressed economies of scale. Trade theory had come back full circle to Adam Smith but now using formal equations.

A crucial implication of the new trade theory was that trade would often, indeed usually, involve imperfect competition; that is, if there are economies of scale, firms with large output will have more efficient production, and so only a few firms will exist in each sector. Krugman (1992) has argued that much of the trade theory literature in previous decades tended to eliminate economies of scale through assumption because this phenomenon was intractable mathematically. Only with more recent operational models of imperfect competition (especially Dixit and Stiglitz 1977) did it become possible to return to the profession's early emphasis on scale economies.

Strategic Trade

As an outgrowth of the new trade theory, Brander and Spencer (1985) proposed a theory based on insights about strategic behavior by oligopolistic firms gained from the industrial organization literature. Strategic trade theory emphasized that the location of comparative advantage for a given industrial product could be arbitrary—Japan might just as well develop the comparative advantage for video cassette recorders as the United States. What mattered was which country seized the initial lead in the product. That pattern in turn could reflect the process of signals, threats, responses, and counter responses known as strategic behavior by noncompetitive firms. Unlike perfectly competitive firms, such firms are large enough to affect the market. Their decisions are like moves in a chess game and depend on the moves of other players.

Brander and Spencer argued that such product sectors tend to have potentially high oligopoly profits. They suggested in particular that a government could shift the advantage to its own producers in the market game by being prepared to subsidize them or provide tariff protection for them. In particular, home country firms could then stake out an aggressive position in the contested market by announcing that they intended to hold a large market share and would cut the price however far was necessary to enforce that share. With the support of their government, the firms' claim would be credible to foreign rivals and would discourage their entry.

The theory of strategic trade was tailor-made for those who saw the practices of such nations as Japan as systematically unfair. The new theory seemed to prove that free trade was an archaic concept. These perceptions gave the strategic trade theory surprising prominence in business and policy circles normally unfamiliar with the technical economics literature. However, strategic trade theory has many difficulties in application.

The theory is subject to unstable results. Grossman (1986) has shown that a small change in the assumptions about firm behavior can sharply alter the model's results. Brander and Spencer had assumed a type of behavior technically known as Cournot, which has each firm reacting to the quantity of production set by the other until the market reaches an equilibrium. A government subsidy to the home firm's output strengthens the credibility of the company's claim that it plans to stake out a large quantity share of the market. However, Grossman noted that the policy implications could reverse if an alternative behavioral assumption, Bertrand behavior, were applicable instead. In this alternative, each firm reacts to the price set by the other firm until the market reaches equilibrium. The home firm promises to keep its price high, thereby helping secure high profits for itself and the foreign competitor. The government intervention needed to ensure credibility of this pledge consists of taxing the export to insure that it bears a high price (Grossman 1986, pp. 53–54).

Another questionable assumption of the Brander-Spencer strategic trade model is that the good in question is not consumed in the domestic market of either the home country or the country of the rival producer but only in third-country markets (as noted in Krugman 1992, p. 432). This assumption is necessary to allow monopolization of the market to confer welfare benefits on the home country. Otherwise, such benefits for home producers would come at the expense of home consumers. Yet these must be very strange goods indeed: they are of no use to U.S. or Japanese consumers (the rival producing countries), but instead are attractive only to the Hottentots and some trade theorists.

As if there were not enough problems with strategic trade at the theoretical level, in practical application at the policy level, there is a tendency to lapse from the formal economic definition of strategic—gamelike interactive behavior among rival firms—to a more generalized notion of strategic that the authors of the theory did not intend. To the layman, "computer chips are more important than potato chips;" but that importance is not strategic in the formal economic sense unless computer chips are produced by large oligopolistic firms and potato chips are produced by numerous firms too small to affect the market individually. In the formal terms of the theory, cigarette production is more strategic than milk production because large oligopolistic firms produce cigarettes and countless dairy farms produce milk, yet the American Medical Association would call milk more strategic and more important than cigarettes.

The risk of degrading the technical concept of strategic in practice also makes the theory susceptible to capture by interest groups. In the context of trade politics in most countries, the traditionally powerful political lobbies for protection would soon claim their industries were strategic and required protection or subsidies. Agriculture would be called strategic in France and Japan; computers in Brazil; steel, automobiles, sugar, and textiles in the United States; and coal in Germany. After all, Japanese rice reduces vulnerability to embargoes, and German coal reduces reliance on Gulf oil. Yet, these industries would mostly have no claim to government intervention under the formal strategic trade theory.

As policy prescription, the notion of government intervention to support home-country industries fails to recognize that such intervention would be subject to emulation and retaliation by governments of other countries. Indeed, existing rules on subsidies adopted in past trade negotiations would explicitly permit countervailing duties by foreign countries in response to attempts to support a strategic industry using subsidies.

Infant Industry

A more traditional argument for exceptions to free trade is the infant industry argument. Here the notion is that future or dynamic comparative advantage may be different from present or static comparative advantage, and if a government intervenes to support a nascent industry with bright future prospects, the country can develop a comparative advantage in the product. There are examples of such success, arguably including such instances as automobiles in Brazil. In industrial countries, Japanese intervention to support earth satellites and French intervention in favor of national computers have essentially been infant-industry policies.

Figure 3.1 illustrates the concept of the infant industry and the difference between static and dynamic comparative advantage. In the figure, there is a production possibility curve, QQ, showing the alternative amounts of coffee and steel that Brazil can produce. At the international price line PP, the country's optimal production point is at x, where it produces a large amount of coffee and relatively little steel. However, if the government intervenes and shifts the production point

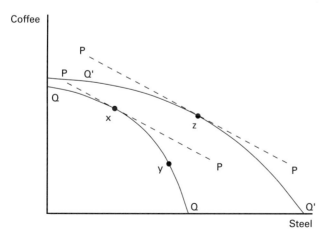

Figure 3.1
Dynamic comparative advantage

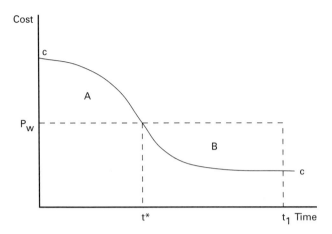

Figure 3.2
Infant industry cost recovery

to y, where there is more steel output and less coffee production, then by learning by doing, the country will eventually be able to shift its production possibility curve to $Q'Q'$. The new production possibility frontier permits much greater output of steel but only slightly more potential coffee output. At the same international price line as before (PP), the country will now tend to specialize in steel rather than coffee. Thus, Brazil will have had static comparative advantage in coffee but dynamic comparative advantage in steel.

The principal problem with infant industry protection has been that in practice the infants never grow up. Essentially, the production possibility curve does not shift out to $Q'Q'$. Latin American nations maintained high tariffs and inefficient production in many industrial sectors for decades in the name of infant industry protection. Moreover, technically the theory does not lead to protection but to a government subsidy. Protection distorts price signals, whereas the government subsidy lowers production costs but leaves relative prices at their efficient international levels. Of course, few governments have spare cash to spend so that protection is typically applied rather than subsidies.

Even if subsidies are available, the efficiency conditions for infant industry stimulus are demanding. Technically, the country's production cost eventually has to fall well below the world level to justify the excess cost paid early in the horizon. Thus, in figure 3.2, the country's marginal cost in the infant industry follows path "cc." Early in the time horizon, this marginal cost exceeds the world price, and the government provides a subsidy equal to the difference. At some point (time t*), domestic marginal cost falls to the world price level. In the ideal case, marginal cost continues to fall below the world level. By the end of the planning horizon (t_1), the total (time-discounted) area below the world price line (area B) must equal or exceed the total area above the world price line (area A). Otherwise, the country will have made a poor investment in the infant industry and will experience net losses. Yet, if marginal cost merely falls to the world level, area B disappears, and the infant has been strictly a burden costing area A.

Industrial policy is a modern version of the infant-industry argument. Those who favor active government intervention in favor of some industrial sectors implicitly believe that those sectors are infant industries that can turn into future areas of comparative advantage. The debate on industrial policy has centered on whether in practice it is possible to pick winners. Japanese economic development is widely perceived as having involved industrial policy, with the Japanese government intervening to support individual sectors, although such intervention is far smaller today than in the 1950s. Traditionally, industrial policy has been seen with more skepticism in the United States, where it tends to be interpreted as a form of central planning.

Of course, in a country with systematic industrial policy, the industries not fortunate enough to be designated as infant industries worthy of support will suffer an indirect discrimination. Some industries can be favored only if others are disfavored because otherwise, the favor has no effect. Disfavor emerges in such forms as higher taxes to finance subsidies to the favored sectors or in higher input costs because unfavored firms must purchase costly domestic inputs from favored sectors rather than obtain them at the world price. As in the case of the strategic trade argument, the infant industry argument lends itself to abuse by special interest groups.

The election of Bill Clinton to the White House brought some shift in U.S. policy in the direction of industrial policy, although how far was unclear. The chairperson of the new president's Council of Economic Advisors, Laura Tyson, was associated with the view that the government should intervene cautiously to encourage high technology industries (Tyson 1992). In its first year, the administration announced that the U.S. government would engage in cooperative research with the big three U.S. automobile companies to help develop a highly fuel-efficient car for the twenty-first century, and the long-term budget proposal had funding for such high technology endeavors as a magnetically levitated train. However, intervention in practice remained at least initially limited. Moreover, the amount of high technology support endorsed by the intellectual mentors of the strategy tended to be small. Thus, after a careful consideration of the implications of the new trade theory for trade policy, Krugman (1992) came to the conclusion that perhaps $10 billion annually in research and development subsidies could be justified—less than one-fifth of one percent of GDP.

Optimal Terms of Trade

The other traditional exception to free trade concerns the possibility that a large country can depress the world price of its import good, thereby improving its terms of trade. Thus, an import tariff would reduce the country's import volume, and foreign firms would find that they had to reduce their price.

The optimal terms of trade argument has broadly been considered a theoretical curiosity rather than a realistic policy alternative. The principal reason is that, if the few countries large enough to have global market power, such as the United States, were to embark on a campaign of higher protection to depress the price of their imports, they would soon face retaliation by other countries and trading blocs, such as the EU. The end result would be losses of the potential gains from trade on all sides rather than terms of trade gains for a single large nation.

Theory Overview

The gains from free trade remain central to economic theory, as well as the policy principles theory has to recommend for practical action. These gains are firmly embedded in the concepts of comparative advantage, along with gains from economy of scale and specialization, which have held up for two centuries. However, particularly in the United States in the 1980s, there was growing concern about fair trade and increasing sentiment that economists were naive to believe in free trade because, although the United States might practice it, other countries did not. The call for fair trade was strengthened by the introduction of strategic trade theory and its seeming new academic respectability for government protection, subsidy, or other intervention. The new theory invoked oligopoly theory to add a new argument to the other principal case for intervention in the past, the infant industry argument. As discussed in chapter 4, the new strategic approach had its most acute manifestation in negotiations with Japan, in which by 1993, U.S. officials were speaking of the desirablity of market share targets.

The quest for fair trade is really a desire to achieve reciprocity—a time-honored concept in international trade negotiations. Ensuring that free trade is fairly pursued on both sides, or reciprocal, is the rationale for trade negotiations. Otherwise, countries could unilaterally lower their protection without bothering to negotiate with trading partners. The economic content in reciprocity is essentially the terms of trade concern: if country A frees imports but country B does not, then country A is likely to experience some terms of trade loss that partly offsets its efficiency gains from liberalization. That is, country A will now demand more imports from country B in view of the unilateral tariff removal, and the import price will be bid up, worsening the terms of trade. If B liberalizes its imports in turn, however, its demand for A's goods will rise, bidding up their price symmetrically, and terms of trade will tend to remain unchanged.

The Uruguay Round

Most countries have come to recognize the need for mutual negotiation to liberalize trade. The historical lesson of the 1930s showed that increased protection caused the depression to deepen and spread worldwide. In the postwar period, there have been several rounds of international negotiations. One of the most important was the Kennedy Round of the 1960s, in which nations substantially cut tariffs. Lower tariffs were a key objective of the United States because it faced being locked out of the European market after the European Common Market, formed in 1960, established free trade behind a common tariff wall. By the 1970s, as tariffs subsided, however, the problem of nontariff barriers had emerged. The Tokyo Round of the 1970s thus concentrated on developing new codes of conduct on such barriers (including discriminatory government procurement, product standards, subsidies, and dumping—or selling at much lower prices abroad than at home).

The succession of postwar trade negotiations fostered rapid growth in international trade, at rates on the order of 6 to 7% annually or about twice the rate of GDP growth. The open trade atmosphere was crucial to developing countries who sought to achieve economic growth on the basis of growing exports of manufactures, including such success-ful cases as South Korea and Taiwan.

The Bicycle Theory (Bergsten and Cline 1982, p. 71) holds that trade policy needs the forward momentum of negotiation toward deeper lib-eralization if it is to avoid a collapse back into protectionism. As new suppliers abroad make inroads into traditional domestic industries, there is a need for the counterbalance of expanding opportunities for exports to offset pressure toward protection.

In the United States in the early 1980s, the bicycle theory seemed to apply. Especially as the dollar strengthened, there was growing protec-tionist pressure. The free trade coalition found it needed to broaden its support to stem these pressures. The solution was once again to push the frontiers of open trade further. This time a new round of negotia-tions would seek to liberalize new areas: services, such as banking; intellectual property, such as patent protection; and foreign direct in-vestment, in which there was a need to limit performance require-ments, such as forced export targets for U.S. automobile firms in Mexico. In this way new advocates of liberalization could be added to the coalition: such services as the credit card companies, the banks, and insurance companies and such seekers of patent protections as the pharmaceutical firms.

In September 1986, the members of the General Agreement on Tar-iffs and Trade (GATT) agreed at Punta del Este to launch the Uruguay Round of trade negotiations. The round was to incorporate the new areas of services, intellectual property, and investment for the first time. However, from the outset, it was clear that the round would have to go much further. These new areas were primarily subject to protec-tion in the developing countries. To interest these countries in liberal-ization of these areas, it would be necessary to liberalize trade in some of the older areas that had proven particularly difficult and were of special interest to the developing countries. These areas especially in-cluded agriculture and textiles, both of which had largely been set apart from the past GATT liberalization and were subject to severe restrictions and subsidies. Moreover, there was other unfinished busi-ness left over from the Tokyo Round.

Figure 3.3 shows the principal interests of each of the major groups of players in the Uruguay Round. U.S. negotiators were primarily in-terested in liberalizing agriculture and opening trade in the new areas. The European Community too had an interest in the new areas, al-though perhaps less interest in services than the U.S. negotiators, who for example, considered U.S. financial services to have a comparative

Player	Seek to obtain	Need to offer
United States	Liberalization in agriculture (grains), intellectual property, services, investment	Liberalization of textiles, nongrains agriculture
European Community	Liberalization in intellectual property, investment	Liberalization of agriculture, textiles
Japan	Avoidance of new protection, liberalization of intellectual property, investment	Liberalization of agriculture
Developing countries	Liberalization of agriculture, textiles, tighter disciplines on safeguard protection	Liberalization of services, intellectual property, investment

Figure 3.3
Major player stakes in the Uruguay Round

advantage. Japan had an interest in the new areas but primarily saw success of the round as important because it could avoid new protective barriers that might otherwise be set up against Japan. The developing countries principally sought the liberalization of markets for their agricultural exports and for textiles. They also wanted new disciplines on the practice of imposing safeguard protection, especially voluntary export quotas, against products from newly industrializing nations.

Each of the major players also knew there was an area in which it would have to liberalize. The United States and the EC had extensive quotas against textile and apparel imports under the Multi-fiber Arrangement that would have to be liberalized. The United States also had some specialized farm products that stood to lose protection, e.g., dairy products, sugar, beef, and peanuts. For the EC, by far the largest sacrifice, or offer, that would have to be made was liberalization of agriculture under the Community's Common Agricultural Policy (CAP). For Japan too, agricultural liberalization, especially in rice, was the most painful. For their part, the developing countries would have to accept liberalization in their markets for services trade, adopt improved intellectual property protection, and limit performance requirements imposed on foreign investment.

An examination of figure 3.3 suggests that perhaps the slimmest gains and the largest sacrifices applied to the same major player, the European Community. Agricultural protection under the CAP has long been considered the glue that holds the Community together. At the same time, Europe was concentrating primarily on its own internal move to a single market and to European Monetary Union (see chapter 7), and international liberalization in the new areas was of less interest than to the United States.

Agriculture

Agriculture proved to be the most difficult and important of the negotiations, as well as the key to their success or failure. U.S. negotiators insisted that Europe cut protection in three areas: export subsidies (a requested cut of 70%), domestic farm supports, and restrictions on imports. EC negotiators initially offered only to seek to reduce an aggregate measure of support (AMS) in all areas with no explicit commitment to reduce in a particular area, such as export subsidies. The Europeans offered to reduce its AMS by 30% from the 1986 base, but as it had already cut support in that year, the effect was to offer only a modest 15% cutback. In addition, however, the Europeans wanted rebalancing in agriculture, which in practice meant increasing protection against soybeans and other oilseeds. The latter had not been important imports in 1960 when the EC negotiated its CAP with the United States and so had been left relatively free of restrictions. As oilseed imports became massive over the next two decades, the EC wished to correct this oversight, or more charitably, to achieve a more balanced degree of protection across farm products. The community had already proceeded to subsidize rapidly growing domestic production of soybeans.

More broadly, EC negotiators saw the new U.S. adamancy on agriculture as an unrealistic, high stakes gamble, out of keeping with past special treatment of agriculture. U.S. negotiators countered that the developing countries could not be brought along to liberalize in the new areas if agriculture was off the table.

In December 1990, the Uruguay Round negotiations temporarily broke down over the agricultural impasse. Important developing country members of the Cairns Group of agricultural exporting nations, such as Argentina and Brazil, walked out of the negotiations at their crucial phase because European negotiators refused to make further concessions on agriculture.

Japanese negotiators were also nervous about agricultural liberalization and content to hide behind the U.S.-EC impasse. The proposed liberalization would convert quotas into tariffs, and these could be as high as 700% for Japanese rice, a politically conspicuous and embarrassing revelation of just how costly protection was to Japanese consumers.

By late 1991, the German government began to make statements distancing itself from the more unyielding position of the French. At the end of that year, the chairman of the GATT, Arthur Dunkel, issued a "chairman's text" on all areas of the negotiations, including agriculture, and this compromise document provided a vehicle to reopen the negotiations. Nonetheless, the agricultural obstacle caused the negotiations to drag on without much progress through most of the next year.

Only a late-1992 retaliatory threat by the United States managed to break the U.S.-EC agricultural impasse and clear the way for completion of the round. In November 1992, in the Blair House Agreement in Washington, D.C., negotiators from the European Community agreed to cut the volume of their subsidized agricultural exports by one-fourth. However, in 1993, the new Balladur government in France insisted that the Blair House Agreement was not acceptable, thereby keeping the Uruguay Round on the brink of collapse.

Textiles

Since the 1970s, world trade in textiles and apparel has been subject to a regime of bilateral quotas under the Multi-fiber Arrangement (MFA). The charter of the Uruguay Round pledged to reintegrate textiles into the GATT, which meant a commitment to phase out quotas and return to tariffs, the only form of protection formally permitted under GATT. There was considerable progress toward agreement by the time of the Dunkel text draft. Existing quotas were to be successively expanded, with past quota growth rates increased by 15% in the first three years, 20% in the next three, and 25% in the final four years of a decadelong adjustment. Thus if recent growth of U.S. textile import quotas for Korea had been at 2% annually, the rate would rise to 2.3%, then 2.8%, and finally 3.5%. At the end of the decade, quotas would be eliminated and textiles and apparel would be subject to tariff protection under GATT rules.

The textile formula raised some obvious problems. It was likely to leave protection still high at the end of the decade and thus require a sudden jolt of adjustment at that time. The political credibility of that outcome was somewhat suspect, although incorporating textiles into overall Uruguay Round negotiations instead of leaving them in the stand-alone MFA framework meant that there would be cross obligations, such as developing country liberalization in services, that could be invoked at the end of the decade to block any attempt to get out of the requirement to eliminate quotas. Moreover, the normal GATT provisions would permit safeguard protection for any textile sectors suddenly inundated by imports at that time.

For the United States, the draft agreement formula implied overall import growth of about 7% per year (with quota-controlled growth at about 4% and with possible high growth of 10 to 15% for uncontrolled categories). To achieve a smooth transition out of quotas, in contrast, would require total import growth of 9% annually (Cline 1990b). Nonetheless, the firm commitment to quota elimination at the end of ten years represented the most promising opportunity for dismantling MFA protection in the past quarter-century.

By late 1993, textile interests in the United States and Europe were arguing that liberalization should only apply to imports from countries that in turn liberalized their own markets. Because many developing countries have high protection on textiles and apparel, there was considerable logic to this view. Moreover, with modern technology, the textile fabric sector has become capital intensive and naturally suited to comparative advantage for industrial countries. By contrast, apparel is difficult to mechanize and continues to require intensive hand labor operations. Thus, there is a natural division of labor in which the industrial countries are likely to specialize in textile fabric and the developing countries in apparel using imported fabric from the industrial countries as an input. Such a regime would require liberalization on all sides.

Tariffs

The Dunkel draft agreement called for a 30% cut in tariffs, and thus, for example, a 10% tariff would fall to 7%. Most tariffs are already low in industrial countries, but they remain high in some sectors (e.g., textiles) and tend to be higher in developing countries.

At the Tokyo Summit in July 1993, the G-7 industrial countries agreed to a market access initiative that would eliminate tariffs in some sectors and cut them by 50% rather than the standard 30%, in other sectors where they were high. Whether these deeper cuts would apply to textiles, however, continued to divide the U.S. and EC negotiators by late in the year.

New Areas

The proposed Uruguay Round agreement provided for codes of fair treatment in services. Although the United States sought liberalization of perceived barriers in financial services in such countries as Japan, its insistence on exemption for the U.S. shipping industry posed a problem. As the negotiations developed, moreover, it became clear that the financial services sector in the United States was disappointed by the absence of strong reciprocity requirements for liberalization in developing country markets.

In intellectual property, industrial countries sought strong, standardized protection of patents. If the United States and other industrial countries were to liberalize imports that would further erode their sunset industries, such as footwear and clothing, they needed opportunities to expand exports in their sunrise, high technology sectors. The pharmaceutical and computer software industries were important examples of sectors with great concern about violations of intellectual property. Negotiators also sought to curb the practice of counterfitting name-brand products. Initially, delegations from the developing countries had feared that tighter protection of intellectual property would reduce technology transfer from North to South, but increasingly, key developing countries came to the conclusion that patent rights were important for the development of their own technology as well.

In investment measures, the negotiations sought to limit export performance requirements, mandatory production agreements, local content requirements, and other distortions. It was an irony, however, that the United States seemed to be moving gradually toward adoption of some investment requirements of its own. In early 1992, the Bush administration reached an agreement in which Japan pledged to increase its imports of U.S. automobiles and parts to $10 billion annually by 1995. Sales of U.S. parts makers to the transplant Japanese auto firms in the United States were to count as part of this target, an implicit performance requirement for local content of production.

Other Issues

The pending agreement also addressed the question of safeguard protection. The draft proposal provided that there would be no more voluntary export requirements, and any safeguard protection would have to be in the form of tariffs. Moreover, new disciplines were to be imposed on the safeguards, especially timetables for phaseout. However, largely at European insistence, selective safeguards were to be allowed, whereby protection could be imposed against a handful of countries with the largest increases in market penetration. This compromise eroded the earlier GATT requirement of most favored nation application to all countries across the board. The previous GATT rule against selective safeguards was designed to exert maximum pressure on the importing country, forcing it to eliminate temporary protection by affecting all suppliers. However, most countries had simply ignored the GATT safeguard provisions and concluded bilateral voluntary export restraint agreements.

In the area of subsidies, the emerging agreement provided for stronger disciplines that limited application of countervailing duties in exchange for broader coverage of practices considered to be in violation of subsidy rules, such as exports supported by subsidies to depressed geographic regions within a country. In antidumping measures, there was to be tighter control over the calculation of these penalties, as the United States and the EC were perceived as using procedures that exaggerated the antidumping duty. In return, there was to be more complete coverage of dumping practices, for example an end to the circumventing of antidumping penalties by importing most of the product at a nearly finished stage and adding only minor production steps at the end ("screwdriver" assembly).

In most of these areas, a difficult problem from the Tokyo Round persisted: whether to make the codes apply to all countries (most favored nation, MFN) or instead to limit benefits to code signatories who explicitly undertook corresponding obligations. The Tokyo Round had opted for the latter, conditional MFN alternative, but many had been disappointed that in important nontariff barrier codes, numerous countries had failed to sign up, especially among developing countries. In the end, the Uruguay Round opted for MFN inclusion, largely because of disappointment with experience under the conditional MFN codes of the Tokyo Round, which the developing countries had frequently ignored.

End Game

On the eve of the 1992 U.S. election, agreement still had not been reached to break the impasse between the EC and the United States (and other Cairns Group members) over agricultural liberalization. The issues had narrowed, for example, as to whether export subsidy limits would apply just to values or also to physical quantities. The United States raised the stakes when it threatened retaliatory tariffs on $1 billion worth of imports from the EC because of the EC's subsidized support of soybeans and other oilseeds. The EC was willing to cut production but not as far as the United States wanted.

In November 1992, U.S. and EC negotiators finally reached agreement on the issue of oilseeds subsidies, as well as the much wider set of issues concerning liberalization of EC agricultural trade. The Blair House Agreement came only after severe tension between France and other EC members, and it remained possible that France would exercise its veto right under the EC's Treaty of Rome to block agricultural liberalization, although to do so could abort not only the Uruguay Round but also progress toward European economic and monetary union.

The year 1993 was one of historic opportunity for international trade. After acrimonious domestic debate, in November 1993, the United States Congress passed NAFTA, the North American Free Trade Agreement (see chapter 4). The stage was then set to secure a final agreement in the Uruguay Round, forced by the December 15, 1993, expiration date for U.S. fast track congressional authority to approve the negotiation outcome without amendments.

The international macroeconomic context was not favorable for trade liberalization, as Europe and Japan were in severe recession and the U.S. economy was only weakly entering into recovery (see chapter 1). Nonetheless, and in part because of the risk of aggravating world recessionary tendencies further by a collapse in the round, U.S. and EC negotiators finally reached agreement immediately before the December 15 deadline. The Uruguay Round was completed and to be signed at Marrakech, Morocco, on April 15, 1994. The epilogue to this book provides a brief summary of the final outcome.

Bilateralism versus Multilateralism

During the 1980s, the question of regional free trade areas (FTA) reemerged as a dominant issue after a quarter century of dormancy. The last time regionalism was at the center of trade debate was in the formation of the European Common Market in the late 1950s.

The revival of the forces of regionalism stemmed from frustration with the slow pace of multilateral trade liberalization. In 1982, at the GATT ministerial meeting of trade negotiators, U.S. Trade Representative William Brock proposed a new round of multilateral liberalization and was rebuffed by the Europeans and others. U.S. authorities then began to consider an alternative strategy. If the world trade regime could not be moved ahead, then perhaps it was time for deeper liberalization within more limited groups of like-minded nations. Such efforts would at least liberalize some trade, the argument went, and might even prod the other nations to go along with multilateral liberalization.

The first fruit of the new move toward limited free trade arrangements was bilateral but not regional: in 1985, the United States and Israel reached a free trade agreement. Then, in 1988, the United States and Canada entered into a free trade agreement, a logical outgrowth of earlier sectoral free trade in automobiles and of the Canadian desire to assure that process protection in the United States (e.g., through antidumping and countervailing duties) did not close off the crucial U.S. market in the future.

In early 1990, after a trip to Europe where he became convinced that European investors were preoccupied with Eastern Europe and would have little time or money for Latin America, Mexico's President Carlos Salinas Gortari proposed that the U.S.-Canada agreement be expanded to include Mexico. The U.S. administration of President George Bush was immediately enthusiastic and later suggested in its Enterprise for the Americas Initiative that free trade throughout the western hemisphere was the appropriate longer-term goal. By the time NAFTA was finally passed by Congress in November 1993, there was already talk of a Pacific-Asia Free Trade Area, highlighted by the first summit meeting of leaders from the new Asia Pacific Economic Cooperation (APEC) grouping in Seattle.

For both trade theorists and policymakers, the move toward bilateralism and regionalism posed serious questions. The principal issue was whether regionalism would serve as a stimulus or a roadblock to more rapid multilateral liberalization. The most extreme risk was that a move toward bilateralism and regionalism would create an archipelago of mutually exclusive fortress trade blocs.

The classic test in trade theory for whether a free trade area is desirable or undesirable for the international trading system is whether its effect is primarily trade creation or trade diversion (Viner 1950). If trade creation dominates, then a free trade area is a second-best arrangement: not as good as completely free trade but better than no liberalization at all. If trade diversion dominates, the arrangement actually reduces economic welfare as compared to the situation with no regional liberalization.

Suppose two countries both have a tariff of 20%. They grant free trade to each other but keep the tariff against goods from other countries. Trade will be created to the extent that inefficient production in each country is replaced by more efficient production in the partner country and to the extent that consumers purchase more at lower prices as the consequence of the tariff reduction. However, trade will be diverted to the extent that the only change is that each country switches its import purchases from the rest of the world to the new partner country.

Appendix 3A presents a graphical analysis showing that there are welfare gains from trade creation but welfare losses from trade diversion. The partner countries themselves lose on trade diversion because previously their governments collected tariff revenue that is now gone and because their mutual costs of production exceed the world price on goods diverted from outside suppliers. The other countries, of course, lose export opportunities as the consequence of trade diversion.

Bhagwati (1992) has been the sharpest academic critic of the new move toward bilateralism and regionalism. He considers the European Community to be the prime example of economic integration gone wrong. In his view, the EC is effectively protectionist, especially in agriculture. By implication, he considers the EC to have involved more trade diversion than trade creation. Most of the earlier studies of the EC, such as Balassa, ed. (1975), were more charitable to the common market and in particular tended to conclude that the new export opportunities for outside countries gained on balance from the European Common Market because integration stimulated economic growth of the European countries and therefore their demand for imports generally.

Bhagwati, however, recognizes the strong emerging forces for regionalism and thus proposes reforms of the GATT to ensure that new trade blocs cause as little trade diversion as possible. He proposes that GATT no longer permit the formation of free trade areas but only allow customs unions, or common markets, instead. A customs union has a common external tariff applied by all partners, while a common market additionally permits the free movement of capital and labor within the group. In contrast, an FTA permits each country to retain its original tariff structure while adopting free entry for goods from partners. This arrangement then requires rules of origin; otherwise, goods from the outside could enter the country with the low tariff on the item in question and be transshipped to other partners. Yet rules of origin can be a source of quasi-protective effects (as discussed in chapter 4 with respect to NAFTA). Moreover, the FTA enables each partner to keep its high tariffs rather than forcing each member country to move to intermediate levels.

Bhagwati also proposes that the GATT require new customs unions to set their common external tariff structure at the lowest level for each tariff category among the preexisting tariffs of the partner countries rather than at the average of the previous tariffs as is more commonly the case. The two proposals would undoubtedly make new trade blocs more liberalizing and also would presumably reduce their political appeal. However, these proposals seem unrealistic on the heels of the formation of NAFTA, which would meet neither criterion.

The ideal would of course be that major multilateral liberalization in the Uruguay Round, and perhaps subsequent rounds, would reduce most favored nation tariffs and protection (i.e., those applicable to all countries generally) so far that there would not be much difference from the free trade within the FTAs and therefore little trade diversion. In any event, by late 1993, the political dynamics of bilateralism versus multilateralism suggested that the two might be complements rather than substitutes. In the United States, the NAFTA debate had become a general symbol for open trade versus protectionism, and the European and Asian observers watching the battle agreed that, if NAFTA failed to pass Congress, the message would be that the United States was shifting toward protectionism, with such a message having adverse implications for GATT and the Uruguay Round as well.

Trade and Income Distribution

By the early 1990s, another key issue was emerging for trade policy: the possible impact of open trade on domestic income inequality. As discussed in chpater 1, in the 1980s, the real wage of unskilled workers in the United States fell substantially, and the wage gap between skilled and unskilled workers widened. The NAFTA debate revealed great anxiety within the United States that the hard times of unskilled workers were due in considerable part to international trade.

Economists are sensitive and schizophrenic on this issue. They favor free trade and do not welcome arguments that can be seized upon politically in favor of protection. They are quick to point out that, even if trade did hurt unskilled workers, the solution would be training programs rather than protection. They can point to empirical analyses showing that U.S. domestic factors rather than trade seem to account for the widening wage gap (Bound and Johnson 1992). Furthermore, even unskilled workers gain from free trade in their role as consumers who benefit from lower prices. An analysis of textile and apparel protection shows that it is the lowest-income groups that suffer the most from higher clothing prices imposed by protection (Cline 1990b, p. 202).

The awkward problem for economists is that their own mainstream theory predicts precisely that free trade will worsen the distribution of income between unskilled workers on the one hand and capital and skilled labor on the other hand for a country like the United States where unskilled labor is the scarce factor. Indeed, under certain assumptions, Heckscher-Ohlin trade theory and the associated Stolper-Samuelson theorem lead directly to the conclusion that free trade will equalize factor payments across countries, meaning that in principle U.S. wages for unskilled labor would eventually fall enough to equal those in China and India, where wages would rise.

Obviously that outcome has not occurred in the past, and most economists have tended to regard the factor price equalization theorem as a curiosity rather than an iron law of things to come under free trade. One reason is that the numerous simplifying assumptions of the theory are unrealistic: that there are identical production functions everywhere, identical quality of factors, zero transportation costs, incomplete specialization, only two factors of production, and so forth.

The most careful empirical study of the issue so far (Lawrence and Slaughter 1993) rejects the hypothesis that trade was responsible for the falling absolute and relative wage of unskilled U.S. workers in the 1980s. The authors find that two key requirements of the Stolper-Samuelson theorem are contradicted by the data. First, import prices of labor-intensive goods were not falling, and second, the number of skilled workers relative to unskilled workers was rising in all sectors rather than falling as predicted by the theory. The first of these conditions follows from the fact that the way trade reduces the price of the scarce factor is by reducing the demand for the good that intensively uses it, that is, unskilled wages in footwear production are driven down by a falling price for footwear and weaker demand for domestic production. The second condition is more subtle and counterintuitive.[1]

The Lawrence-Slaughter results are important but less than conclusive,[2] and it seems likely that debate on this issue will intensify in the 1990s. The core issue is essentially whether the public at large should redistribute some portion of the consumption gains it receives from free trade to lower-skilled workers in compensation for any downward pressure that trade may place on low-end wages. Like the theoretical issue, this policy issue seems likely to be hotly debated in the coming years.

APPENDIX 3A: SOME TRADE ANALYTICS

Comparative Advantage

Suppose that in England, one worker can produce either 2 bottles of wine or 4 yards of cloth in a given period. In contrast, in Portugal one worker can produce 1.95 bottles of wine or 1 yard of cloth in the same period. English workers are more efficient than Portuguese workers in absolute terms in both products. Nonetheless, it will pay England to concentrate on the production of cloth, which can then be exchanged for wine imported from Portugal.

In England, the price of cloth stated in bottles of wine is 2 yards per bottle, the price given by an identical amount of labor to produce one product or the other. In Portugal, the price of cloth is about 0.5 yards per bottle of wine, again based on the relative amounts that can be produced by one worker. Thus, cloth is relatively cheaper in England, where a lot of cloth may be obtained for one bottle of wine, than in Portugal, where little cloth can be purchased with one bottle.

If the two countries enter into trade, the international price will settle somewhere in between the national levels, or for example, at 1 yard of cloth to 1 bottle of wine. It is obvious that Portugal can do better to trade its wine for English cloth because England is a more efficient cloth producer. Although not as obvious, it is also beneficial for England to trade for Portugal's wine because, in England, it is only possible to obtain one-half bottle of wine for each yard of cloth (the English home price is 2 yards per bottle), while by trading, England can obtain wine at the international price of 1 bottle per yard of cloth.

Suppose a worker in England spends one labor-period worth of wages. If he does so without trade, he can buy either 2 wine; 4 cloth; or 1 wine and 2 cloth. Suppose he chooses the latter. Now England opens the borders to trade. Then the worker can produce 4 cloth, keep 2 cloth, and exchange 2 cloth for 2 bottles of wine. In isolation without trade (autarky), the best he could do was 1 wine and 2 cloth. With free trade, he can obtain 2 wine and 2 cloth, and he is unequivocally better off.

Gains from Trade

Figure 3.4 illustrates the gains from trade using a production possibility curve. This curve shows the alternative combinations of wine and cloth that the worker can produce in Portugal. This curve is concave to the origin of the diagram, that is, it looks like the perimeter of a ball rather than that of a radar dish (convex). The reason for the shape is diminishing returns. As more cloth is produced and less wine, larger and larger sacrifices of wine are required to obtain an additional yard of cloth because the special inputs necessary for cloth become relatively more scarce.

In figure 3.4, when Portugal is in autarky, its production point is at a, where there are e units of wine produced and g units of cloth. Now, suppose that England and Portugal open their borders to trade, and

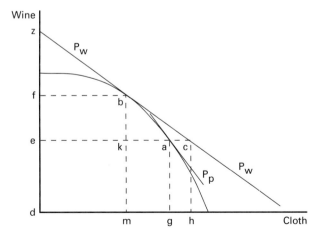

Figure 3.4
The gains from trade

suppose that the international free trade price line settles along P_wP_w. The slope of this line tells the number of bottles of wine (vertical distance) that are equivalent in value to a given amount of cloth. For example, consider point c on the price line. Here the horizontal distance ec tells the amount of cloth that has the same value as the vertical distance ez in bottles of wine. This international price line places a lower price on cloth than does the domestic Portuguese price line at the original production point a. The domestic price line is more steeply sloped so that it equates fewer yards of cloth with a larger number of bottles of wine. Cloth is more expensive while wine is less costly in Lisbon than internationally before trade is permitted.

Under free trade, the optimal production point for Portugal moves upward to the left: more wine and less cloth. The international price line is tangent to the production possibility curve at b, so that this point represents the highest-value output combination available to Portugal. The country will now produce amount df of wine and amount dm of cloth at home. It is easy to demonstrate that this outcome is superior to the original autarkic position because Portugal can have just as much wine to consume as before but enjoy a larger amount of cloth. It can do this by exporting the extra amount of wine now being produced, ef. At the international price line, this amount of wine exports, equivalent to vertical distance bk, can be traded for the horizontal distance kc of wine. All that is needed to make Portugal just as well off as before is the amount ka of wine because then Portugal has de wine to consume and $ea = dg$ cloth to consume just as before. In addition, however, it now receives ac extra cloth from trading because its exports of bk wine may be exchanged for the entire amount kc of cloth. The additional yards of cloth, ac, are the gains from trade.

A similar diagram for England would show a production possibility curve more gently sloped, with a larger cloth production potential and a smaller, or equal, wine production potential. After free trade, England would find it advantageous to move to a production point to the southeast—more cloth and less wine than in isolation. It too would gain from trade because it could consume just as much cloth at home as before, produce extra cloth, and trade the extra cloth for more wine than it could have produced by itself. The difference between the two countries in product specialization is determined by Portugal's comparative advantage in wine and England's comparative advantage in cloth.

Production Functions and Heckscher-Ohlin Trade

Suppose that a product can be produced by alternative combinations of labor (L) and capital (K) according to the following formula:[3]

$$Q = K^a L^b.$$

For simplicity, suppose that $a = 0.5$ and $b = 0.5$. This means that the production function becomes: $Q = \sqrt{K}\sqrt{L}$. Figure 3.5 shows an isoquant, a curve showing alternative combinations of labor and capital that will produce a given quantity of the product.

Consider point A, where 25 units of labor are combined with 9 units of capital. Production is: $\sqrt{9}\sqrt{25} = 15$. Similarly, at point B, 25 units of capital are combined with 9 units of labor to obtain production of: $\sqrt{25}\sqrt{9} = 15$. With the same output, point B is on the same isoquant as point A.

Figure 3.6 then shows two different products with their corresponding isoquant fields. Moving further out in the field of either one corresponds to producing more of the product in question and to using larger amounts of capital and labor inputs.

In figure 3.6, the optimum combination of labor and capital occurs where the isoquant is tangent to the price line showing the relative price of capital and labor, PP. Thus, price line PP equates the amount of labor L_o with the amount of capital K_o. At this price, thirty units of

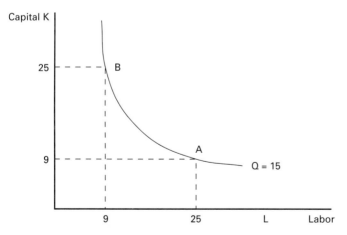

Figure 3.5
The production function isoquant

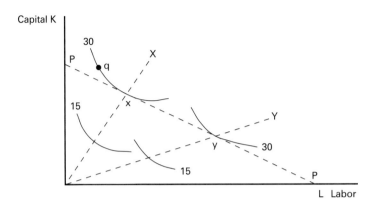

Figure 3.6
Capital intensive (X) and labor intensive (Y) goods

product X will most cheaply be produced using the combination of capital and labor shown at point x, where the isoquant for thirty is tangent to the factor price line. Any other combination, such as at point q, would correspond to a factor price line that is further out from the origin and therefore represents greater total cost. Similarly, the optimal production point for good Y at a volume of thirty units will be at point y, where the isoquant is tangent to the factor price line.

In the figure, product X is a capital-intensive good, and product Y is labor intensive. The reason is that, at a given factor price ratio (a given slope of the factor price line), the path of optimal production points for product X will be a ray from the origin that has strictly higher capital/labor ratios, while the corresponding path for product Y will have strictly lower capital/labor ratios.

It makes sense that, if India has a large amount of labor and relatively little capital, it will tend to specialize in product Y. Otherwise, if India specializes in product X, the country will tend to run out of capital before it employs all of its available labor. On the other hand, the United States with a relatively large amount of capital and small amount of labor will tend to specialize in product X.

The conclusion about concentration in the product that uses each country's abundant factor would follow even if both countries had identical factor price ratios (i.e., the same slope along the factor price line). However, typically they do not. In India, the factor price line is flatter (labor is relatively cheaper), whereas in the United States, it is steeper (capital is relatively cheaper). This divergence in factor price ratios reinforces the tendency for India to specialize in the labor-intensive good and for the United States to specialize in the capital-intensive good.

Trade Diversion and Trade Creation[4]

Consider a country with original tariff rate t_o that imports from the world market as shown in figure 3.7. The country pays price P_w for the good, although consumers must pay the price including tariff, $P_w (1 + t_o)$. Total consumption of the good is $0c$ of which $0b$ is produced at home and bc is imported.

The country joins a common market, or customs union, freeing imports from partners who supply the good at price P_c. Importation expands to Q^M_1 as more is demanded at this lower price and less is produced at home in view of the lower domestic price. The increase in total imports, $Q^M_1 - Q^M_0$, represents trade creation. Its welfare benefits are the two triangles, $A + B$. The first represents the savings from released domestic resources originally producing the good. The opportunity cost of producing a unit of the good is given by the supply curve

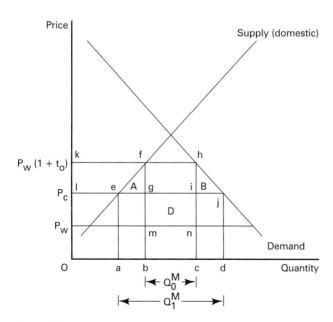

Figure 3.7
Trade creation and trade diversion

so that, although domestic resources worth *aefb* went to produce *ab* of the good, this quantity may now be imported for *aegb*, a savings of *A*.

The second triangle, *B*, represents the gain in consumers' surplus[5] net of the loss of producers' surplus[6] and original government tariff collections. Movement down the demand curve from *h* to *j* has transferred to consumers the total area *lkhj* in new consumers' surplus at the expense of a loss of *lkfe* for producers' surplus and of *gfhi* in foregone government tariff revenue, leaving net social gain of *A* + *B*, of which we have already counted *A*. Note that the transfer away from producers and government toward consumers contains political implications: the trade creating effects of common market formation may not be popular to the politically organized groups—producers and bureaucracy—although they are beneficial to the consumers.

While total trade creation was $Q^M_1 - Q^M_0$, the integration also involved a switching of import supply from the rest of the world to a partner. That is, the partner supplied nothing before and everything, Q^M_1, after integration, while the world market supplied Q^M_0 before integration and nothing after. There was, therefore, trade diversion away from the supply of the rest of the world (ROW) to the supply of partner in the amount Q^M_0. There is a welfare cost for this diversion, represented by rectangle *D*. Thus, the country previously imported Q^M_0 at price P_w, but it has now switched this portion of imports to partner supply at the higher price, P_c. The loss is also equivalent to the gross loss of tariff revenue (originally *mfhn*) minus that portion of tariff revenue transferred to consumer surplus (*gfhi*).

It is illuminating to consider who gains and who loses from trade diversion. The government loses, and the loss comes wholly out of tariff revenue. However, the producers of exports in partner countries gain because they will now sell goods previously purchased from the world market.

Suggested Readings

Krugman (1992), Bhagwati (1992), Schott (1994), CBO (1993a).

4   Trade Policy Case Studies: Japan and NAFTA

For much of the 1980s and early 1990s, conflict with Japan over fair trade was one of the dominant issues in U.S. trade policy. By 1993, the question of whether the United States should join Mexico and Canada in a free trade area had exploded into one of the most bitter controversies of American economic policy in recent memory. The two issues provide fertile ground for the application of analytical techniques in reaching policy decisions.

The U.S.-Japan Trade Controversy

One of the most persistent problems in international economic policy has been the issue of perceived trade protection by Japan, resulting in trade conflict between the United States and Japan. Already, in 1979, former U.S. Treasury Secretary John Connally was insisting in the Republican primary campaign that, if Japan did not open its markets to American goods, the United States should leave the Toyotas rusting at the docks. As the overall and bilateral U.S. trade deficit soared with the strong dollar in the early 1980s, the pressure intensified. In 1985, the U.S. Senate passed without opposition a resolution condemning "unfair Japanese trade practices." The emerging Omnibus Trade Bill narrowly missed including an amendment proposed by Congressman Richard Gephardt (D, Iowa) that would have imposed import quotas on countries with large bilateral surpluses with the United States (read especially Japan). The bill did include a "Super 301" clause that mandated a threat of trade penalties for countries declared by the U.S. trade representative to be priority foreign countries for unfair trade practices (again, read especially Japan) (Destler 1992). By 1993, after eight years of intensive bilateral negotiations, the new Clinton administration was again pushing Japan to open its markets, this time through the use of quantititative targets, possibly including market shares for imports.

Both microeconomic and macroeconomic influences caused this chronic trade conflict. At the micro level, there was a widespread belief among businessmen in the United States and other countries that the Japanese market was effectively closed to imports through collusive private sector practices difficult to identify. At the macro level, however, matters had repeatedly been severely aggravated by an exchange rate regime that had permitted the Japanese yen to become undervalued and the U.S. dollar overvalued, leading to the predictable result of a high Japanese surplus globally, as well as bilaterally with the United States.

Macroeconomic Influences[1]

By the late 1980s, there was much disappointment with the ability of traditional macroeconomic tools to resolve the U.S. trade deficit, especially the bilateral deficit with Japan. The exchange rate had moved from 260 yen per dollar in February of 1985 to 125 yen by the end of 1987, but the bilateral deficit stood at $57 billion in 1987 and was still $50 billion in 1989 when the overall U.S. trade balance had made a much greater correction. The resiliency of the bilateral U.S. deficit with Japan seemed to many to confirm the dominant belief that the Japanese market was heavily protected by invisible barriers.

Despite this public perception, a closer examination shows that Japan's trade, including that with the United States, has in fact responded to the standard macroeconomic influences and, in particular to the real exchange rate and rate of domestic and foreign growth as set forth in chapter 2.

Exchange Rates and Relative Growth
Figure 4.1 demonstrates that U.S.-Japan bilateral trade has responded closely to changes in the real yen/dollar exchange rate. The dotted line (plotted against the left scale) shows the number of real yen per real dollar, deflating by wholesale prices. When this index is high, the dollar is strong. The solid line (plotted against the right scale) shows the Japanese surplus in bilateral U.S. trade, expressed as a percentage of bilateral exports plus imports. Each observation on this line is plotted for the period two years subsequent to the year indicated on the hori-

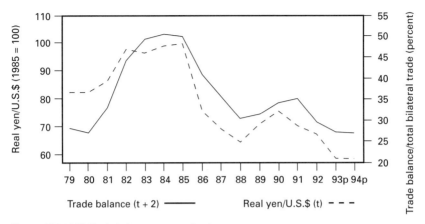

Figure 4.1
Japan's trade surplus with the United States and the strength of the dollar against the yen

zontal axis to take into account the lag from the exchange rate price signal to the trade consequences.

It is evident that the two lines move closely together, indicating that there is a close correlation between the real strength of the dollar against the yen in year t and the bilateral trade imbalance in year $t + 2$. Thus, the strong dollar in 1984–85 led to the large Japanese bilateral surplus of about 50% of bilateral trade in 1986–87. The weak dollar by 1988 led to a sharp reduction to this bilateral imbalance, falling to about 30% of bilateral trade by 1990. Unfortunately, the dollar took an inappropriate upward excursion against the yen in 1989–90, and the U.S. bilateral deficit suffered the penalty two years later (rising once again to about 35% of the bilateral trade base). The proposition that the exchange rate matters for the bilateral trade imbalance would thus seem verified, contrary to the popular notion that the yen-dollar exchange rate has exerted little or no effect on trade with Japan.

Japan's global trade balance also responds to the real strength of the yen. Figure 4.2 shows the ratio of Japan's nonoil imports to its exports (percentage shown on the right scale), plotted jointly with the strength of the yen against sixteen industrial country currencies (deflating by wholesale prices) two years earlier (left scale).[2] The higher the import/ export ratio, the lower Japan's non-oil trade surplus relative to the

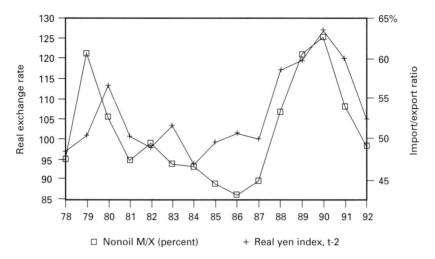

Figure 4.2
Japan's trade and exchange rate

trade base. It is evident in the figure that there is an extremely close correlation beween the level of the real exchange rate and the import/ export ratio two years later.

Similarly, figure 4.3 shows that the U.S.-Japan bilateral trade balance is responsive to the differential between the two countries' domestic growth rates, just as suggested in chapter 2. Thus, the bilateral surplus was relatively low as a fraction of bilateral trade in 1990–91 when U.S. growth was low and Japan's growth was high. However, the surplus was relatively high in 1984 when U.S. growth was high and Japanese growth was low. A similar response can be seen for Japan's global surplus in relation to the differential between Japanese and OECD growth (Cline 1993d).

These three figures strongly suggest that Japan's trade responds to the normal macroeconomic influences of real exchange rate and growth in the domestic and foreign markets. By implication, if Japan's market has special protective restrictions, they must operate parametrically rather than absolutely—for example, by restraining imports by a given percentage from levels that they would otherwise reach based on the macroeconomic influences rather than limiting them to a rigid absolute level. In contrast, in the extreme case of protection with the same effect as a fixed quota, there would be no response of imports to changes in the real exchange rate and growth rate.

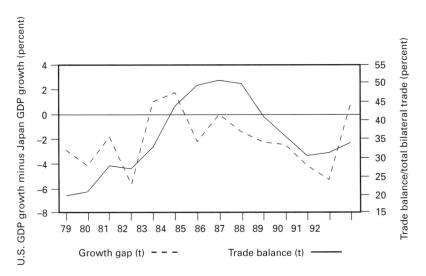

Figure 4.3
Japan's trade surplus with the United States and its relative growth rates

Japanese versus European Trade Response
A common argument pointing to Japanese protection is that, after the decline of the dollar in the late 1980s, the U.S. trade balance with Europe adjusted from a deficit to a surplus while the bilateral balance with Japan failed to adjust. This argument is wrong because it erroneously judges adjustment by the absolute trade balance rather than by the proportionate change in the underlying trade flows.

As shown in table 4.1, there was a large real depreciation of the dollar against the European currencies and the Japanese yen from 1984–85 to 1989–90. Allowing for a two-year trade flow lag, there was a large corresponding adjustment in U.S.-EC and U.S.-Japan trade flows. Thus, from 1986–87 to 1991–92, U.S. exports rose by 82% to Europe and by 74% to Japan. Similarly, import growth from both markets was low in this period: 17% over five years from the EC and 15% from Japan during the same period. Considering that the real dollar depreciated somewhat less against the yen than against the EC currencies (26% versus 34%), the sensitivity of the U.S.-Japan adjustment was actually somewhat higher (coefficient of adjustment in table 4.1).[3]

It is true that the absolute U.S. trade balance with the EC shifted from a deficit of $26 billion to a surplus of about $7 billion, whereas the bilateral deficit with Japan changed very little (from $59 billion

Table 4.1
U.S. bilateral trade and exchange rates

	EC	Japan
Real exchange rate		
(1985 = 100)		
1984–85 average	99.8	99.5
1989–90 average	65.6	73.2
A: percent change	−34.3	−26.4
U.S. exports ($billion)		
1986–87 average	56.7	27.1
1991–92 average	102.9	48.0
B: percent change	81.5	73.9
U.S. imports ($billion)		
1986–87 average	82.2	86.8
1991–92 average	96.3	99.9
C: percent change	17.2	15.1
Trade balance ($billion)		
1986–87 average	−25.5	−59.2
1991–92 average	6.6	−51.9
D: percent change	undefined	−12.3
U.S. exports/imports		
1986–87 average	0.690	0.318
1991–92 average	1.069	0.480
E: percent change	54.9	50.9
Coefficient of adjustment		
F: $= -E/A$	1.60	1.93

to $52 billion). The explanation for this paradox between comparable proportionate change and divergent change in absolute trade balance is simply that the initial trade gap factor was much larger in U.S. trade with Japan than with Europe. Thus, in 1986–87, the ratio of U.S. exports to imports in trade with the EC was approximately two-thirds, whereas in trade with Japan this ratio was only about one-third (table 4.1). This divergence, in turn, reflected the influences of triangular trade and of Japan's high savings rate, as discussed below.

The central point here, however, is that the proper analysis of trade adjustment, using proportionate change in the trade flows rather than the absolute difference between exports and imports, shows that U.S.-Japanese trade responded just as well to exchange rate adjustment as did U.S.-EC trade. Once again, this conclusion suggests that, if Japan is uniquely more protective than Europe, its protection is of a parametric form that does not obstruct the workings of exchange rate adjustment.

Oil and Fiscal Adjustment

Japan actually had a current account deficit in 1979–80 and only a small surplus in 1981–82. Its large current account surplus only began to emerge by 1984 when it reached 18% of exports of goods and services. After peaking at 38% in 1986, the surplus fell to 11% of exports of goods and services by 1990, although rebounding to 31% by 1992.

The decline in oil imports played a major role in the emerging surplus. Oil imports fell from 39% of exports of goods and services in 1980 to only about 10% in 1986–92 (Cline 1993c). The collapse in oil prices in 1986 was one reason, but in addition, major energy conservation efforts in Japan sharply reduced the volume of oil imports, especially relative to GDP.

There was another important macroeconomic influence in the 1980s that contributed to an emerging external surplus. The government systematically eliminated its fiscal deficit, which had been almost 5% of GDP in 1979–80 and fell to zero by 1986–87. Private saving and investment both fell modestly (by 2% and 3½% of GDP, respectively) so that the net effect was that the saving-investment gap rose by some 6% of GDP, largely because of the elimination of government dissaving. This change translated into a corresponding rise in the external balance (chapter 2). Viewed in this light, it was fiscal tightening that converted the windfall gain of lower oil prices into a rising trade surplus rather than higher imports. Without tighter fiscal policy, the oil price decline would have induced higher consumption and imports through the terms of trade effect on real incomes in Japan. In short, the combination of lower oil prices and lower fiscal deficits drove the rising Japanese trade surpluses in the 1980s (Cline 1993c).

Structural Bilateral U.S.-Japan Deficit

American politicians frequently say outright or imply that unless the bilateral deficit with Japan disappears, the United States should impose trade policy pressure on Japan and perhaps retaliate with U.S. protection. However, there are two reasons why even under equilibrium conditions we should expect a sizeable U.S. trade deficit with Japan.

The first reason is that because of high saving in Japan and low saving in the United States, it is reasonable to expect a modest but chronic external surplus for Japan and external deficit for the United States. As discussed in chapter 2, the external balance equals domestic saving minus domestic investment so that high saving tends to generate an external surplus. To some extent Japan has been saving a large amount because of its demographic composition, which is aging rapidly and by the early twenty-first century will be characterized by a large retired population. By that time, dissaving by the aged is likely to reduce the national savings rate and external surplus. Whatever the reason, for the period 1975–91, gross national saving averaged 18.1% of GDP in the United States and 32.3% in Japan (OECD 1993, p. 213).

Low U.S. saving and high Japanese saving suggest that in equilibrium, there will be a chronic external deficit for the United States and surplus for Japan. A benchmark for safe levels of these imbalances is probably on the order of 1% of GDP for the U.S. deficit and 1½% of GDP for Japan's surplus.[4] From this source, one should expect a chronic bilateral trade imbalance that essentially reflects each country's share in the other country's overall imbalance.

The second reason for a chronic bilateral trade imbalance is triangular trade. Japan has minimal natural resources and must import all of its oil, as well as most other raw materials. The United States has large deposits of many natural resources and produces half of its oil at home. As a result, Japan must import more heavily from Saudi Arabia and other suppliers of oil and raw materials. Japan must export manufactures to pay for these imports. The natural trade triangle that results is that Japan exports manufactures to countries such as the United States that are more self-sufficient in natural resources. Correspondingly, the United States gains export sales indirectly rather than directly, for example when countries such as Saudi Arabia use their earnings on oil sold to Japan to buy goods from the United States.

The combined magnitude of these two components of the structural imbalance is substantial. Bergsten and Cline (1985, p. 40) estimated the equilibrium bilateral trade imbalance at about $25 billion annually. A more recent estimate (Bergsten and Noland 1993) places the figure in the range of $40 to $50 billion annually. It is thus a mistake for politicians to seek balanced bilateral trade as the proof of fair trade with Japan.

Protection and the Trade Balance

Economists like to point out that macroeconomic forces determine the overall trade balance, not microeconomic influences such as sectoral protection. As a result, they stress, if Japan suddenly did eliminate all of its protection, the result would be an increase in both imports and exports, leaving the trade balance unchanged.

This admonition contains much truth but is probably overdone. Just as causation can be shown to run in both directions between the saving-investment identity and the behavioral equations relating imports and exports to the real exchange rate and activity at home and abroad, causation can run from protection to the saving-investment identity. Indeed, the simplest way to incorporate protection is to add a protection variable in the import equation:

$$M = f(ER^*, T, Y_D),$$

where T is the tariff equivalent of tariff and nontariff protection.

If it is true, as suggested in chapter 2, that an exogenous change in the real exchange rate ER^* can affect the trade balance and influence the saving-investment balance, then surely there is some room for the same point to hold with respect to the level of protection. Implicitly the standard macroeconomic point about protection assumes that any change in T will be offset by a change in ER^* so that the trade and saving-investment balances will be left unchanged. But that view assumes an overly rigid role for a given current account position in determining the exchange rate. Instead, we have seen large ranges of the exchange rate consistent with alternative current account balances. Indeed, by analogy, when Japan cut its oil imports through energy conservation, the real exchange rate should have appreciated enough to prevent the current account balance from rising. That did not happen, nor is it likely that a major elimination of protection would be wholly offset by exchange rate depreciation, leaving the trade balance unchanged.

Instead, the truth of this macroeconomic proposition is simply that there is likely to be a substantial, though not complete, offset of a reduction in protection through an induced real depreciation of the exchange rate, so that the trade balance will not decline by the full extent of the initial rise in imports resulting from liberaliation. By implication, there will be some increase in exports of other products. This phenomenon does mean that if Japan has high protection and removes it, U.S.

markets can expect some increase in the pressure from still more exports from Japan in other sectors.

Japan's External Surplus in the 1990s
After declining from 1986 to 1990, Japan's current account surplus was, by 1993, at an all-time high of about $135 billion. At about 3 percent of GDP, the surplus was only modestly smaller than the record surplus in 1986 (4.3% of GDP). The lagged effect of real yen depreciation in 1989–90 and the severe Japanese recession in 1993 were the driving forces behind the renewed large surplus. But whatever its causes, the large surplus contributed to renewed trade tension and U.S. pressure for quantitative import targets and other unconventional means of opening the Japanese market.

U.S. negotiators reportedly insisted that Japan should reduce its external surplus to a range of 1 to 2% of GDP. Ironically, calculations using a multicountry trade model (Cline 1989b; Cline 1993c) projected that by 1995, Japan's external surplus should be well below $100 billion and probably comfortably below the 2% of GDP ceiling proposed by the United States. The principal reason was the massive real appreciation of the yen, which rose in real terms by about 25% against the dollar and deutschemark from 1990 to mid-1993. After the standard two-year lag, this rise was highly likely to reduce the trade surplus. A second reason was that sooner or later Japan's domestic growth was likely to return to at least the range of $3\frac{1}{2}\%$, adding further to import growth. For these reasons, it seemed likely that Japan's external adjustment was already in the pipeline by 1993. Curiously, projections by the international agencies (IMF 1993b) showed no prospective reduction in Japan's surplus.

Some economists argued that the large rise of the yen in 1993 (from 125 to the dollar at the beginning of the year to about 107 in the second half) was counterproductive for reducing Japan's trade surplus. The supposed reason was that the yen shock was so unfavorable for economic growth that Japan's imports would fall by considerably more than they might rise as the consequence of yen appreciation. However, this argument is basically wrong, especially if a two-year horizon is considered.

At a strictly logical level, the stronger yen adversely affects domestic output by reducing exports and raising imports. Suppose the change in the trade balance is 100. The induced reduction in imports equals the marginal propensity to import times 100, or perhaps 20. So whether or not the rise in the yen depresses the economy, it is almost impossible for it to do so by enough to cause an indirect reduction in imports that exceeds the initial reduction in the trade surplus.

As an empirical matter, the model discussed above finds the following parameters. A 1% rise in the real value of the yen causes a reduction of about $3½ billion in Japan's current account surplus. A change in Japan's domestic growth rate by 1 percentage point for one year causes a change of $5 billion in the current account surplus. Thus, real appreciation of at least 20% from 1990 to 1993 meant potentially a reduction of some $70 billion or more in the current account surplus. It would take some 14 percentage point-years of reduced Japanese growth to offset the exchange rate influence. There was no conceivable way the strong yen could depress the domestic economy this much.

By late 1993, the key conditions for reducing Japan's external surplus were thus maintenance of the strong yen, thus avoiding a backslide to depreciation (as happened in 1989–90), and effective implementation of the large packages of fiscal stimulus that had been announced (chapter 1).

The Nature of Japan's Protection

It is widely recognized that, except in agriculture and a few manufactured products such as footwear, Japan's overt protection is low. Protection of manufactured goods was high in the 1950s and 1960s, and the government used discriminatory procurement and other protective practices to stimulate postwar industrial development. By the late 1970s, and especially the 1980s, however, most explicit barriers had been removed, and by the late 1980s, the government was promoting rather than discouraging imports in an attempt to defuse trade conflict with the United States. By the 1980s, tariff averages were slightly lower than in most other industrial countries. In contrast, agricultural quotas are highly restrictive. Japan's agricultural prices are about 150% above world levels, even higher than the excess price in Europe because of the CAP.

The central issue is invisible protection. There is a large body of anecdotal evidence suggesting the presence of informal barriers (see, for example, Prestowitz 1988). The question is whether complaints about Japan's informal barriers stem from actual restrictive practices or whether instead such complaints principally reflect the frustration of foreign competitors seeking to compete with a highly efficient manufacturing nation that frequently has lower-cost production.

Lawrence (1993, pp. 6–7) has summarized the arguments and evidence pointing toward unusual protection in Japan:

> Japan has an unusually low share of manufactured goods imports: 5.9 percent of domestic consumption in 1990, versus 15.3 percent for the United States and 15.4 percent for Germany. Japan also has an unusually low share of intra-industry trade . . . An unusually high share of Japanese imports from the United States are shipped by Japanese foreign affiliates to their Japanese headquarters . . . and an unusually low share is shipped by U.S. firms. Surveys indicate that foreign brand products are more expensive in Japan than elsewhere . . . Although Japan is officially open to foreign investment, Japan also displays an unusually small share of domestic sales accounted for by foreign-owned firms—1 percent versus 10 percent for the United States and 18 percent for Germany—and an unusually small share of these firms are majority owned. . . . The U.S. foreign investment position in Japan is not only unusually small, but unusually concentrated in wholesale trade . . . Japan accounts for just 5 percent of U.S. foreign direct investment, but 35 percent of all U.S. receipts of royalties and fees from unaffiliated foreigners . . . [suggesting that] foreign firms with know-how are induced to license and engage in joint ventures rather than to set up majority-owned affiliates.

A low ratio of manufactured imports to consumption is, of course, just what one would expect for a country that is the quintessential case of comparative advantage in the manufacturing sector. As discussed above in connection with triangular trade, Japan has minimal natural resources and must export virtually nothing besides manufactures to pay for its raw materials imports.

Part of the explanation of low manufactured imports is that Japan has relatively low intra-industry trade, which tends to dominate North-North trade as discussed in chapter 3. Thus, while Germany imports Peugeots from France and sends back Volkswagens in return, Japan has massive exports of automobiles and imports very few. However, the test of intra-industry trade can be ambiguous. We would expect a country like Germany to have intense intra-industry trade with its immediate neighbors, and we would also expect less of such trade between extremely distant countries. Japan is extremely distant from all other industrial countries. Similarly, we would expect a large economy that enjoys economies of scale in its own domestic market to conduct less intra-industry trade than a small nation. From this standpoint too, we should expect Japan to have less intra-industry trade than any other country except the United States, the only single country with a larger GDP.

Saxonhouse (1993) notes that, if the European Community is treated as an aggregate and if an adjustment is made in the measure of intra-industry trade so as to take into account a country's overall trade imbalance, then Japan's intra-industry trade looks closer to that of the United States and of the EC than is usually estimated, and its index of intra-industry trade is rising more rapidly than the U.S. and EC measures.[5]

With respect to the other features listed by Lawrence, the meaning of the price tests is discussed below. As for direct investment, the question is whether there are explicit practices that discriminate against foreign investment.

The empirical literature on invisible Japanese protection has come to resemble a shoot-out at the econometric corral. Like other famous econometric shoot-outs, such as the statistical tests of whether the Keynesian or monetarist model better fit the behavior of the economy, this one seems to have left numerous casualties but no clear victory for either side.

The first volley was fired in the mid-1980s, as several trade economists conducted statistical tests to examine whether Japan was an outlier, or aberrant country, that imported less than should be expected in view of its economic characteristics. Saxonhouse (1983), Bergsten and Cline (1985), and Leamer (1988) found that the answer was no; Japan does not import less than should be expected. Bergsten and Cline applied a simple test at the macroeconomic level relating the import/GDP ratio to the size of GDP. Saxonhouse and Leamer both used Heckscher-Ohlin trade frameworks that relate sectoral imports and exports to a country's endowments of labor, capital, and natural resources. The models also took account of transportation cost, although typically with such less-than-satisfactory measures as distance, and natural resources. This first round of tests found that Japan's trade adhered to international patterns.

By 1985–86, the growing view among economists was that the U.S.-Japan trade problem was mainly a macroeconomic issue that should be resolved by exchange rate changes and fiscal adjustment. However, soon there was a revisionist literature that provided new statistical tests reaching the conclusion that Japan did indeed import too little given its economic characteristics. Lawrence (1987) used the Helpman-Krugman model of intra-industry trade to calculate that Japan's manufactured imports were too low by about 30%. Statistical tests by Petri (1991), including a variable for the *keiretsu* (large groupings of companies), found that the presence of these groups significantly reduces a sector's imports. Using the same data set, Lawrence (1991) found similar results.[6] For his part, Noland conducted statistical tests showing that Japan was an outlier in its low imports (Balassa and Noland 1988, appendix C; Noland 1992). Business groups in the United States were quick to seize on the revisionist estimates as evidence that Japan had been shown definitively to be using invisible barriers to restrict imports (ACTPN 1989).

However, the revisionist volley proved no more definitive than the initial set of studies. Thus, although the underlying Helpman-Krugman theory had implied that the share of imports in consumption for a given sector should be a linear function of the sector's competitiveness abroad, Lawrence (1987) had used a logarithmic relationship, and with Goto's reestimatation the equations using the linear relationship, the finding of Japanese underimporting disappeared (as cited in Saxonhouse 1993, p. 34). Similarly, Saxonhouse (1993) has been just as critical of the Noland findings as Noland has been of the Saxonhouse findings (Bergsten and Noland 1993). Two observers of the debate (Srinivasan and Hamada 1990) concluded that there were enough statistical problems with all of the models that neither side of the debate could be considered definitive, although they singled out the Leamer study as the most appropriate methodologically.

Refreshingly, Lawrence (1993, pp. 10–11) has acknowledged methodological problems with his earlier study. Already in an earlier paper, in recognition of the difficulties in reaching a definitive statistical test of invisible protection, Lawrence (1991) suggested a more direct test: compare prices in Japan to international prices. If prices in the Japanese market are far above world levels, then there is protection even if formal barriers are low. He and others cited price surveys showing that prices of manufactured goods were indeed higher in Tokyo than in New York.

Using the same data source, however, I have found an important distinction (Cline 1990c). It turns out that imported goods from the United States and Europe are indeed more expensive in Tokyo than in New York by about 60%. However, Japanese brand products are about the same price in Tokyo and New York.[7] One interpretation of this finding is that foreign firms face special barriers in the distribution system that increase their costs and force them to sell at unusually high prices in the Japanese market. That influence may be particularly relevant where existing distributors are exclusively tied to Japanese manufacturers and where newcomers must not only deliver their product but also start up distributorships. This burden can be especially high when the outlet requires a lot of land, which is extremely expensive in Japan. Many argue that automobiles are a key example, although a few foreign firms such as BMW have gone to the trouble to develop independent distribution networks in Japan.

An alternative interpretation has quite different implications. It is possible that foreign firms simply pursue a high-profit, low-volume strategy in the Japanese market. If they believe that the price elasticity of demand for their product is low, they will maximize profits by charging high prices in the expectation that the luxury market will buy despite the price premium because of the prestige associated with the product. There are indications that the main Japanese importing firm for foreign automobiles, Yanesa, has traditionally done exactly that. In any event, in this interpretation, the prices of foreign goods are high because of a conscious strategy of foreign firms rather than because of invisible Japanese protection.[8]

At the same time, the price test would seem to rule out classic protection of the domestic market for Japanese goods. If Japanese firms were taking advantage of a protected domestic market, we would expect to see them charge prices well above the world level for their goods rather than about the same price as they charge abroad.[9]

In sum, the econometric literature on Japan's invisible protection is ambiguous and so are the price survey data that provide a more direct test of protection. Perhaps for this reason, in 1992, a study by the GATT secretariat concluded that protection by the *keiretsu* "may be less important than often claimed" (GATT 1992).[10]

Managed Trade and Bilateral Negotiations

The dominance of the view that Japan's restrictive mutual purchasing from affiliate firms within *keiretsu* groups and/or that other invisible barriers restrict market entry, has already led to two major instances of managed trade between the United States and Japan. In the late 1980s, U.S. negotiators secured a commitment from Japanese representatives that Japan would seek to increase the share of U.S. firms in the Japanese semiconductor market to 20%, about double the previous level. This agreement was justified as a substitute to the imposition of antidumping penalities on Japanese exports to the U.S. market so as to avoid imposing a burden on U.S. computer producers.

Although the market share did subsequently edge up to the high teens and met the 20% target in late 1992, the arrangement allowed Japanese semiconductor producers to increase their prices sharply at a time when American computer companies needed large volumes of low-price chips to take advantage of changing technology for personal computers (Flamm 1990). As often happens with restrictions, the result was to increase Japanese profits. Nonetheless, Tyson (1992) and Bergsten and Noland (1993) have characterized the agreement as a success with respect to its market-share objectives, while criticizing the early floor-price aspect of the agreement.

The semiconductor agreement raises many issues. One of the most important is the validity of the initial justification for intervention to remedy protective behavior. In her long chapter on the sector, Tyson (1992) never demonstrated that the Japanese semiconductor industry was engaging in oligopolistic practices that had the effect of restricting imports. The closest anyone ever came to such evidence was a 1983 chart provided by the U.S. Semiconductor Industry Association, showing that the share of imports in Japanese consumption had been mysteriously constant at about 11% of the market over several years despite several trade opening initiatives (Destler 1992, p. 128). Yet, it is plausible that Japan had simply achieved world-class competitiveness in the sector. It is also not particularly relevant that the U.S. share in the Japanese market was lower than in other markets because that is just what one would expect with a manufactured product for which both Japan and the United States had comparative advantage relative to the rest of the world. This is especially the case considering that the bulk of Japan's semiconductor production was in simple DRAM chips used intensively in the consumer electronics industry, an industry that the U.S. producers had abandoned in the 1980s.

Another issue is whether the market share agreement worked. U.S. semiconductors have been the strongest in the more sophisticated microprocessor chips. It is possible that the rise in the market share by 1992 had more to do with the ascendancy of these, including the extremely successful INTEL 486 chip, than with pressure from Japanese bureaucrats on Japanese firms.

In a second major episode of managed U.S.-Japan trade, in early 1992 U.S. President George Bush travelled to Japan with an entourage of U.S. automobile executives. Bush secured a pledge from Japanese automobile firms (including transplant firms in the United States) that they would purchase $19 billion in automobile parts from U.S. firms by 1994 (Bergsten and Noland 1993, p. 113).

By 1993, the Clinton administration seemed to be moving toward more voluntary import expansion (VIE) agreements in its negotiations with Japan. The rationale seemed to be a simple conclusion that the Japanese market is demonstrably different so that normal market mechanisms do not work.

Trade theory, including that for strategic trade, would say that an approach far preferable to VIEs would be to begin to address the underlying causes of invisible protection, if and where it exists. The principal cause of such restraints is attributed to noncompetitive practices by oligopolistic firms and affiliate groups. The best approach would thus be to pursue antimonopoly enforcement in specific cases of such behavior rather than abandon hope that the market process can work and mandate trade shares established by government officials.

Bergsten and Noland (1993, pp. 194–95) point out several risks of VIEs. These agreements are subject to political capture; they lead to a rigid U.S. retaliation threat, whereas forces beyond the Japanese government's control may affect market share, undermining the credibility of the threat; and they invite abuse by powerful trading countries, and thus, by implication, emulation by the EC. Further attempts to coordinate imports will "inevitably lead to cartelization of the industry," and any quantitative targets are arbitrary. Nevertheless, the two authors suggest that there is a role for the cautious use of VIEs as a transitional, second-best mechanism for compensation of unbalanced trade structures resulting from past protection in Japan and for *keiretsu* market distortions (pp. 196–97).

The fundamental issue regarding VIEs in U.S.-Japan trade is: who bears the burden of proof of unfair action, and how high is the threshold of proof? Where such proof seems conspicuous, as in the case of rigged bidding in Japanese public construction contracts—a practice that was vividly revealed because of its role in the corruption exposés that eventually brought down the LDP government—it is difficult to oppose a VIE, although if possible, reforming the practice in question is preferable. However, where the only evidence is that imports have a low market share, the normal standard for Anglo-Saxon jurisprudence, namely, innocence until guilt is proven, would seem to be missing. As suggested above, it is doubtful that the semiconductor industry would have stood a rigorous test of illegal behavior on the part of Japanese firms. An associated risk is that in adopting a VIE strategy, U.S. negotiators could lose the high ground of adhering to free trade, market-oriented principles. These considerations merely underscore the Bergsten-Noland point that VIEs should be pursued only with great caution. Moreover, as suggested here, VIEs should be contingent upon persuasive evidence that specific collusive, restrictive, or discriminatory practices by industry or government are present.

As one example of the risks of applying the VIE approach, take the case of *keiretsu* firm behavior. It is by no means evident that the mere presence of a *keiretsu* is proof of restrictive behavior. Saxonhouse (1993, p. 39) cites a study by Weinstein and Yafeh showing that the higher the proportion of *keiretsu* firms in an industry, the more competitive the industry is (as measured by lower price-cost margins). This evidence suggests that imports are low in *keiretsu*-intensive sectors because competition is intense in these sectors.

In contrast to the risks of incipient managed trade, there have been other more promising areas of bilateral negotiations. The first was the MOSS (market-oriented, sector-specific) talks in the late 1980s. These negotiations had liberalized Japan's imports in telecommunications, medical equipment, pharmaceuticals, and electronics, with impressive subsequent results for U.S. exports. The second was Super 301 negotiations undertaken after the U.S. government identified Japan as a country systematically restricting trade under procedures required by the 1988 U.S. Trade Act. These negotiations focused on earth satellites, supercomputers, and wood products, the main cases where U.S. negotiators were able to identify tangible barriers, such as government procurement discrimination or unusually high tariffs.

The third area was the SII, the structural impediments initiative, undertaken in 1989. These negotiations cast a much wider net and sought to reform fundamental aspects of economic structure. U.S. negotiators urged liberalization of Japan's retail trade regulations and land zoning laws, and tighter enforcement of antimonopoly laws against the *keiretsu*. Many Japanese citizens welcomed the U.S. pressure for liberalization of a system often closed even to domestic Japanese firms, and they even invented a name for this pressure, *gaiyatsu*. For their part, Japanese negotiators called for the United States to reduce its fiscal deficit and take measures to increase domestic saving. The negotiations reflected a sophisticated understanding of the underlying macroeconomics behind the trade imbalance, as well as a surprising willingness to open essentially domestic structural matters to international discussion. Japanese authorities did facilitate entry into the distribution system, but progress on the other SII commitments, including U.S. fiscal adjustment, was less evident.

The common thread of these negotiation results was that where U.S. negotiators had a concrete complaint on a specific practice that could be changed, there was usually progress. However, where the complaint was that for some unspecified reason, U.S. exporters did not have a fair share of the Japanese market, either little was accomplished or it was necessary to resort to practices that violated the Americans' own principles of favoring market-oriented rather than command-and-control solutions.

U.S.-Japan Overview

There has been important progress in sectoral and structural trade negotiations between the United States and Japan. However, by 1992–93, there was a dangerous trend toward managed trade. A midcourse correction was necessary that would have focused trade demands on "smoking gun" protection where specific restrictive practices could be identified. The next phase of trade cooperation also needed to concentrate on reducing monopoly practices. At the macroeconomic level, there was reason to believe that by late 1993, the large real appreciation of the yen and the eventual recovery of the Japanese economy would substantially reduce the large external sector surplus that had once again soared in 1992–93.

North American Free Trade Agreement

Besides multilateral negotiations in the Uruguay Round and bilateral U.S.-Japan trade tension, the other major trend in trade policy as the 1990s opened concerned regional trade areas. The European Community was adopting its more complete free trade under the single market by 1992 (see chapter 7). As discussed in chapter 3, as early as 1982, U.S. authorities had indicated that if the EC and others were unprepared to move ahead rapidly on trade liberalization, the United States might pursue bilateral and regional pacts with a more limited number of countries willing to liberalize faster. The U.S.-Canada Free Trade Agreement of 1988 was a consequence of that approach. By August of 1992, the heads of state of the United States, Canada, and Mexico had agreed to enlarge that pact to include Mexico in a North American Free Trade Agreement (NAFTA).

Objectives

Mexico's President Carlos Salinas de Gortari had concluded earlier that with attention turned toward newly democratic Eastern Europe, policymakers and investors in Europe would have little interest in channeling capital to Mexico. Thus, Mexico's best chances lay in casting its lot with the United States. Mexican policymakers also wanted the same thing from the NAFTA as Canada had sought: assured future access to a U.S. market susceptible to rising process protection. But perhaps most of all, the Salinas team sought to use the NAFTA as a vehicle to lock in its historic reforms in Mexican economic policy and in the bargain secure large capital inflows of direct investment geared to production for the entire North American market.

For their part, U.S. negotiators had several important objectives in free trade with Mexico. The collapse of the Mexican economy during the debt crisis of the 1980s had served as a warning about the danger of having an unstable economy and impoverished population along the U.S. border. Through open trade, the United States could help Mexico help itself, thereby reducing the long-run prospects of massive immigration and potential Mexican political instability. U.S. firms had already lost exports to Mexico during the debt crisis, an illustration that Mexico's economic health was important for the United States in more direct ways.

There was also the consideration that the Mexican economy offered considerable complementarity to that of the United States. There were concerns about long-run scarcity of unskilled labor in the U.S. economy and about the loss of production to lower-wage competition in Asia. An economic alliance with Mexico offered a remedy for both. At the same time, liberalization would open a substantial market for U.S. firms in such areas as Mexico's banking and insurance industries and in at least the peripheral components of the Mexican oil industry (e.g., petrochemicals).

Provisions

The NAFTA agreement, signed in December 1992 and ratified by the U.S. Congress in November 1993, called for elimination of all tariffs and quotas among the three countries over a maximum of fifteen years—sooner for most products. Sensitive items on the slowest time-table included textiles and agricultural products. NAFTA was to go even further than the Uruguay Round in providing free trade in services and guaranteeing intellectual property.

There were to be strict rules of origin for goods qualifying for free trade. Thus, in textiles there was a yarn forward rule—a product had to be made not only of North American fabric to qualify, but the fabric itself also had to be made from North American yarn. Similarly, with automobiles, there had to be 60% local content for vehicles to qualify for free trade.[11]

The tight rules of origin were one of the elements of the agreement most criticized by trade economists (Hufbauer and Schott 1993). The analytics of rules of origin are subtle. In a world in which there are only final goods (no intermediate inputs), it is impossible for strict rules of origin to have the effect of increasing protection. In such a world, the rule of origin merely prevents transshipment, entry of a third-party good through the partner with the lowest tariff for the purpose of selling to the partner with the high tariff.

Rules of origin can become protective when intermediate inputs are important. The reason is that the intermediate input from a third party now faces essentially a double tariff: once when it enters the member country for transformation into the final product and a second time when it is exported to the other partner and has triggered disqualification for free entry. In such circumstances, the intermediate good from the third party bears not only its preexisting protection barrier but also the full force of the protection on the final good in the market of ultimate destination. This increase in de facto protection is a case of trade diversion, albeit a more disguised case than a simple instance of an explicitly higher tariff imposed on a final good.

A related protective effect of tight rules of origin is that they can distort the pattern of direct investment. For example, a Japanese firm that, in the absence of NAFTA, might invest in Mexico to export to the U.S. market, would tend to import components from Japan. With NAFTA, the firm would be unlikely to invest because these imported components would disqualify the product from free trade status. Under these circumstances, the effect would be to increase the barrier to third party direct investment in Mexico and correspondingly provide an advantage to U.S. and Canadian investment there. Traditional trade models would ascribe no welfare cost to such investment distortions, but an approach more in line with strategic trade theory would tend to conclude that the investment diversion can impose costs not unlike those of trade diversion.

Economic Impact and Political Debate

In part because of relatively tight rules of origin in textiles, automobiles, and some other sectors, U.S. business strongly supported the pact, although with the protest that Mexico's oil sector should have been opened to foreign investment as part of the deal. Labor groups, however, opposed the agreement. U.S. Congressman Richard Gephardt proposed that a tax of 2% be levied on U.S.-Mexico trade to raise funds for adjustment for workers displaced by the agreement and for environmental cleanup in Mexico, especially along the U.S. border.

In the NAFTA debate within the United States, the initial emphasis was on the question of whether the agreement would create or destroy jobs. H. Ross Perot argued that Americans could hear a "giant sucking sound" of jobs being siphoned to locations south of the border. In contrast, Hufbauer and Schott (1992) estimated that the NAFTA would create about 250,000 new export jobs in the United States and displace about 110,000 jobs in import-competing goods, for net job gains of 140,000. Their calculation was premised on the view that Mexico's market-oriented economic reforms could only be sustained with the institutional change of NAFTA and that, with the reforms, there would be large ongoing capital inflows, resulting in a large U.S. trade surplus with Mexico. It seemed more likely that the Salinas administration and its presumably handpicked successor would adhere to the market-based reforms even without the NAFTA. Nonetheless, the assumption of large capital inflows associated with the production for the North American market was surely appropriate and was already being validated by capital flows in 1991–92.

Several other economic studies also calculated effects of the NAFTA. Most predicted small effects for the U.S. economy, primarily because the Mexican economy is only 5% of the size of the U.S. economy.[12] Although the studies generally showed positive effects for both the U.S. and Mexican economies, estimates by Leamer (1991) using a Hecksher-Ohlin framework found that the NAFTA could reduce the annual wage for unskilled U.S. workers by $1,000.[13]

Leamer's estimate highlighted one area in which one should not necessarily expect effects to be small: those for unskilled labor. Mexico's labor force is nearly one-fourth as large as that of the United States, and there is a larger fraction of unskilled workers in Mexico than in the United States. There was thus a legitimate need for attention to labor adjustment, either through programs specially related to NAFTA or through new broader U.S. programs for retraining and placement. Unfortunately, out of eighteen economic models that had featured importantly in the U.S. debate on NAFTA (as surveyed in CBO 1993b), only one disaggregated labor into skilled and unskilled.[14] Most of the models thus missed a crucial point, that is, the need to examine whether NAFTA would contribute to a further widening of the wage gap between unskilled and skilled workers in the U.S. economy.

The studies tended to show larger effects for the Mexican economy than for the United States. In one of the larger impact estimates, the Congressional Budget Office calculated that NAFTA would raise Mexico's GDP by 6 to 12 percentage points above baseline within a decade (CBO 1993a, p. 22). The crucial analytical assumption behind this large estimate was the concept of a high risk premium present in Mexico's real domestic interest rates that would be removed as the consequence of confidence building from NAFTA. The study assumed that NAFTA would reduce this risk premium by 10 percentage points, thereby causing investment and GDP to rise in Mexico. This estimate probably overstated the risk premium effect, but in qualitative terms, the study was almost certainly correct that the largest economic effects would arise from induced investment, especially from abroad, rather than from the welfare triangles of traditional trade theory (see appendix 3A).

At the sectoral level, studies tended to show that the U.S. automobile sector would gain from NAFTA. In the past, Mexico had maintained major barriers to automobile imports and required export performance goals for foreign firms manufacturing automobiles in Mexico. Mexican agriculture was another sector with large expected effects, as liberalization was likely to reduce domestic corn production. NAFTA was expected to increase U.S. exports of grains to Mexico and U.S. imports of Mexican fruits and vegetables. Accounting for about one-fourth of Mexican employment, agriculture seemed likely, on balance, to be a significant source of displaced workers who might cause a temporary bulge in immigration to the United States until the postive growth effects of NAFTA on the Mexican economy could cause a more than offsetting influence. Nonetheless, agricultural liberalization was to be phased in slowly and in any event was already part of the Mexican government's reform agenda with or without NAFTA.

Environment

NAFTA raised legitimate environmental concerns, although these were susceptible to being exaggerated and exploited as a disguised form of protectionism. Although Mexico's environmental laws are about as tough as those in the United States, the Mexican government has lacked resources for rigorous enforcement. A free trade area is a more intense economic relationship among nations than that of most favored nation (MFN). As such, it legitimately involves a higher threshold of mutual expectations, which can appropriately include environmental practices that otherwise should be left to individual nations' discretion (see chapter 8). The legitimacy of this interest especially applies insofar as plant location is likely to be affected, and there was considerable fear among the environmental community in the United States that free trade with Mexico would encourage U.S. firms to locate in Mexico to escape environmental controls. However, these fears were probably exaggerated, in part because environmental protection expenses tend to be only a small fraction of production costs (CBO 1993a, p. xvii).

In 1992, the Bush administration and Congress haggled over how much funding should be made available for U.S.-Mexico environmental improvement and in what form. By 1993, President Clinton negotiated side agreements to NAFTA on environment and labor standards, designed to calm the fears of U.S. environmental groups and labor unions opposed to the pact. The environmental side agreement allowed firms or groups to bring suit against a member government for failing to enforce its own environmental laws. A panel comprised of one representative from each of the three countries was to judge whether such a complaint required remedy, with the provision for trade sanctions in the absence of remedial action.

In the United States, the NAFTA debate reached fever pitch in the autumn of 1993. The issue transformed into a symbolic debate on whether America's future lay with turning inward and protectionist or with deciding to "compete rather than retreat" (in President Clinton's words) and accepting the challenge of an ever more open and integrated world economy. The successful passage of the pact depended heavily on Republican support of the Democratic president and threatened to leave lasting scars on the relationship between the administration and organized labor.

The reaction of the rest of the world to NAFTA was mixed. At first, the principal question was whether the new entity might become an exclusive trading bloc. More generally, there was rising concern by the beginning of the 1990s that world trade was headed toward division into mutually exclusive blocs. However, NAFTA did not impose new protection against outsiders. Although any free trade area involves some trade diversion from third parties, the traditional issue for outsiders is whether they gain an offsetting increase in exports because of the stimulus of the free trade area to economic growth of member countries. In the case of NAFTA, Mexico's growth was highly likely to receive a favorable boost so that outsiders stood to gain in this regard. In any event, by the last phase of the NAFTA debate, the issue had become whether the United States was going to embrace open trade or protectionism. In this context, other nations came to see passage of NAFTA as crucial to the future of world trade and especially the prospects for a successful conclusion of the Uruguay Round.

Western Hemisphere Free Trade?

NAFTA had arisen in the broader context of U.S. trade and investment initiatives toward Latin America. In 1990, the Bush administration had launched its Enterprise for the Americas Initiative, which involved a series of open trade framework agreements with Latin American nations, the prospect of forgiveness of official debt for lower-income countries, and a new Multilateral Investment Fund of $1.5 billion to be administered by the InterAmerican Development Bank. There was a strong hint that at some future date there could be free trade "from the Yukon to Tierra del Fuego."

Pragmatism suggests that that date could be later rather than sooner. The domestic U.S. political turbulence associated with NAFTA had been sufficient that it seemed likely that there would be a waiting period for its effects to be digested before other countries could enter free trade with the United States, either through a docking clause in NAFTA or independently. Chile was first in line after Mexico and was well qualified by its open economy and market-oriented reforms. However, it seemed likely that even U.S. free trade with Chile could face delay, in part because this Latin American country had no domestic U.S. constituency comparable to the Mexican-American population.

As for the possibility of a broader Western Hemisphere Free Trade Area, the timetable is likely to be even slower. One reason is that some countries, such as Argentina and Brazil, have high shares of trade with Europe and Japan, in contrast to the dominance of the United States in Mexico's trade. Another is that an immediate push for free trade throughout the western hemisphere would be seen by U.S. labor unions as rubbing salt in their NAFTA wounds. U.S. trade strategists also have to keep in mind that if the rest of the world gets the impression that the United States is turning inward to the western hemisphere, there could be a backlash that would hurt U.S. exports, and in economic terms, Latin America remains too small to compensate U.S. exporters for any broader loss of markets in Europe, Japan, and elsewhere.

Suggested Readings

Lawrence (1993), Saxonhouse (1993), Bergsten and Noland (1993).

5   The International Debt Problem

The developing country debt crisis erupted in 1982 when Mexico suspended payments, and the problem was still not fully resolved a decade later. In its acute period, 1982–83, it was a crisis of global proportions that threatened the world banking system. The large (money center) U.S. banks had exposure to developing countries that amounted to 150 to 200% of their capital, primarily in Latin America where the crisis was centered.

Intensive international coordination to manage the crisis avoided a global financial disaster. The banks protected themselves by building up capital and setting aside loan loss reserves. However, most of the debtor countries suffered prolonged recession, and by the end of the decade, the debt problem was one of recovery and economic development rather than global financial crisis.

By the early 1990s, it had become clear that country policy was the central determinant of the outcome. Such countries as Chile, Mexico, and Venezuela that had followed good economic policies had put the debt problem behind them. Indeed, the countries with the strongest policies managed to avoid the crisis altogether, including South Korea and Colombia (despite the bad neighborhood effect on the latter). In contrast, countries, such as Argentina (through 1990), Brazil, and especially Peru, where there had been unstable policies lagged behind.

Origins of the Crisis

The debt crisis stemmed from both external and internal forces.

External Causes

The oil shock of the 1970s meant much higher trade deficits for oil-importing countries, such as Brazil. The governments of industrial countries could provide little direct help to the developing countries hit by the oil price increase, but they gave encouragement to financial recycling of OPEC money through bank lending. The banks in turn were eager to lend, in order to invest the large deposits they had received from OPEC nations. By the late 1970s, there was some concern that developing countries were building up too much debt, but the dominant view was that the modern international capital market, and particularly the innovations of syndicated bank lending at variable interest rates based on the London Interbank Offer Rate, LIBOR, was admirably rising to the task posed by the oil shock. Yet, the solution to one problem was sowing the seeds for another. Ironically, important oil-exporting countries such as Mexico were also building up debt as they invested heavily using oil as collateral for loans.

The international interest rate shock of 1981–82 pushed LIBOR as high as 17%. Loans that had been viable when interest rates were 7% and world inflation was 7 to 10% in the mid-1970s turned oppressively burdensome when interest rates rose far above inflation. Broadly speaking, a debtor could manage well if the dollar value of its exports was rising more rapidly than the nominal interest rate because then the export base would grow faster than the inherited growth of debt from interest on past debt. This comparison was favorable in the 1970s when commodity export prices were soaring, but it was highly unfavorable by 1982 when interest rates were high and commodity prices falling. The world recession of 1982, the worst since the 1930s, further aggravated the race between exports and interest on debt because it meant a sharp decline in the industrial countries' demand for imports from debtor countries.

Internal Causes

Imprudent domestic management was another major cause of the crisis for many countries. For example, when the price of coffee tripled in 1975–77, some exporting countries such as Brazil and Costa Rica used the gains as leverage to borrow more abroad, whereas the more cautious Colombians refrained from taking on more loans despite the banks' enthusiastic offers.

Fiscal imbalance was the most common area of mismanagement. Mexico, for example, had large government spending programs for public investment, as well as food subsidies, that brought the budget deficit to 14% of GDP in 1981. Chile and Colombia were the main exceptions, as their fiscal policy was much more cautious. Large budget deficits translated into large borrowing abroad by both central governments and state firms, in part because domestic capital markets were thin.

Financial distortions that led to capital flight were another internal source of debt buildup. Thus in the late 1970s and early 1980s, Venezuela kept domestic interest rates below domestic inflation and below international interest rate levels while holding a fixed exchange rate that looked increasingly unsustainable. Citizens had a strong incentive to place money abroad to earn higher interest and possibly profit from a devaluation. Dollars that left the country in capital flight were not available to purchase imports or service foreign debt.

Development strategy was perhaps the most fundamental internal distortion. For years, the key Latin American countries had pursued the model of import substituting industrialization, which sought rapid industrial development behind high protective barriers against imports. This model eventually led to inefficient production and frequently domestic monopoly. It had a serious side effect of discouraging export development. Firms could sell in the domestic market at the world price plus a high import tariff ($p_d = p_w + t$) but only at the world price in the export market (p_w). It is no accident that Korea and other East Asian countries, which had followed export-oriented development strategies, did much better than most Latin American countries in withstanding the debt crisis.

The outbreak of the crisis was preceded by a warning sign in the spring of 1982 when Argentina suspended debt payments to the United Kingdom during the war over the Falkland Islands. The real crisis erupted in the summer of 1982, however, when Mexico experienced a run on the peso. The price of oil was falling, and short-term lenders were refusing to renew credit. In mid-August the government announced it would have to defer payments, thereby inaugurating the debt crisis. At first it looked as if other countries, such as Brazil, might be able to differentiate themselves from Mexico and keep renewing loans. By the autumn, it had become clear that the banks were cutting off new lending to most of the Latin American countries because of the shock of the Mexican suspension.

Walter Wriston, the chairman of Citibank, had said in earlier years that there was no such thing as sovereign risk because countries do not disappear. The events of mid-1982 provided a rude awakening for creditors that sovereign risk did exist. Moreover, they quickly became acutely conscious that, unlike mortgages and other domestic loans, sovereign loans provided no physical collateral that could be called in the event of nonperformance. The stage was set for a protracted process of bargaining and workout between two primary parties—the debtor countries and the foreign banks—with the participation of industrial country governments and the international financial agencies.

Phases of International Debt Policy

The debt strategy passed through three phases. Each successive phase represented a more radical approach, based on the evolving view that the debt problem was more resistant to solution than previously thought.

Phase I: Emergency Finance and Concerted Lending, 1982–84

The initial policy response to Mexico's suspension set the pattern for the strategy over the next three years. Led by the U.S. Treasury and Federal Reserve, the official international agencies and the commercial banks implemented coordinated lending packages to enable debtor countries to resume payments. Typically, the International Monetary Fund entered into a stabilization program with the country, usually for eighteen months but later in three-year Extended Fund Facility arrangements. The IMF could lend moderate amounts based on the country's quota in that organization. More importantly, the IMF's seal of approval gave the green light for the banks to provide new lending on a coordinated basis. The standard arrangement provided for a rescheduling of principal payment, plus new loans that covered a moderate portion of interest coming due. The reschedulings were relatively short-leash, postponing repayments only for the next two years or so and setting fairly short new maturities (e.g., six to nine years).

There were three intellectual underpinnings to the strategy of coordinated lending. First, the strategy rested upon the diagnosis that most countries were facing a temporary cash flow (illiquidity) problem rather than one of permanent insolvency. As discussed below, this view was based on the prospect that conditions would improve as the international economy recovered and other key macroeconomic influences returned to more normal levels. Recovery from world recession would boost debtor country exports, world interest rates would be likely to fall from unusually high levels, and both of these developments would be likely to increase commodity prices. Moreover, the dollar—seriously overvalued by 1984—seemed likely to fall, and it was plausible that a falling dollar would further boost the dollar price of commodities so as to maintain their real prices against a basket of currencies. A time-honored tradition is that the central bank lends to an illiquid member bank but not to an insolvent bank, whose liabilities far exceed assets even including illiquid ones. By analogy, it made sense initially to address the debt problem by providing new lending rather than moving to the equivalent of bankruptcy proceedings.

Second, lending strategy recognized that there was a severe free rider problem in mobilizing new lending. No individual bank had an incentive to lend new funds, but the banks as a group could benefit if new loans were made and default was thereby avoided. The crucial role of the IMF was to act as the centralizing agency that internalized for the group the individual banks' external economies of providing new lending, thereby overcoming the free rider problem. To this end, the IMF took the position that it would lend none of its own money to a country until there was a critical mass of new lending from the banks.

Third, the lending strategy assumed that, if countries honored their debts, albeit on rescheduled timetables and with the help of coordinated bank lending under IMF and official pressure, they would in later years enjoy a credit reputation that would enable them to reenter capital markets on a basis of voluntary lending. Moreover, the strategy anticipated that, over a period of a few years, country adjustment and global economic normalization would bring the trade balances, debt/export ratios, and other indicators of creditworthiness back into line with traditionally safe thresholds.

For their part, the banks as a group had an incentive to provide new loans, as may be analyzed in the calculus of involuntary lending (Cline 1983a). Let $p_D{}^0$ be the initial probability of default without new loans; $p_D{}^{1'}$ the (lower) probability after the provision of the new loans; D, the amount of loans outstanding; and L, the amount of new lending. The banks as a group had an incentive to lend so long as the expected cost of the new loans was less than the expected benefit of increased security of the old loans. This test was met if:

$$p_D{}^1 L < \{p_D{}^0 - p_D{}^1\} D.$$

Thus, the expected loss, if any, on the new loans was the afterpackage default probability multiplied by the amount of new loans. The expected gain on old loans was the reduction in default probability, $(p_D^0 - p_D^1)$, multiplied by the previous total of outstanding loans. As long as the amount of new lending was moderate and the country was likely to be willing and able to honor its debt with the help of the new loans, this condition was met. The international financial agencies soon coined the more harmonious term concerted lending in preference to involuntary lending, but it was the same thing.

Phase II: The Baker Plan, 1985–88

The year 1984 seemed to validate the initial debt strategy. There was a strong recovery in the world economy. Economic growth returned to Latin America, the main center of the debt crisis, after two years of recession. However, by early 1985 there were increasing strains on the approach. Leaders of major Latin American countries were frustrated that although they had devalued exchange rates, cut trade deficits, and paid the price of recession, voluntary lending was not resuming. Serious inflationary pressures were affecting their economies, in part because of devaluation necessitated by the need to close the trade gap. Two major countries, Argentina and Brazil, returned from military to democratic rule, and there were populist pressures for higher wages and a tougher line with the banks. In the same year, a devastating earthquake hit Mexico City, imposing a reconstruction bill of several billion dollars.

In September of 1985, U.S. Treasury Secretary James Baker proposed a new strategy for the debt problem. The Baker Plan called for a more structural approach that treated debt as a longer-term development problem rather than one of temporary illiquidity. It proposed that debtor countries pursue fiscal adjustment and in addition carry out structural reform in three areas: liberalization of trade, liberalization of policies on direct foreign investment, and privatization of state enterprises. The proposal to privatize state firms seemed intrusive at the time, yet within five years a wave of privatization had swept Latin America.

The Baker Plan set forth targets for lending by the banks and the international agencies. For a group of fifteen large, troubled debtor countries (later expanded to seventeen to include Costa Rica and Jamaica, whose political salience exceeded the size of their debt), the banks were asked to make new loans amounting to $20 billion over three years. As total bank claims on these countries amounted to about $250 billion, this proposal meant new money of about 3% of existing exposure each year, or about enough to cover one-third of the interest coming due. In view of the structural-developmental diagnosis of the problem, lending was to be at longer maturities and rescheduling was to cover more years in advance (multiyear rescheduling agreements, MYRAs), and terms were to be lightened by narrowing the spread above LIBOR (e.g., from 2% to 1%).

The Baker Plan also pledged to increase the lending of the multilateral development banks (Mdbs), primarily the World Bank and Inter-American Development Bank, by $10 billion over the three year period. However, the plan gave no explicit attention to IMF lending, yet repayments of IMF loans made at the outset of the debt crisis were scheduled to come due so that much of the increased MDB lending would be offset by reflows back to the IMF. Nonetheless, the targets for MDB lending represented a more formal commitment of public sector effort to match the adjustment efforts of the debtor countries and the new lending undertaking by the banks.

In implementation, the Baker Plan eventually employed an important innovation in financial engineering, the menu approach. It had become increasingly clear that different types of banks had different objectives. Large money center banks that planned to remain in the Latin American business had more reason to lend new long-term money, while small, regional banks with relatively little exposure had an incentive to get out as fast as possible so that they could say their books carried no Latin American paper (a purity worth something in price-earnings ratios for bank stocks).

The menu approach (Cline 1987) introduced the notion of the exit bond for the small banks, an option of accepting a lower-interest, long-term bond in exchange for the bank's claim rather than participate in new money packages of additional loans. The menu also included the idea of new-money bonds, under the argument that bonds had been treated more favorably and thus this form of lending might acquire implicit seniority, facilitating bank participation. Debt-equity swaps were another important option on the menu. Banks could accept local currency, at some discount from face value of their claim, for use in the purchase of shares in businesses.[1] Discounted buybacks were yet another option and were analogous to exit bonds but involved steeper discounts in return for payment in cash (and in foreign exchange rather than local currency).

Soon after the Baker Plan was launched, an international event occurred that dealt it a heavy blow: the price of oil fell by half in 1986. The early analysis of the debt crisis had warned that a collapse of oil prices would damage prospects for emerging from it (Cline 1984) because the debtors that were oil exporters (such as Venezuela, Mexico, and Ecuador) had a much higher share of oil in their exports than the share of oil in imports of oil-importing debtors (Brazil) and because the debtors as a group were large net exporters of oil.

Among the Baker-seventeen countries, there were three groups. In the first, five oil-exporting nations (Ecuador, Mexico, Nigeria, Peru, and Venezuela) accounted for 39% of the total external debt in 1985. In this group, oil represented 76% of export earnings in 1985 (calculated from IMF 1991a). In a second group of oil importers, nine countries (Brazil, Chile, Costa Rica, Ivory Coast, Jamaica, Morocco, Philippines, Uruguay, and Yugoslavia) accounted for 47% of the debt. These countries on average spent 22% of their export earnings on imported oil. The third group consisted of countries with oil self-sufficiency: Argentina and Colombia. Their debt was 14% of the total. In all, countries accounting for about 60% of the debt were oil importers or self sufficient and had limited or negligible direct benefits from lower prices. Countries accounting for about 40% of the debt depended massively on oil exports.

Especially after the collapse of oil prices in 1986, the Baker Plan faced severe difficulties. As always, Mexico was a leading country for the evolving debt strategy, and after the collapse of oil prices, Mexican authorities were convinced that something more forceful than the Baker Plan would be required. In a populist phase, Brazil went into extended arrears on interest, and Argentina later followed. Latin America was in severe recession by 1988–89, and it was easy to blame external debt even though often the fundamental problem was fiscal imbalance and high inflation that discouraged investment.

By 1987–88, critics in industrial countries were arguing that the debt strategy had been too one-sided and had not involved enough sacrifice by the banks. Congressional critics stressed that U.S. export jobs had been lost because of undue attention to the banks' interests. Such criticisms, however, missed the underlying point that the existing strategy was not designed to comfort the banks, but to maximize the chances of the debtor countries to have future access to credit markets and to remain integrated into the world economy by avoiding a messy divorce from the international banking system as a consequence of default.

Further, by 1988 a growing view in policy circles was that the banks had failed to deliver on their part of the Baker Plan. Their exposure to the debtor countries had stagnated or declined, thereby seeming to indicate that they had not lent the new money pledged. In fact, the banks did enter into new money packages that amounted to about $13 billion out of the $20 billion target (Cline 1989a). Their reported outstanding claims failed to rise only because they were selling off debt in the secondary market or because they were conducting debt-equity swaps and discounted buybacks. The latter two phenomena were helpful in solving the debt crisis, even though they gave the appearance of backsliding by the banks because their exposure to debtor countries fell rather than rose.

For their part, the MDBs lent considerably less than intended under the Baker Plan. The reason was primarily that key countries had entered into periods of policy disarray and did not meet IMF conditionality requirements. If the swing to repayments to the IMF is taken into account, there was a major decline rather than an increase in net capital flows from international agencies to major debtor countries under the Baker Plan. Similarly, industrial country export credit agencies were reducing their net lending.

With the benefit of hindsight, a case may be made that despite its difficulties, the Baker Plan could well have proven sufficient to resolve the bulk of the debt problem if it had not been for the collapse of the price of oil. Even as matters turned out, two important Latin American debtors, Colombia and Chile, did not require the next phase of intensification of debt policy, partial forgiveness of debt under the Brady Plan. Moreover, if the arithmetic rather than the psychology is considered, neither Mexico nor Venezuela would have needed debt reduction (forgiveness) if oil prices had not fallen in 1986. Mexico lost about $6 billion in annual oil export earnings from lower oil prices and gained only about $1.5 billion annually from the eventual interest and debt forgiveness of the Brady Plan. As for the largest non-oil-exporting debtor countries, Argentina and Brazil, the essential problem was one of poor domestic economic policies rather than an unmanageable debt burden that required debt reduction.

Nevertheless, market conditions by 1988–89 offered an opportunity for voluntary, market-oriented debt reduction that could help not only the countries hurt by the oil price collapse but also those that had lagged behind because of weak domestic policies (at least, so long as the latter were prepared to adopt policy reforms). The essence of this opportunity was that many banks were so disheartened that they were prepared to accept a substantial write-down in the debt in exchange for either immediate cash or long-term bonds that had a meaningful guarantee. This market opportunity set the stage for the next phase in debt strategy.

Phase III: The Brady Plan, 1989 and After

The preconditions for this next phase began to be set in place in 1987. In that year, Brazil's suspension of interest payments prompted its largest creditor, Citibank, to set aside substantial loan loss reserves. This action came as a shock to the financial community because Citibank had been in the lead in supporting new lending, and the implication was that, if this lender no longer considered the claims worth full face value, how could anyone else? Other banks soon followed suit, and as interest arrears persisted, U.S. regulators made such reserves mandatory. As banks built up loan loss reserves, they created a cushion that would eventually facilitate debt reduction agreements. With the banking system less vulnerable, debt forgiveness as a conscious part of the strategy became more plausible.

The second development that pointed in the same direction was the growth of a secondary market in claims on troubled debtor countries. Banks wishing to be free of such tarnished assets sold them to investors, often at extremely low prices. Investment banks, even the lead money-center banks, helped make markets in these claims, and prices began to be quoted regularly. Prices in the range of twenty to forty cents on the dollar were common. As these secondary market prices gained attention, they began to be interpreted by many as evidence of what the claims were really worth. It was not a large leap from there to the view that it would be fair to reduce the debt through a forgiveness that would cut the claims by some amount reflecting the depth of the discount observed in the secondary market. There was, however, a major catch: sales in the secondary market gave the seller immediate cash. If claims were written down but still remained payable at some future date, the real value to the seller would be much less than the secondary market price because of the continuing risk.

This situation was ready-made for entry of a third party to provide the comfort of a guarantee. With a guarantee, the banks that were prepared to sell at deep discounts in the secondary market would be content to accept a significant, though less deep, cut in long-term claims. Under these conditions, there could be a high return to the use of official resources from industrial countries and international agencies in the form of guarantees in a package of voluntary debt reduction (Williamson 1988; Cline, 1988).

In the 1988 U.S. election, candidate George Bush hinted at more extreme measures to deal with the debt problem. A Texan, he had a keen political interest in Mexico. Within Congress, there were calls for a new international agency to buy up the debt and to pressure banks to sell it at a major discount. When riots in Caracas led to at least 300 deaths in February of 1989, seeming to demonstrate that economic adjustment programs imposed to deal with the debt crisis were causing unacceptable suffering and political instability, the last piece of evidence that a new debt strategy was necessary seemed to be in hand, and by March, Treasury Secretary Nicholas Brady launched the Brady Plan.

The new plan replaced concerted lending with debt reduction as the centerpiece of the debt strategy. The reduction of debt was to take place on a voluntary, market-oriented basis. Public funds for enhancements, or guarantees on the debt, were to provide the incentive for banks to accept reduced claims. Somewhat confusedly, the plan initially also stated that further new lending should continue as well. However, for any given bank, new lending and debt reduction were far more likely to be mutually exclusive options.

The new phase did not go to the radical extreme of forcing banks to accept prescribed write-downs. Debtor countries had concluded early in the crisis that unilateral default, certainly in the form of repudiation, was counterproductive. Even lapsing into arrears had been shown to have the adverse side effect of causing short-term trade credits to run down. As for the option of an international official effort to force and to administer the equivalent of uncompensated default, the impact on the debtors was not likely to be much better. It was unclear, as well as being relatively unlikely, that governments could legally force their banks to forgive claims. Moreover, forced forgiveness would leave a bad image in international credit markets for the country in question for years to come, even if it was the governments of industrial countries that did the forcing of their respective banks.

For their part, the banks distinguished between countries that truly needed debt reduction in a workout and those that did not. J. P. Morgan was reported to have once said, "Willingness to pay is more important than ability to pay." Banks and credit markets were more likely to return to a favorable credit rating for a country if the extent of any debt reduction seemed to be related closely to a reasonable evaluation of what was necessary after the country had made its own best efforts at adjustment, than if the demand for reduction was more politically based and not seen as necessary.

By mid-1989, Mexico had tentatively reached agreement on a Brady Plan debt reduction. There were three basic options. Banks could exchange their loans for thirty-year par bonds that kept full face value but paid a fixed interest rate set at about one-third below the previous LIBOR-based rate. Another option was discount bonds that paid the full LIBOR plus a spread of 13/16% but cut the principal by 35%. Finally, they could choose new money, by retaining their full claim but lending an additional 25% of exposure over four years. The conversion bonds had guarantees on principal and on eighteen months' interest; new money had no guarantee. Most banks chose the guaranteed conversion bonds, although in retrospect, the few banks that chose new money look prescient. The agreement effectively cut the equivalent of $15 billion off of the banks' $50 billion loans (excluding short-term) to Mexico. The IMF, World Bank, and Japanese Export-Import Bank lent Mexico $5 billion for use in purchasing guarantee assets, U.S. Treasury zero-coupon bonds coming due in thirty years.

By the end of 1990, Venezuela had negotiated a similar agreement with the banks. The Venezuela agreement set 30% as the depth of cut. It included the option of cash buyback at forty-five cents on the dollar. More banks chose the new-money option in the Venezuelan case. The Philippines also reached a Brady Plan agreement that involved buybacks at fifty cents on the dollar and new money. However, Philippine authorities promptly said further reduction would be necessary.

In contrast, Mexican officials praised the new accord and insisted that Mexico had put the debt crisis behind it. This psychology proved crucial because it soon became apparent that the indirect effect from improved confidence was at least as important as the direct effect of lower debt service payments. Figure 5.1 shows the interest rate the Mexican government was paying on its domestic peso treasury bills. Note that inflation was running at about 20% per year in 1989. The treasury bill rate was 55% immediately before the agreement in principle, plummeted to 34% after tentative agreement was reached, and reached about 25% within a few months after actual signing of the agreement. World Bank experts have estimated that the total effect of the Brady Plan agreement was to increase Mexico's prospective growth rate by 2 percentage points annually for 1990–94 (Van Wijnbergen 1991). Of this gain, half was from the direct effect of lower interest payments on external debt (a reduction of about $1.5 billion annually), but fully half came from the indirect effect of higher confidence and

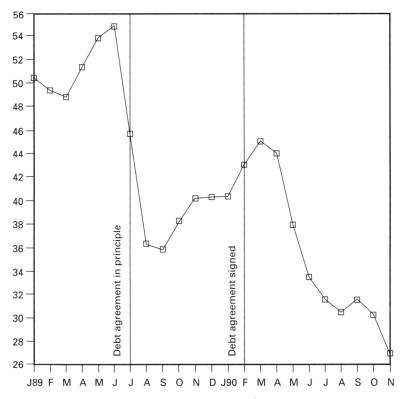

Figure 5.1
Mexico: average rates on three-month treasury bills (percent per year, uncompounded)

lower domestic interest rates. By 1991–92, Mexico was enjoying favorable economic growth, relatively low inflation, and a massive inflow of foreign capital in the form of portfolio and direct investment. By all accounts, the Brady Plan for Mexico was a stunning success, even though some critics had initially called for substantially deeper debt reduction (Sachs 1989).

The Economics of Voluntary Debt Reduction

Economists were developing the analytics of voluntary debt reduction prior to the Brady Plan. One concept many emphasized was the notion of a debt overhang. The argument was that domestic and multinational investors would not invest in a country until its excess debt was eliminated because they feared that future governments would have to tax the output from their projects in order to pay the debt. Krugman (1989) noted that this argument amounted to a Laffer curve for debt, referring to the curve made famous by Arthur B. Laffer, who had argued in the early 1980s that a lower tax rate would stimulate activity so much that the absolute tax revenue might increase.

Figure 5.2, panel A, shows the debt Laffer curve. The horizontal axis shows the face value of the country's debt. The vertical axis shows the expected value of repayment as perceived by the banks. Up to a moderate amount of debt, the two are equal, and the curve lies along the 45° line. As the debt builds up further, however, creditors begin to doubt full repayment, and the expected value of repayment falls short of face value of debt. After a maximum, or turning point (D_1), expected value actually falls as further face-value debt is added. If the country has debt of D_0, then both the debtor and the creditor can be made better off by reducing debt back to D_1. The amount $D_0 - D_1$ is excess debt, or the debt overhang.

The extreme argument for voluntary debt reduction thus invokes the case where the country is to the right of the maximum on the debt Laffer curve. However, cross-country statistical tests relating the secondary market price to relative indebtedness (e.g., debt/GDP) indicate that this situation has been rare (Cline 1990a). In cases such as that of Mexico, it is indeed difficult to imagine that a creditor would gain $1.01 in expected value of the remaining claim by forgiving $1.00 from the existing total. External debt is simply too limited a part of the total economy, and for that matter, bank claims were only about half of external debt in the Mexican case. Where investment is depressed, the main reason is more likely to be unstable expectations caused by high inflation, and although the devaluation and interest burden associated with the debt crisis are part of the reason for inflation, they are unlikely to be as important a source as the chronic domestic policy distortions, such as an inadequate tax structure, losses of state enterprises, and populist subsidy programs. Countries at points such as D_0 in figure 5.2(A) are likely to be limited to extreme cases, such as that of the Sudan, where debt was about twenty times exports in 1988–89.

For most of the large, middle-income debtor countries experiencing debt difficulty, the situation is more likely to be as shown in panel B of figure 5.2. In this instance, it is impossible to make both the debtor and the creditor better off by simply reducing debt. Any movement backward along curve RR benefits the country but reduces the expected value of repayment to the banks. However, it is still possible to achieve mutually beneficial debt reduction if the ingredient of a guar-

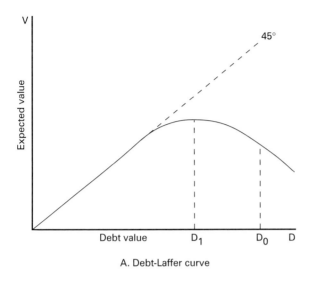

A. Debt-Laffer curve

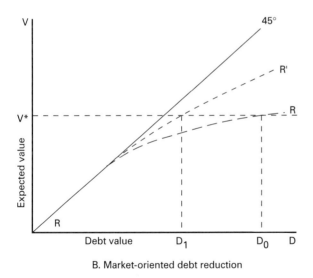

B. Market-oriented debt reduction

Figure 5.2
Nominal value of debt (D) and the expected repayment (V)

antee is added. Suppose a Brady Plan guarantee of principal plus eighteen months' interest is added. Then any given face value of debt has a higher expected repayment value, and the debt curve shifts up to RR'. It is now possible to reduce the face value of the debt from D_0 to D_1, which benefits the country, without reducing the expected value of repayment to the banks. In figure 5.2(B) this expected value remains unchanged at V^*. Essentially, the guarantee has provided a substitute that compensates for the reduction in the face value of the claim. Importantly, if the country fully intends to honor the debt after the restructuring, the guarantee will never be called upon, and the international agencies that have provided it will not have experienced any real cost or loss because the debtor country is paying them interest for the guarantee funds. Indeed, if the international agencies are confident of this outcome, there is no shifting of any loss to the public sector from the banks and the debtor country. Figure 5.2(B) thus shows the essence of Brady Plan debt reduction for most middle-income debtor countries.

This debt reduction is clearly market related because the depth of the cut is geared to the extent of the guarantees (as shown by the amount by which the debt curve swivels from RR to RR') and geared to the initial extent of the secondary market discount (the amount by which curve RR falls short of the 45° line at D_0). In the spirit of market-oriented debt reduction, country negotiators cannot seek to reduce debt all the way down to the secondary market price unless they are prepared to pay outright cash or provide complete guarantees. Instead, the extent of the discount shown by the secondary market price is shared between the debtor and the creditor. In the Mexican case, the secondary market price in 1988–89 was forty cents on the dollar. The agreement settled at sixty-five cents on the dollar, which shared the discount at thirty-five cents for Mexico and twenty-five cents for the banks. The banks were willing to accept the thirty-five cent forgiveness because they considered it compatible with the amount of security, which altogether, including set-aside Mexican reserves, stood at $7 billion or about one-seventh of face value and one-fifth of after-reduction value. To induce the banks to accept a deeper cut would have required more guarantees or else a departure from market orientation and a shift toward a forced solution.

The Brady Plan deals have also generally been voluntary in that they have typically included the option of lending new money. A bank confident of the country's future can choose to keep its entire claim and lend additional money. As noted, the few banks that did so for Mexico look clever in retrospect because, by 1992, Mexico seemed likely to be able to honor its remaining debt fully.

Growing Out of Debt

The need for Brady Plan debt reduction meant that the initial debt strategy was insufficient. However, the depth of debt reduction has been moderate. Mexico's 35% cut for banks amounted to only 15% for overall debt because half of the debt (primarily that owed to international agencies and bilateral export credit agencies) was excluded. If Mexico was able to recover fully with a reduction of only 15% in its debt, despite the oil price collapse, then the initial strategy must not have been too far off the mark. As noted, the cases of Chile and Colombia show that for some important cases the initial strategy was sufficient.

The essence of the strategy through the Baker Plan was that countries would grow out of their debt problem by adopting economic reforms that would increase the export base and the productivity of the overall economy. The ratio of debt to exports is a useful summary indicator of the degree of success in this effort. A country begins with a high debt/export ratio, but by increasing exports, it reduces the ratio over time, even though the absolute debt volume may be rising from new money packages. The debt/export ratio comes down faster if the country manages to run a trade surplus so that funds are available to repay the debt or at least cover most of the interest. The ratio also improves if the country can obtain direct investment because that form of capital does not increase debt. The entire process is helped if international conditions are favorable: low interest rates, high growth in industrial country markets, and rising commodity prices.

Appendix 5A sets forth a simple model of the strategy of growing out of the debt crisis. In this model, the growth rate of the debt/export ratio may be projected as follows:

$$g_d = i - \beta/d - k - [\dot{p}_w + \epsilon g_{YDC} + c],$$

where d is the ratio of debt to exports, i is the world interest rate (LIBOR), β is the trade surplus as a fraction of exports, k is annual direct investment capital inflow as a fraction of debt stock, $\dot{p}_w$ is world inflation, g_{YDC} is the growth rate of industrial countries, and c is a constant specific to the country. The logic here is that ideally the growth rate of the debt/export ratio will be negative so as to reduce the ratio over time. The growth rate of this debt burden indicator will be lower if there is a lower component of inherited debt buildup from interest rates (lower i), favorable access to foreign capital in the non-debt-creating form of direct investment (high k), a high propensity to run a trade surplus (β) to eat away at the debt, and high export growth (the entire final bracketed expression) in order to increase the denominator of the debt/export ratio. For its part, nominal export growth depends on world inflation, growth in industrial country markets, and country-specific factors.

With this equation for the debt/export ratio, it may be seen how a country can grow out of its debt problem under reasonable conditions. A typical value for the debt/export ratio at the outset of the crisis was 300%, or $d = 3.0$. A target debt export ratio for return to creditworthiness would be 200% ($d = 2.0$). World interest rates including spread were on the order of 9% in the late 1980s ($i = .09$). Latin American countries were typically running trade surpluses of say 20% of exports ($\beta = 0.2$). A country the size of Brazil with $100 billion in debt could expect to get say $3 billion annual inflow from direct investment and repatriation of flight capital, or $k = .03$. World inflation was on the order of 4% annually (.04). The income elasticity of industrial country demand for Latin American exports (ϵ) has been on the order of, say, 2.0. Industrial country growth was close to 3% ($g_{YDC} = .03$); and the exogenous export growth component might be, say, 2% annually ($c = .02$). With these central values, we would have:

$$g_d = .09 - 0.2/3.0 - .03 - [.04 + 2 \times .03 + .02] = -0.13.$$

Thus, the debt export ratio would decline at an annual rate of 13%. After one year, it would fall from 300% to 260%, the next year it would stand at 230%, and by the fourth year, it would be down to 200%, the creditworthiness threshold. In short, under reasonable assumptions, the country could export its way out of its debt crisis.

It is also easy to apply the model to show the influence of unfavorable external conditions and bad domestic policy. Suppose an overvalued exchange rate turns the country intercept for export growth to $c = -.02$ and leads to a trade deficit such that $\beta = -.2$. Suppose world growth is sluggish at $g_{YDC} = 0.01$, and there is no direct investment inflow ($k = 0$). With all else unchanged: $g_d = 0.12$. Thus, the debt/export rises at 12% annually instead of falling at 13%. Clearly, where it was possible to combine good policy with good luck, it was much more feasible to grow out of the debt crisis.

What Went Wrong?

Figure 5.3 shows that, for the seventeen Baker Plan countries, the ratio of debt to exports rose from an average of about 275% to about 375% from 1982–85 to 1987 before turning down again. In terms of the debt model just considered, the single largest reason for this adverse trend was the collapse in the price of oil and consequently in the value of oil

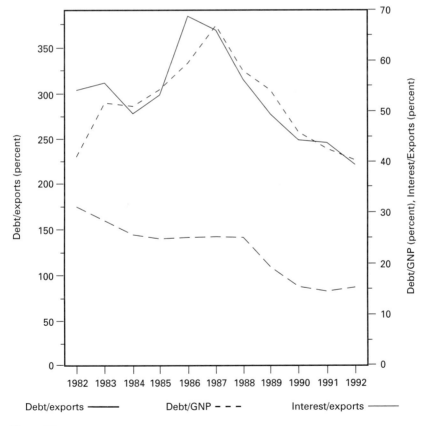

Figure 5.3
Debt ratios for seventeen heavily indebted countries

exports. However, after initial gains in 1983–85, there was also deterioration in the debt/export ratio for such nonoil countries as Argentina and Brazil. One reason was that commodity prices fell, for example, those for Brazilian coffee and Argentine wheat. This decline was contrary to expectation because, if the real commodity price had remained unchanged, nominal dollar commodity prices should have risen both because of general world inflation and because of the decline in the value of the dollar against other major currencies after 1985.

Some analysts have hypothesized that the export-oriented debt strategy contained the seeds of its own destruction because it induced a large outward shift in commodity export supply and thus depressed commodity prices. However, the evidence shows little correlation between debt and increased commodity export volume. In the case of grains, other factors, such as European export subsidies, were more important. More generally, the experience of the 1980s seemed to confirm the earlier Prebisch-Singer thesis that there was a long-term trend toward declining terms of trade (export price relative to import price) for commodity exporters (Ardeni and Wright 1992).

Still, most of the other elements of the scenario for favorable emergence from the debt problem (Cline 1983a; 1994) fell into place. World economic recovery occurred, and LIBOR fell to the range of 8% from its earlier high levels. Ironically, one outcome less favorable than expected was that world inflation fell to the range of 3 to 4% or even lower as measured by wholesale prices rather than remaining at the 6% pace of the early 1980s. Because the debtor countries were in trade surplus, lower inflation meant a smaller dollar value of the trade surplus for a given physical volume of exports and imports and therefore a smaller nominal value for the export base.[2] Viewed another way, lower inflation meant less inflationary erosion of the existing debt.

However, where the debt recovery scenario went wrong for nonoil countries, the principal reason was typically weak domestic policies rather than disappointing international developments. The most vivid illustration is the contrast between Peru and Chile. From 1982 to 1987, fiscal deficits and an overvalued exchange rate brought an 18% reduction in Peru's exports and a rise in inflation from 65% to nearly 700%. In contrast, Chile's exports rose by 90% over the same period even though its principal export product was the same as Peru's, copper. Chile's inflation stayed within the range of 15% annually.

Internal versus External Transfer

Increasing exports and achieving a favorable trade balance were necessary but not sufficient conditions for countries to emerge from the debt crisis. These balance of payments aspects dealt with the external transfer part of the problem, namely the challenge of temporarily transferring resources back to creditors to reverse the buildup in debt. However, there was an additional task: mobilizing the internal transfer from the citizenry to the government so that the government could afford to make its debt service payments. The internal transfer required a sound fiscal performance.

By the late 1980s, most of the external debt of Latin America was owed by governments. Therefore payments to foreign creditors required taxation of the domestic public. In several countries, it had been public borrowing that built up the foreign debt in the first place. In others, the debt had not started out that way. In countries such as Chile and especially Argentina, soon after the outbreak of the debt crisis the governments had guaranteed or assumed direct responsibility for private debt owed abroad. From the banks' perspective that seemed only fair because it was government exchange restrictions that made private clients unable to transmit payments. However, frequently the conditions under which the government took responsibility imposed a lasting burden on the public sector. Thus in Argentina in 1982 when the government took over private external debt, it did not obtain a comparable domestic asset in return from the private sector, in part because private banks and firms were near bankruptcy following chaotic domestic economic conditions. The result of this action was to impose both an internal and an external transfer problem onto the government.

Later in the 1980s, the distinction between the two types of transfers became vivid in Argentina and Brazil. Both countries ran large trade surpluses, thereby generating the foreign exchange to make the external transfer. However, both had large fiscal deficits, and the governments decided not to pay interest on foreign debt, in part because they did not have enough tax revenue. The broad result was that a fiscal deficit wound up forcing capital flight. The government was unable to purchase the trade surplus, so it went to the private sector, which largely placed it abroad again in dollar assets.

There were important interactions between the internal and external transfer. When governments devalued exchange rates in the early

1980s to stimulate exports and to pay debt service, the result was to shrink domestic GDP expressed in dollars. The dollar value of debt service did not shrink, however, so foreign debt service rose substantially as a fraction of GDP. Correspondingly, the fiscal primary surplus, excluding interest, necessary to service the debt rose relative to GDP, increasing the burden of the internal transfer.

These exchange rate swings could be huge. The Argentine economy had typically been of a size of some $80 billion annually. With severe devaluation in 1989, the economy shrank to $60 billion in dollar terms. Then, when the exchange rate appreciated again, the economy ballooned to $140 billion by 1991. The amount of interest coming due on foreign debt remained about the same at some $5½ billion per year. But the internal and external transfer was far more manageable when this amount represented about 4% of GDP (1991) than when it stood at 9% (1989).

Another key interaction was the impact on domestic interest rates. In the Mexican case, the uncertainty associated with the debt crisis, as well as the risk that there would be a breakdown in negotiations and a run on the peso, meant that domestic interest rates had to be held at a high level, that is, they incorporated a high risk premium. External debt thus had an indirect internal transfer burden attributable to the increase in interest payable on the government's domestic debt.

Resource Transfers

At the beginning of the 1980s, Latin America was receiving some $40 billion annually in capital inflows, largely in syndicated bank loans at floating interest. The debt crisis cut capital inflows to a level of some $10 billion annually in 1983–88. As the interest coming due on debt (plus dividends on direct investment) was about $35 billion annually, new capital inflows were no longer enough to cover interest, and there was an outward transfer of resources as exports of real goods and services had to exceed imports to pay for the interest not covered by new capital. In traditional models of economic development, this resource outflow meant a lower growth rate.

The Harrod-Domar growth model is one example. It postulates that growth results from the increase in capital, which is the consequence of investment. Investment can be financed by domestic saving or by foreign saving, the inflow of foreign capital matched by foreign goods and services. In this model, the growth rate for the economy equals the savings rate as a percentage of GDP divided by the incremental capital output ratio. A typical value for the incremental capital output ratio is 4, meaning that $100 million in new investment generates an annual flow of $25 million in output. Typical savings ratios are on the order of 20% of GDP, meaning that, without foreign capital, growth rates can typically be around 5% annually (20% ÷ 4).

The decline of some $30 billion annually in Latin America's capital inflows for most of the 1980s meant a reduction in inward resource transfers by about 6% of regional GDP, which averaged on the order of $500 billion. With a decline in foreign saving equal to 6% of GDP and an incremental capital output ratio of 4, one could have expected annual growth to decline by about 1.5 percentage point. The actual decline was greater. From 1978 to 1980, Latin American growth averaged 5.7% annually. From 1982 through 1988, the average was 1.4%, a decline of about 4 percentage points. The strong implication is that, while the debt crisis reduced potential growth rates in the 1980s, the actual deterioration far exceeded what could be attributed to external debt because of additional problems of domestic policy distortions. Once again, the strong growth performances of such countries as Chile and, to a lesser extent, Colombia with more stable domestic policies, but comparable compression of external finance availability, provide evidence.

Debt Policy for the 1990s

By 1992, the international debt crisis was largely over, one decade after it began. There was no longer a threat to the international financial system. Banks had built up their capital and set aside loan loss reserves. For the nine largest U.S. banks, debt owed by the seventeen "Baker Plan" debtors had fallen from 194% of capital in 1982 to only 63% in 1992. As figure 5.3 indicates, the debt indicators revealed steady improvement for these countries after 1987. The weighted average of net debt (deducting reserves) to exports of goods and services fell from a high of 375% in 1987 to 225% by 1991, and net debt relative to GDP fell from 67% to 44% over the same period. A better measure of the debt burden is the interest/exports ratio because it considers not just the amount of debt but also its price (the interest rate). On this measure, the setback after the oil price collapse was almost wholly offset by falling interest rates, and figure 5.3 shows that interest fell from 27% of exports in 1982 to a plateau of 23% in 1984–88 and then declined

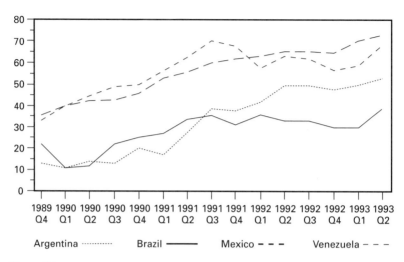

Figure 5.4
Secondary market values (cents per dollar)

further to 17% by 1991. Rising exports, falling interest rates, and a roll-
back in debt from debt-equity swaps and Brady Plan reductions
brought the aggregate indicators back close to levels traditionally associated with creditworthiness by the end of the debt crisis decade.

Further evidence of improvement was present in the secondary market prices of Latin American debt, as seen in figure 5.4). The price of
Venezuelan and Mexican debt had risen from thirty-five to forty cents
on the dollar in early 1989 to sixty-five cents on the dollar, or nearly
full face value of the conversion bonds considering that they incorporated an effective reduction of thirty to thirty-five cents on the dollar.
The price of Argentine debt had soared from eleven cents on the dollar
in early 1990 to fifty cents on the dollar. Brazilian debt remained at
thirty-five cents on the dollar, a reflection of the greater ongoing problems of domestic economic instability in that country.

Moreover, economic performance was improving. For the Baker
Seventeen countries, average growth had been negative in 1982–83,
had then temporarily rebounded to about 3% in 1984–87, and had
fallen to below 2% in 1988–90. By 1991, growth had returned to 3.2%.
In Latin America, inflation had reached an average of about 1,000% in
1990, but by 1992, it was down to about 25% annually if Brazil were
excluded. As noted below, the capital markets had rediscovered Latin
America in a big way by 1991, in part because interest rates were unat-
tractively low in the United States.

By mid-1992, there were tentative Brady Plan agreements for Argentina and Brazil, in addition to those reached in 1990 for Mexico and Venezuela. These four countries alone represented 75% of bank claims on the seventeen heavily indebted Baker countries. Perhaps the largest doubt remained about the Brazilian case because domestic inflation remained high, over 20% per month and restoring fiscal balance required fundamental reform, including constitutional change.

Three principal areas of unfinished business remained for the international debt strategy. First, there were numerous small countries, such as Peru and Ecuador, for which Brady Plan agreements had not been reached. Second, there was the ongoing problem of debt in sub-Saharan Africa. Third, there was a new problem of dealing with the debt of Russia and other former Soviet republics. Beyond these three areas, there was the question of whether the extraordinary debt relief granted to Egypt and Poland had any implications for other countries.

There is every reason to expand Brady Plan agreements to the smaller countries when and where they have entered into adequate economic reform programs. One possibility would be greater scope for discounted buybacks for these countries because the amounts are small relative to bank capital.

The debt problem of sub-Saharan Africa, in contrast, is qualitatively different from that of Latin America. Most African debt is owed to industrial country governments rather than commercial banks. The African debt problem basically stems from the fact that past assistance should have been extended on a grant basis rather than as loans. The problem is one of development aid policy, not private capital market stability and incentives. There is much to recommend the British and Canadian proposals of deep reduction of official claims on sub-Saharan African countries. However, economic policy distortions have been so serious in the region in the past that it makes sense to make official debt forgiveness conditional on the types of policy reforms that the Latin American countries have undertaken.

The cases of Egypt and Poland illustrated the high political component of international debt policy. In 1991, the industrial countries forgave 50% of official claims on both countries. For Egypt, this measure was a reward for sending troops to the front lines in the Gulf War. For Poland, it was a reward for being in the vanguard of Eastern European democratization (and for having numerous relatives who lived and voted in the United States). The simplest way to evaluate the Polish and Egyptian debt reductions is that, when the debt is primarily owed to governments, politics rules the decision. It is a perfectly acceptable and understandable expression of the political will of western governments to undertake special debt forgiveness for special friends. The problem becomes more complicated when the debt is owed to the private capital market because then the creditors respond to shareholders and not voters, and the debtor country must look to its future credit rating when it considers pressing for deep forgiveness. The likelihood was that Poland and Egypt would remain as special cases rather than represent the pattern of things to come in the 1990s.

Implications for the Former Soviet Union

The new debt problem of the 1990s is that of the former Soviet Union (FSU). As discussed in chapter 6, by 1993, the Russian republic had assumed responsibility for most of this debt, which amounted to approximately $80 billion (World Bank 1993). It is instructive to ask what lessons have been learned from the 1980s debt crisis that can help in the management of the FSU debt. One set of issues concerns the economic adjustment policies Russia and other FSU countries will need to pursue. Another concerns the proper conceptualization and implementation of the international policy response. On the latter question, a major issue is whether the FSU debt requires forgiveness, as in the Brady Plan, or merely restructuring and relending, as in the Baker Plan.

The Latin American debt crisis showed that domestic economic policy reform is the central requirement for normalizing external debt. In part, this reform is necessary because of the internal transfer problem: without fiscal adjustment, the government cannot be counted on to service its external debt, and foreign creditors, especially private, are unlikely to resume lending. As discussed in chapter 6, fiscal imbalance has been a severe problem for the new Russian economy.

Another 1980s debt lesson is that capital flight is a potentially large source of weakness for debt management. And indeed, the Russian case in 1991–93 showed signs of major capital flight, estimated at more than $7 billion for 1992 alone (World Bank 1993, p. 138).

The Latin American experience also showed the importance of achieving export growth, in part through the pursuit of realistic exchange rate policies. Here again, the Russian case showed signs of serious trouble as the new nation's hard currency exports stagnated in 1992–93 because of economic disorganization, as well as a decline in the oil sector in particular, and as the central government increasingly lost control over export revenue earned by state firms. Although the ruble was seriously undervalued rather than overvalued in 1991–92, and thus not the source of export erosion, it was by no means clear that a permanent exchange rate policy was in place that would assure realistic exchange rates in the future.

With respect to the issue of debt forgiveness, the relevance of the Latin American experience is limited. In the Russian case, only about $25 billion out of the $80 billion total of external debt is in the form of long-term claims by commercial banks. There was thus less potential for overall relief as a consequence of reduction of commercial bank debt, which was the principal vehicle of the Brady Plan. Nor was there an established secondary market for bank debt owed by Russia, yet this market had been an important signal for setting the parameters of debt relief in the Brady Plan for Latin American countries. In addition, commercial bank claims on the FSU had been heavily concentrated in German banks, in part because of German government encouragement of lending, so that reduction of bank claims would imply an unusually concentrated creditor country distribution of relief.

These considerations suggest that Russian debt in the 1990s would more appropriately be addressed through the rolling over of official credits, perhaps with coordinated new lending by existing commercial bank creditors, rather than through debt reduction along the lines of the Brady Plan. The more fundamental lesson from Latin American experience was that there would be no true resolution of the external debt problem in the absence of domestic economic reform and stabilization. Chapter 6 further examines the problem of FSU external debt.

Capital Market Recovery

In contrast to lingering debt problems in Africa and the new debt problem of the former Soviet Union, by the early 1990s, the major countries in Latin America were able once again to borrow on bond markets and were experiencing large capital inflows. Private investors had poured so much money back into the region in 1991 that finance ministers worried about excessive buildup in reserves. Share prices on Latin American stock exchanges doubled and tripled, although they subsequently fell back by a third or more from their peaks. By 1991–93, capital inflows to the region were back up to $35 billion annually (IMF 1993b). This time the finance was in direct investment, bonds and repatriation of flight capital rather than syndicated private bank loans in the 1970s. Nevertheless, market access was back.

There was some concern that the capital reflows would prove vulnerable to the first sign of a revival of interest rates in the United States, where the lowest rates in thirty years were encouraging investors to search for returns elsewhere including in Latin America. However, even the renewed capital flows to the region were small in the context of the global capital market, and it seemed likely that, even if there were a return of interest rates to somewhat higher levels, countries in the region that maintained sound policies would be able to sustain their renewed access to the capital market.

For the moment, the problem was actually an embarrassment of riches for some countries. Thus in Chile, capital inflows were so high by 1992–93 that the country resorted to a modest real appreciation, removal of restrictions on capital outflows, and finally a 30% deposit requirement on foreign deposits to moderate the inflows, which were placing pressure on the domestic money supply and inflation. Mexico and Argentina had large current account deficits associated with buoyant capital inflows and explicit strategies to use fixed exchange rates as an anchor against inflation, and at some point, increased domestic productivity and fiscal restraint were likely to be essential to hold these deficits within prudent bounds. Encouragingly this time, the external deficits were driven by private sector investment decisions rather than by government fiscal deficits.

Overview

By 1993, it was still premature to print the epitaph for the international debt crisis, but it was perhaps time to prepare the draft text. Impressive domestic policy reforms had swept much of Latin America, and the region had reestablished access to capital markets. As for the industrial country banks, by the early 1990s, the irony was that their biggest problem turned out not to be Latin American debt but domestic loans to real estate.

Overall, the debt crisis of the 1980s represented a historically important example of the successful evolution of an internationally coordinated policy to deal with a systemic threat. The policy was a case of learning by doing, making successive reformulations and intensifications of policy as previous-stage remedies proved inadequate. In broad terms, the strategy of concerted lending coupled with domestic policy reform under the Baker Plan proved adequate for countries such as

Chile and Colombia with good policy and adequate luck on external influences. It proved inadequate for countries, such as Mexico, with good policies and bad luck. The Brady Plan provided additional relief for these latter countries. Additionally, in cases where countries, such as Argentina and potentially Brazil, had finally adopted economic reforms, it provided a market-based alleviation for those countries that for several years previously had been unable to meet debt payments primarily because of weak domestic policies rather than because of bad luck on external developments. Neither the Brady Plan nor any other was likely to resolve the debt problem for countries that remained locked in domestic economic impasse from severe fiscal deficits, high protection, overvalued exchange rates, and other policy distortions.

The Baker and Brady Plans achieved what had not been possible in the debt crisis of the 1930s: an early return of debtor countries to capital markets. The widespread defaults of Latin American countries in the 1930s had locked these countries out of capital markets for four decades. There was no international financial system in the 1930s comparable to the Bretton Woods system of the International Monetary Fund and World Bank to facilitate an international response. In addition to the availability of these institutions in the 1980s, however, the choice of the strategy was also important to the outcome. The Baker and Brady plans were oriented toward a market-based, cooperative solution. Much more sweeping, forced forgiveness, or more confrontational approaches, would have been likely to delay reentry of countries into the capital markets for much longer.

The importance of the cooperative, market-oriented approach was evident in cross-country comparisons of early return to the capital market. Countries that had been more cooperative and that had achieved more successful adjustment were paying more favorable rates to borrow by the early 1990s. By 1993, Chile, which had been foremost among Latin American countries in fiscal, trade, and other structural reform and which had not requested Brady Plan debt forgiveness, was paying spreads of only 150 basis points above U.S. treasury bonds. In contrast, Brazil, which had gone into extended interest arrears in the late 1980s and had continued to experience severe problems with fiscal deficits and inflation as high as 30% per month, was paying spreads of over 700% (Cline 1994).

It is an open question whether the debt crisis could have been handled better. Some policy analysts argue that the Brady Plan came far too late, and its delay caused inexcusable human suffering in debtor countries. That issue provides interesting grist for the mill of economic historians. They, in turn will have to consider that it was not until 1987 and later that the banks had set aside a cushion of reserves or that a secondary market had developed to provide some signal for market-oriented debt relief. They will have to take into account the fact that, prior to the oil price collapse, the economic case for debt forgiveness was much weaker in the case of the major oil-exporting countries. And the historical reassessment will have to ask whether the policy reform that swept Latin America in the late 1980s would have been forthcoming if easier and earlier solutions had been available. To a considerable degree, some of the emerging democracies in Latin America probably needed to pass through a learning period before the public recognized that populist solutions were unsustainable. Debt forgiveness prior to that transformation would have been unlikely to provide a lasting solution.

APPENDIX 5A: A MODEL OF DEBT RECOVERY

Define d as the ratio of debt to exports:

$$d = D/X. \tag{5.1}$$

Define g as a growth rate, and then considering that the growth rate of a quotient equals the growth rate of the numerator less that of the denominator, the debt/export ratio will grow at:

$$g_d = g_D - g_X, \tag{5.2}$$

that is, the debt export ratio grows at the rate of debt growth minus the rate of export growth.

For its part, the export growth rate will typically equal some constant rate c characteristic of the country (this intercept, for example, would be high for Korea), for example, plus an income elasticity for exports, ϵ, multiplied by the growth rate of income in industrial country markets, g_{YDC} plus the rate of world inflation to convert real export growth into growth in nominal dollar terms. Thus:

$$g_X = c + \epsilon g_{YDC} + \dot{p}_w. \tag{5.3}$$

This formulation, with world economic growth as the driving force, tends to understate the importance of the country's own efforts through devaluation and structural reform, but these factors may loosely be incorporated by specifying a higher country intercept, c.

Now consider the absolute rise in debt, ΔD. This increase has a passive or inherited component equal to the existing debt times the interest rate, iD. It may be restrained by the country's running a surplus of exports, X, over imports, M, because that surplus can be used to pay interest. Debt buildup can also be limited by acquiring direct investment, I. The debt buildup in a given year thus equals:

$$\Delta D = iD - [X - M] - I. \tag{5.4}$$

We may identify a parameter for the country's ability to run a trade surplus as $\beta = [X - M]/X$. Then we may write:

$$\Delta D = iD - \beta X - I. \tag{5.5}$$

The growth rate of debt equals the absolute increase divided by the initial level, or $g_D = \Delta D/D$. Thus, we may write:

$$g_D = \Delta D / D = \{iD - \beta X - I\} / D. \tag{5.6}$$

If we define k as the ratio of direct investment inflow in a given year to total debt, and keeping in mind that $X/D = 1/d$, this may be rewritten as:

$$g_D = i - \beta/d - k. \tag{5.7}$$

Subtracting the growth rate of exports, equation 5.3, from the growth rate of debt, equation 5.7, we have the growth rate of the debt/export ratio:

$$g_d = i - \beta/d - k - [\dot{p}_w + \epsilon g_{YDC} + c] \tag{5.8}$$

Suggested Readings

Cline (1994).

6

Economic Reform in the Former Soviet Union and Eastern Europe

Our generation has witnessed the historic collapse of Communism in Europe in a period shorter than it took the United States to fight its civil war. Within three years after the fall of the Berlin Wall in November 1989, the ideological struggle that dominated the twentieth century was over, as was the cold war and its risk of nuclear holocaust. Communist regimes had fallen throughout Eastern Europe, and the Soviet Union had broken up into independent republics.

The West has immense stakes in a successful entry of the former Soviet Union (FSU) into the community of democratic nations oriented toward a market economy. It was the intolerable combination of colossal economic failure and the denial of personal liberty that caused European communism to collapse, and it seems likely that economic improvement will ultimately be indispensable if the new freedoms are to last. In 1992–93, Boris Yeltsin's Russia got off to a rocky start in this process of economic transformation. In part because there were no standardized economic formulas for the transition, enormous mistakes were made and more were likely to come.

The extent of the initial setback was staggering (see figure 6.1). IMF data indicated that, over the four year period 1990–93, real production fell by 28% in Eastern Europe and 39% in the former Soviet Union (IMF 1993b). In contrast, for Latin America at the depth of the debt crisis in 1983, real production had fallen by only about 4%. This chapter first considers what economic analysis suggests about the transition to capitalism and then reviews the initial experience of Russia and Eastern Europe in this process.

Microeconomics of Transition to Capitalism

Private property and the right to exchange goods and services freely are the essence of capitalism, even in the mixed-capitalist system

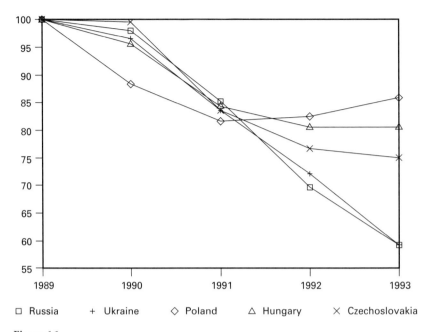

Figure 6.1
Economies in transition: real GDP, 1989 = 100

where there is a major role for the state in providing social welfare and public goods. The price mechanism is at the heart of free exchange of goods and services. Soviet communism was most notable for its failure to allocate resources through a well-functioning price system. The classic symptom of this failure was the frequency of long queues of shoppers waiting to buy scarce goods at state stores.

Most economists, both Eastern and Western, have begun to develop a consensus on the elements of the transition to market capitalism (Fischer, 1992). The key changes include (1) macroeconomic stabilization, that is, fiscal balance and control of credit; (2) price liberalization; (3) the achievement of exchange rate convertibility for goods and services (current account convertibility); (4) privatization of state enterprises; and 5) adoption of a social safety net. Thus, both microeconomic and macroeconomic reforms are necessary.

Price Liberalization

Figure 6.2 illustrates the classic problem of queueing in the command and control economy. Consumers are prepared to purchase the alternative amounts of the good at the alternative prices indicated along

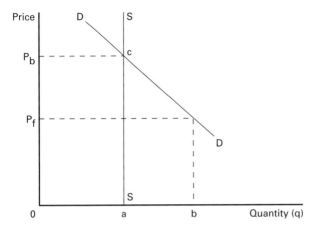

Figure 6.2
Supply and demand command and control with rationing

the demand curve, *DD*. The planning agency sets a price of p_f. At this price, consumers seek to purchase amount $0b$ along the quantity axis, (q). The state firm produces only quantity $0a$, which it sells at the official price p_f. The result is a shortage of amount ab. The frustrated customers in the queue who are turned away would have purchased ab but find it is unavailable.

Figure 6.2 also reveals the analytics of the black market. With the amount of the good fixed at $0a$, a market-clearing price would be where the vertical supply curve *SS* intersects the demand curve, or at point c where the price is p_b. Any informal vendor who manages to obtain a source of supply for the good can sell it at a street price, or black market price (as such transactions were usually illegal), of p_b.

At the beginning of 1992, with the encouragement of the International Monetary Fund and World Bank, the Russian government freed most prices (as discussed below). In the ideal competitive-capitalist economy, this standard reform from the Western agencies' operations manuals would have the effect shown in panel A of figure 6.3. Here, the supply curve is smoothly and gently upward sloping. At the former controlled price of p_f, the state firm produced only $0a$, leaving excess demand (an unsatisfied queue) of ab. With the price freed, a moderate rise in the price to the market level p_m induces consumers to cut back their desired purchases and induces the state firm to increase its output so that the two become equal at amount $0d$, corresponding to the intersection of the demand and supply curves. Suddenly there are no more queues, and the goods reappear on the shelves.

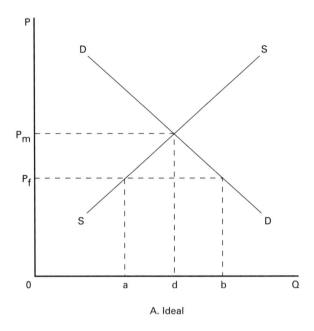

A. Ideal

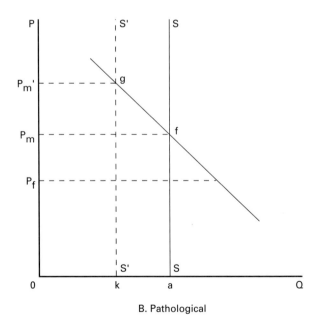

B. Pathological

Figure 6.3
Supply and demand under price liberalization

Suppose, however, that bureaucratic rigidity in the state firms leaves production unchanged at the previous level so that the supply curve is vertical. Then in panel B of figaure 6.3, the effect of price liberalization is to suppress the amount of desired consumption down to what is available, amount $0a$. To accomplish this effect, prices must rise much more than had been hoped—all the way to a higher p_m where the demand curve intersects the vertical supply curve at point f. Or suppose that matters are even worse and that the confusion about input availability and chain of command associated with the collapse of state planning *reduces* the amount of the good that can be produced, shifting the vertical supply curve from SS at amount Oa to $S'S'$ at amount $0k$. In this case, the market clearing price will rise even higher to p_m', where the demand curve intersects the new supply curve $S'S'$. The net effect of price liberalization in this case is an extreme rise in prices and a decline in production. Hence the label pathological.

The initial experience of Russia, as well as much of Eastern Europe, with price liberalization suggests that frequently the pathological case may have been more relevant than the ideal case. One reason is the lack of private ownership. Most of the institutional structure of the state firms remained initially unchanged, yet the smooth, gently upward-sloping supply curve assumes a keen response of producers to price and profit incentives, to which private owners are more likely to respond. Where ownership is not private, managers may be less than enthusiastic about attempting to increase production because they themselves may not benefit from higher profits. The lack of an incentive to respond to price signals will be greater if there is doubt about such basics as the value of the rubles that will be received as the profits. Indeed, if the ruble is suspect, the state firm's manager may consider it advantageous to hoard the output, shifting SS to $S'S'$, rather than to sell more of it in response to higher prices. "Informal privatization" in which managers collude with workers to divert much of the firm's production to their own private use, aggravates the problem further, shifting $S'S'$ further to the left.

Complete price liberalization also raises questions of equity and monopoly regulation. Where prices have been held low on basics, such as bread, liberalization can be regressive. The efficient response is to free prices but to make available special subsidies targeted at the poor. As for monopoly, the economic structure of the centralized economies has been extremely concentrated in a small number of large industrial firms. There may thus be a need for price regulation in the more monopolized sectors, especially after privatization. Eventual breakup of monopoly firms may also be required, unless sufficient competition can be provided by imports to provide price discipline.

McKinnon (1993) has argued that in the Russian case, it was a mistake to free prices in a system in which the state enterprises had soft budget constraints, which has come to denote an economic structure in which the state firms are not allowed to go bankrupt but instead can always secure credit from the central bank to cover their deficits. McKinnon argues that under such a system, there is no equilibrium price level. The state firms can bid for resources without limit. Thus, it is necessary to control the absolute price level to provide a nominal anchor to prices and to avoid runaway inflation.

McKinnon argues that price liberalization worked better in Poland. There, state firms and households both dealt in cash, and there were limits to credit given to state firms. In the former Soviet Union, the state enterprises conducted transactions in quasi-blocked deposit accounts rather than cash and could thus bid for resources without cash in hand. In return, they transferred their profits to the central government. As a consequence, price controls had been a source of government revenue, as the center had kept consumer prices high and wages and raw materials costs low, appropriating the resulting profit of state firms. Eliminating the price controls removed this source of revenue, aggravating fiscal deficits.

Triage: An Alternative Approach

Massive and immediate privatization might seem to be one way to end the problem of no equilibrium price level under soft budget constraints for state enterprises. However, when as much as 90% of the labor force is employed by state firms as was the case in Russia, this option is not a viable one since implementing it means that much of the work force could be out of a job almost overnight. Nor is the mantra of the necessity of implementing a social safety net a convincing reply. Such mechanisms exist only inadequately even in the United States. At the same time, McKinnon's suggestion of a return to comprehensive price controls seems inadvisable as the result could easily be extreme shortages and long queues once again. Far preferable is a clampdown on central bank credit to state firms in order to turn the soft budget constraint substantially harder.

In view of the collapse of production in the transition to capitalism in Eastern Europe and especially the former Soviet Union, it is worth considering whether a different approach would have been less costly and whether an interim shift in strategy could minimize further such losses. One alternative approach would be a strategy of "triage." In French military tradition, wounded soldiers on the battlefield are divided into three groups: those who can walk away after minor medical assistance, those with severe wounds who can be saved with intense medical attention, and those who are judged beyond hope of saving. Field doctors concentrate their attention on the second group rather than spreading their resources thin in an attempt to help the third group as well, thereby jeopardizing the survival of those in the second.

Applied to the economy in transition, the triage strategy would focus on the maintenance of production in key state firms. In the Russian case excessive credit from the central bank to the state firms caused high inflation in 1992–93. However, the absolute cutoff of credit could have caused widespread closure of state firms, even steeper production declines, and massive unemployment.

Under these circumstances, limiting central bank credit to a core group of state firms while cutting off credit to the hopeless firms could reduce inflationary pressure and at the same time preserve crucial production and employment. There would be two criteria for identifying the state firms to assist in this triage approach: their efficiency, which would be based on international competitiveness, and their critical role as suppliers of intermediate goods to other sectors.

The efficiency criterion would amount to an infant industry argument (see chapter 3). Support would be concentrated on firms whose production is reasonably close to international standards of quality and productivity so that the favored infants would stand a good chance of growing up. To evaluate efficiency, it would often be necessary to apply shadow prices on outputs and inputs. These accounting prices in turn would be based on international prices as translated into the domestic currency, the ruble, at a meaningful long-term exchange rate. If the ruble is extremely undervalued, a firm that produces a product that sells domestically at 10,000 rubles each will be mistakenly considered inefficient if a comparable product is worth $20 on the world market and the undervalued exchange rate is only 1,000 rubles to the dollar. However, the firm will rightly be measured as efficient if a shadow exchange rate of 500 rubles to the dollar is applied because then the domestic good is worth $20, the world price, rather than only $10, the domestic price at the market exchange rate.

For its part, the critical supply criterion would apply the lessons of interindustry, or input-output, economics. As set forth in appendix 6A, the economy may be divided into several product sectors. Each sector produces goods that are partly used as intermediate inputs into the production process in other sectors, as well as being partly used for final demand domestically or in exports. Products that are used heavily as intermediate inputs have high forward linkages. Their absence can cause bottlenecks and thus a collapse of output in downstream, user industries.

The efficiency and critical input criteria would provide a basis for selective maintenance of sectoral output. This strategy would, of course, be transitional, as the eventual objective would remain privatization. However, privatization of the larger firms seems likely to take a considerable amount of time.

Some might object that this approach really amounts to a return to central planning, which was shown impossible by the past experience of these economies. An attempt to apply efficiency tests and input-output analysis at the most detailed level almost certainly would in fact be beyond the capacity of the severely strained central bureaucracies. However, it seems likely that such an approach could be applied to, say, the 500 or even 1,000 largest state firms. This set of firms would embrace the bulk of industrial production and employment. Moreover, technical assistance from international institutions, such as the World Bank, could provide expertise to help identify the state firms qualifying for special support and those considered too hopeless to warrant such support (or healthy enough to dispense with it).

There is still another objection to the triage approach: it appears to play into the hands of the old political forces that continue to believe in the centrally planned economy and the communist (or at least *nomenklatura*) political organization. However, the political dangers, including that of a countercoup by precisely these forces, are even greater in an economy in chaos and hyperinflation.

The triage approach contains some important implications. First, it may be necessary to supplement simple price liberalization with special measures to avoid the collapse of production in sectors that are important for supplying intermediate inputs into production elsewhere in the economy.

Second, an implication of the critical supply criterion is that the complete elimination of state direction of output might procede sequentially, first in final consumer goods and only subsequently in the intermediate goods necessary to sustain output across a wide variety of industries. This approach indicates some swing of the pendulum back toward industrial policy, though not a comprehensive command-and-control economy.

Third, where bottlenecks arise because of a breakdown in intermediate supply, it may be desirable to allocate some of the scarce foreign exchange available to purchase imports and break the bottlenecks. And finally, despite the usefulness of input-output and shadow-price efficiency analysis, there should be no illusion that, over the longer term, the full economy can be meticulously planned at highly detailed levels using these or other analytical devices. That option was essentially tried and shown to have failed. Indeed, economists in centrally planned economies were at the forefront in developing mathematical programming techniques in the effort to achieve efficient resource allocation under command and control but by now the consensus is that this task is not feasible.

Institutional Reform

The illustration of backward-shifting supply (see figure 6.2) and emphasis on key intermediate products highlight the need for institutional reform in the FSU structure of production to improve supply conditions. The underlying reform needed is to link production management with profit incentives and property rights. Firming up the basic legal groundwork for ownership rights, including in the area of rights to private land ownership, is an important part of this process. Privatization of state firms is the principal means of implementing reform of the ownership and incentive structure. Where privatization is expected to take place slowly, interim mechanisms are necessary to provide proper production incentives.

Several key areas of institutional reform are necessary if the economies of the former Soviet Union are to achieve successful transition to the market. Legal reform is necessary. There is a need for company law to clarify the rights and obligations of corporations and for capital market law. New laws are needed to regulate the various commercial exchanges springing up.

Enterprise reform is also necessary in order to make state firms truly autonomous rather than continuations of the command and control system. There should be a halt to the spontaneous privatization whereby managers and workers purloin state firm assets. To achieve effective and responsible autonomy, firms should be corporatized. Shares should be issued in the firms, with some fraction, perhaps up to 25%, given to the workers and managers and with the rest sold off to the public. In the case of Russia, corporatization was largely completed in 1992 as a prelude to privatization.

A social safety net is necessary, under the new circumstances whereby the state firm is no longer obligated to maintain employment for its workers. The banking system is in serious need of reform. There is a need for competitive banks that exert discipline on the companies to which they lend. In Russia, in 1991–92, there was a mushrooming of banks, typically owned by the state enterprises to which they began lending. The banks have been in serious trouble from the dubious loans on their books, caused in turn by the weakness of the state enterprises that are their clients. There is a need to streamline banking procedures and to allow direct interbank clearing of payments. In 1992, the banking system was in such disarray, and the delays in check clearing so severe that there was a considerable premium for outright currency as opposed to bank deposits.

Macroeconomic Reform

The challenge of institutional transition to the FSU market is compounded by an additional layer of macroeconomic imbalances of the more mundane variety, familiar from such regions as Latin America. The special features inherited from the centrally planned economy, however, give these macroeconomic imbalances specific nuances.

Monetary Overhang and Inflation

One such peculiarity is the special legacy of the queueing system for the process of price liberalization. Ideally, price liberalization does not cause generalized price inflation. Instead, some prices rise while others fall, and the system of relative prices realigns to provide a better set of signals to the economy for expanding production in some sectors and curtailing it in others.

In the context of the Soviet economy and most Eastern European economies under central planning, however, there had been large pent-up demand in the form of excess savings built up because of the unavailability of goods. The excess savings amounted to a monetary overhang that represented large potential inflation. In Russia, this overhang increased after the Gorbachev reforms of 1987, which gave state enterprises more autonomy. State managers promptly granted themselves and their workers large wage increases, thereby aggravating shortages and the monetary overhang.

In the absence of special measures to immobilize the monetary overhang, the consequence of price liberalization was certain to be generalized inflation. Whereas rationing had previously allocated scarce goods, there would be general bidding up of prices as consumers sought to spend their excess savings on goods, and higher prices rather than queues would be the rationing mechanism. This process would feed on itself as the rise in prices would encourage the public to spend its monetary savings for fear that if left intact, their value would soon evaporate with the eroding value of the ruble.

Transition planners faced several alternative options in dealing with the monetary overhang. The first, and the one they chose in most cases (certainly the Russian), was to inflate away the monetary overhang, simply allow all prices to rise so much that the public's excess savings were wiped out. Thus, in Russia, the ratio of money defined to include savings accounts to GDP stood at a high level of 65% in 1991 but by 1992 had fallen to only 15% as the consequence of inflation, and the resulting rise in nominal but not real GDP.

A broad class of alternatives would have been to have used a comprehensive program of privatization to absorb the monetary overhang. The public could have purchased shares in state firms. The government could have sold apartments, which were owned by the state in Russia, to the families living in them in urban land reform. The state could have sold the land to the farmers working it. All of these measures would have absorbed excess savings by converting the public's assets from financial to real holdings.

A third alternative would have been for the government to carry out a currency reform. The old currency would have been turned in for a combination of new currency and government bonds of, say, ten years maturity in a proportion designed to convert the monetary overhang into the bond holdings. The bonds would then have been made tradable in the market.

Either the privatization and asset sale option or the currency reform alternative, or both, would have been the efficient, stabilizing way to deal with the monetary overhang. Instead, in Russia and other key cases, the governments chose the easier but more costly path of inflating the overhang away. In considerable part, this outcome resulted from the sequencing of the reforms. If massive privatization and currency reform had come first, there would have been little monetary overhang left to cause inflation. Because simple price liberalization came first, the result was a large increase in the general price level.

Fiscal and Quasi-fiscal Deficits

The monetary overhang was a onetime distortion that had to be addressed one way or another. In principle, even the option of inflating the overhang away can be implemented through a once-and-for-all increase in the price level without subsequent ongoing inflation. Whether there is subsequent inflation or even hyperinflation depends on whether there is rapid expansion of the money supply.[1]

Rapid money expansion can arise from two sources. The first is the government's fiscal deficit, or excess of government spending over tax revenue. If the central bank prints money to finance this deficit, the money supply rises much faster than output. With the supply of money rising rapidly and the demand for it only rising apace with output and thus transactions, money becomes in excess supply. The price of money drops so that it commands fewer goods and the money price of goods rises.

Fiscal deficits and their monetization have been the central source of chronic inflation in many Latin American countries. In the Soviet Union in 1991, a huge fiscal deficit, amounting to 20% of GDP, was a driving force behind inflation. A major reason for the deficit was that tax collections fell sharply as states stopped turning over revenue to the center. Monetization of the deficit added to the inflationary pressure from the monetary overhang.

The second source of excessive money growth can be central bank credit to the state enterprises and collective farms. Technically this lending is not a fiscal deficit. However, in practice if no one expects to repay the loans, such lending amounts to the awarding of grants that should be included in the government's budget but are not. Under these circumstances, the central bank soon experiences losses, and the losses of the central bank are what are called quasi-fiscal deficits. In most of 1992 and 1993, a driving force in Russian inflation was the quasi-fiscal deficit brought on by large credits from the central bank to the state firms.[2] Thus, in Russia, the central government budget deficit was 20% of GDP in 1992 and an estimated 10% in 1993, while central bank credit to enterprises amounted to 23% of GDP in 1992—at a real value loss of at least 4% of GDP and potentially up to the full face value of 23% of GDP (IMF 1993b, pp. 86–89).

Similarly, there is a key linkage between the macroeconomic problem of fiscal deficits and the microeconomic problem of ownership structure. When the firms experiencing losses are state enterprises, their losses add to the public sector fiscal deficit. Thus the central government may have a balanced budget, but the public sector as a whole has large deficits. There is ample precedent worldwide, such as the Argentine railways, but the scope for losses by state enterprises is much greater in an economy in transition where the bulk of the economy has not yet been privatized.

The fundamental solution is to carry out privatization. As part of this process, an interim solution is simply to impose the rigors of bankruptcy on state firms and close down those firms that experience large and chronic losses. The problem with this discipline is that, in Russia, the state firms have provided as much as 90% of employment and state farms another 8% and closing the money-losing state enterprises means displacing much of the labor force. Hence the importance of moving to a phase of triage, where there is judgmental discrimination in deciding which firms to maintain.

In the Russian case the trade-off between inflation and job losses as a consequence of privatization may be less than clear cut. The privatization model essentially involves turning over the firm to existing management and workers (albeit with some outside share ownership). This structure builds in an incentive toward a social compact between management and workers, whereby managers implicitly promise not to fire anyone and workers in turn promise not to complain if management appropriates some of the firm's assets for personal gain. In the first instance, then, the workers keep their jobs. The privatized firm then faces the same financial problems as before privatization, and as before, managers approach the central bank for financing. The difference is that the central bank should be in a better position to resist these requests than when the firm was in the state sector; and there is at least some increase in the flexibility to dismiss workers. The point, however, is that privatization does not automatically eliminate inflationary pressures from central bank financing to inefficient firms.

Exchange Rate Convertibility

The exchange rate is convertible when it can be freely traded for dollars and other foreign currency at a single, unified rate. There is current account convertibility when this opportunity applies only for imports of goods and services and additionally capital account convertibility when citizens may freely trade in their ruble financial assets for dollars. Typically the centrally planned economies did not have full or even current account convertibility, and informal street conversion of rubles to dollars was illegal.

Current account convertibility is important for at least two reasons. First, it enables the country to import the regime of relative prices that prevail on the world market, at least for tradable goods. If a television set sells for the equivalent of 200 bushels of wheat on the world market, it will be inefficient for Russia to maintain price controls on wheat and bread that make the price of the television set equal to, say, 1,000 bushels of wheat. To do so would be to discourage domestic production of wheat and encourage excessive production of television sets. Economies in transition can piggyback on the efficient relative prices already worked out through stiff competition in the world markets.

Second, convertibility of rubles into dollars for purposes of profits remittances and interest payments will be important if foreign investment is ever to be persuaded to enter the country in sizeable amounts. Foreign firms invest to make profits for their shareholders. If their profits are all going to be accumulated in dubious, blocked rubles, they will stay at home or invest in other countries.

In contrast, capital account convertibility is a luxury that the economy in transition is unlikely to be able to afford. The great uncertainty and likely price instability associated with the transition mean that, if given the opportunity to do so at a moderate exchange rate, many domestic citizens would convert their ruble bank accounts into dollars for placement in capital flight abroad. The sad experience of such Latin American countries as Venezuela, Mexico, and Argentina in this regard should serve as a warning about the risks of easy convertibility at a central, moderate exchange rate for capital outflows.

By 1991, there was an extreme divergence between the official rate of the ruble—set at 1.6 to the dollar for commercial transactions—and the street, or black market, price, as much as 100 rubles to the dollar. A central question for the transition was what the right exchange rate would be and when convertibility might be established. Setting a new exchange rate at the black market rate would have been extreme and inappropriate. For example, the Russian minimum wage was about 300 rubles per month, and an official convertible exchange rate set at the prevailing black market rate would have had the ridiculous effect of pricing Russian labor at $3 per month.

Living standards were of course not that low, and the Russian case was an extreme instance of divergence between an exchange rate, the black market rate, and the purchasing power parity rate that would prevail if the exchange rate were set on a basis of equal costs at home and abroad. One reason for higher purchasing parity living standards in Russia than revealed by the ruble wage rate was the pervasive influence of low-cost benefits. Rents on apartments owned by the state were so low as to be practically free. Utility charges were so negligible that people controlled the temperature of their apartments in winter by opening the windows when it got too hot rather than turning down the heat. State firm obligations to workers typically included a wide range of health and other worker benefits not counted in the monthly wage. Official prices for bread and certain other basics were extremely low.

Even taking these low-cost benefits into account, there remained an extreme divergence between the black market value for the dollar and a meaningful purchasing power value, which would have set the exchange rate at a much more favorable level, perhaps some thirty or forty rubles to the dollar. The economics of the black market help explain this divergence.

Figure 6.4 illustrates the difference between the official and black market rate. Before exchange rate unification, there is a controlled market and a black market. The controlled market preempts the great bulk of dollars entering the economy through exports and other sources. In panel A, the government sets a low ruble rate per dollar, R_o, for official transactions, such as imports of wheat. The amount of dollars demanded by potential importers at this rate, shown along demand curve DD, exceeds the amount of dollars generated by the export firms, shown along official supply curve S_oS_o. As a result, there is a queue of unsatisfied import demand equal to dollar amount ab. The price that the public would be willing to pay in view of the amount of foreign exchange made available ($0a$) may be determined by considering where the vertical line at that amount intersects the demand curve, point k.

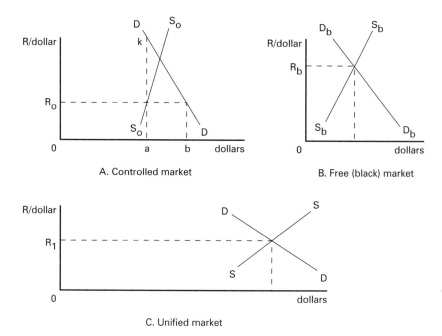

Figure 6.4
Exchange rate convertibility

At the same time, figure 6.4(B) shows that there is a much smaller amount of foreign exchange that makes its way to the black market, along a supply curve $S_b S_b$. The unsatisfied demand from the official market spills over into the black market, where the equilibrium price set by the intersection of the supply and demand curves for dollars, R_b, is at a much higher ruble/dollar price than in the official market. The demand curve in the black market includes demand for capital transactions, that is for capital flight.

In panel B of figure 6.4(C), the exchange market is unified. Whereas some people were prepared to bid an extremely high price for the few black market dollars available, the amount of their demand is relatively modest when compared to the entire pool of foreign exchange earnings. As a result, when the exchange market is unified, the market-clearing price settles at an intermediate price, R_1. This price is perhaps considerably closer to the original official price than to the initial black market price.[3]

In the first half of 1992, only about 5% of the foreign exchange earned by Russian firms was being turned over to the free market. The rest was managed by the government and provided on terms of special access to state enterprises and other official users. Export firms had to pay a tax of 30% and in addition had to turn over another 40% of foreign exchange at official low rates. The result of the thin market left over for free transactions was an extremely high free or black market price, as indicated in panel B of figure 6.4.

In summary, the move to exchange rate convertibility during the transition is likely to have several predictable features. First, many of the nearly free fringe benefits under the socialist state are likely to start bearing considerably higher prices so that they can begin to be provided on a market rather than rationed basis, and consequently, money wages are likely to have to increase. Also, because of these increases, the nearly unimaginable difference between ruble wages and their dollar equivalent at the black market rate is likely to narrow. Second, as more foreign exchange is channeled to the free market rather than preempted for the official, controlled market, the exorbitant price of foreign exchange on the black market is likely to fall.

External Trade and Debt

The former Soviet Union had a substantial external debt, approximately $70 billion. The collapse of the USSR raised two basic questions about this debt: who would be responsible for it, and would the economies of the FSU republics, including Russia, be able to earn enough foreign exchange to service the debt? The latter issue was familiar from Latin American experience in the 1980s.

A new type of problem arose, however, in the area of external trade. Under central planning, much of the trade conducted by the USSR and Eastern Europe was in mutual trade within the Council for Mutual Economic Assistance (CMEA) grouping of socialist nations. This trade was typically payable in rubles rather than hard currency, such as dollars or deutschemarks. Moreover, it was often at preferential prices. In particular, the USSR sold oil to CMEA partners at well below world prices. By 1990–91, it was evident that the key trade problem associated with transition to the market was the breakdown in intra-CMEA trade as members moved to insisting on hard currency payment.

The Debt Problem

Among the republics of the former Soviet Union, only Russia and the Ukraine were major earners of foreign exchange, Russia primarily from its exports of oil and other raw materials and the Ukraine from exports of grains. Thus, Russia had accounted for 70% of exports and Ukraine for 15% (GATT 1992, p. 52). The creditors of the USSR sought to assure that responsibility for external debt would be assured despite the breakup of the Soviet Union. They spent months negotiating joint and several liability of the new republics for the debt of the former USSR, essentially to make sure that Russia would make good on any debts not honored by other republics. In contrast, in other historical breakups of political groupings, such as the Austro-Hungarian Empire, it had been more common to arrive at a parceling out of the debt individually among the new nations, based on regional economic size (Williamson 1992b). Nonetheless, it turned out that Russia did not oppose joint and several liability. Indeed, it even offered to assume the entire debt if it could correspondingly take over the entire foreign exchange reserves of the former union. By 1992, Russia had reached agreement on such zero option accords with eleven of the fourteen other FSU republics, including the Ukraine (World Bank 1993).

There is great confusion concerning Russian trade data. The World Bank (1993, p. 139) reports that FSU export earnings were $83 billion in 1990, but Russia's exports were only $40 billion in 1992. If this collapse had in fact occurred, it might imply that Russia could not hope to carry the burden of FSU external debt. However, using trade data reported by partner countries, it can be shown that FSU exports had never reached above the range of some $45 billion to $50 billion (Cline 1994). What collapsed was the data, not the trade: Russian statistical authorities have evaluated the ruble-denominated exports to CMEA partners in 1990 and before at artificially high dollar values. Even so, by 1993 the ratio of FSU debt to Russian exports was about 200%, a level that has traditionally been considered near the limits of safety.

The OECD countries rescheduled principal due for 1992 and rescheduled principal and interest in early 1993. Although the private banks tried to avoid rescheduling, they rescheduled as well. As suggested in chapter 5, Russia's ultimate ability to honor the external debt will almost certainly be determined by the nation's degree of success in achieving domestic economic stabilization and growth.

Interrepublic Trade and Payments

Soviet planners had been fascinated with large-scale production and had constructed an industrial structure comprised of a network of unusually large individual plants and correspondingly large interregional trade. Interrepublic trade represented 13% of GDP for Russia but about one-fourth of GDP for the Ukraine and one-third or more of GDP for the ten other republics excluding the three Baltic states. Increasingly after the breakup of the FSU, there was a breakdown in interrepublican trade similar to the breakdown that had earlier occurred in CEMA trade with Eastern European countries when that trade was placed on a convertible currency basis in 1990–91. Interruption of intra-FSU trade imposed special hardship on the non-Russian republics with high trade shares in GDP.

Ironically, the initial obstacle to trade was not that the new republics imposed import barriers against goods from other republics. On the contrary, the problem came from export restrictions. Essentially, the various republics were growing increasingly skeptical of exporting goods and services in return for dubious paper money, rubles not convertible into dollars except at inordinately high black market rates. Yet most republics had minimal hard currency export earnings to use in purchases from Russia and other FSU republics.

Williamson (1992b) has suggested that the newly independent states should form a payments union similar to the European Payments Union, which helped postwar European nations maintain mutual trade despite their dollar shortage. A payments union provides a mechanism for clearing balances of mutual trade within the year without requiring hard currency payment at the time of the trade transaction. It could require several billion dollars to finance, however, and ultimately would require a decision on the part of the intra-FSU surplus republics as to how large they would allow their credit balances against the deficit republics to rise.

In contrast, the International Monetary Fund had initially advocated that the republics continue to use the ruble as their currency. While this ruble area strategy might have minimized the problem of a breakdown in interrepublic trade, it caused severe problems in the sphere of monetary policy. Lipton and Sachs (1992) argue that the extension of ruble credit by central banks in other FSU republics was a major reason for monetary destabilization in Russia in 1992.

Russia's New Economic Policy, January 1992

In 1991, inflation had reached 200% in the USSR, and GDP had fallen by 9%. Gorbachev had permitted large increases in controlled prices but did not set them free. Large subsidies were required as the government controlled prices at the consumer level but let them rise at the wholesale level. At the level of republics there were large fiscal deficits, and for the Union as a whole, the fiscal deficit reached 20% of GDP. Tax revenue declined as state enterprise managers and employees diverted funds, encouraged by an atmosphere of lawlessness as the old rules broke down.

There were important proposals for economic reform before the Union collapsed. Gorbachev had considered and rejected the Shatalin Plan for a 500-day transition. In the first 100 days, small businesses would have been privatized and large state firms transformed into corporations with independent boards of directors. In the following 150 days, with macroeconomic balance established and monetary overhang eliminated by the revenue from the initial wave of privatization, prices would have been liberalized, larger firms privatized, and land reform initiated. The plan sought to avoid a price shock at the outset of the transition (Fischer 1992, p. 86). However, it did not anticipate the breakup of the Soviet Union.

The formal dissolution of the USSR took place on December 21, 1991. On January 2, 1992, the government of Russian President, Boris Yeltsin launched its New Economic Policy, which amounted to an orthodox shock treatment (in comparison with the more structuralist, gradualist Shatalin plan).

The centerpiece of the new policy was immediate price liberalization, covering about 90% of goods at the retail level and 80% at the wholesale level. On average, prices surged by almost 300% within a few days. The government left price controls only on energy, transportation, and basic foods, and even for these items, it raised prices by some 250% before setting the new ceilings.

The fiscal program called for a reduction in the budget deficit from 20% of GDP to only 1%. In the face of planned inflation of 150% for the year, it limited increases in nominal government spending to 90%, thereby sharply reducing real spending. The real outlays were to fall by 20% for defense, including a 50% cut in military hardware. Overall, government spending was to fall by an amount equal to 10% of GDP. Fiscal revenue was to rise by nearly an equivalent amount to close the deficit. The central measure was an increase in the value added tax (VAT) from 5% to 28%.

The new economic policy imposed an incomes policy that sought to limit wage increases. Thus, the minimum wage was to rise by only 70%, much less than the 150% inflation programmed in the plan. The plan established a dual exchange rate, with a free, floating rate of around 100 rubles to the dollar for general transactions and a much lower commercial rate for key exports (oil, natural gas, metals, and gold). Export firms were to sell 40% of earnings to the central bank at only half the free market exchange rate.

The trade policy of the new plan was remarkably free. There were no duties on imports, arguably a mistake in view of the possible contribution of import tariffs to badly needed fiscal revenue during the transition. In effect, rather than trade barriers, the need to purchase foreign exchange at the extremely expensive free market rate for all but privileged imports acted as the vehicle to suppress imports.

By August 1992, the government added another element to the plan. Each adult Russian citizen was to receive a voucher in the amount of 10,000 rubles ($100 at the free rate) for use in the purchase of state enterprise shares in a general program of privatization. The amount was calculated in principle on the basis of the value of all state firms, although inflation quickly eroded the value of the vouchers.

The implementation of the new policy underwent two distinct phases. In the first, January through March 1992, economic policy was austere. In the second, beginning in April and lasting through most of the year, there was a major relaxation of economic policy and an intensifying conflict between the reformist economic team, led by Prime Minister Yegor Gaidar, and a coalition of the labor unions and the managers of state enterprises, which sought a slowdown in the reforms.

By March 1992, the combined effects of price liberalization and restrictive fiscal-monetary policies had caused a 50% reduction in industrial output from the level of a year earlier. The government had succeeded in cutting the fiscal deficit to 5% of GDP in the first quarter. However, it had done so through a large cut in subsidies, investment, and military and social spending. In contrast, the planned increase in revenue had not materialized because of evasion of the VAT, exclusion of some sectors from the tax, and the low level of activity and thus of revenue.

By the second quarter of 1992, the government was forced to relax fiscal and monetary policy in the face of the collapse of production. This was a critical turning point at which the political infeasibility of economic shock therapy broke down, leaving a much looser policy than perhaps might have resulted if the initial plan had been less severe. There were strikes in the health and education sectors, and the government was forced to grant a threefold increase in wages. The fiscal deficit rebounded sharply. Credit from the central bank soared as its president declared that his chief obligation was to assure that state firms did not close down. Lobbying power rather than efficiency or crucial supply role determined the distribution of central bank credit.

Mau (1994, p. 436) argues that the summer of 1992 was the most dangerous point for the reformers. For a time, there was a threat that opposition among industrialists, farmers, trade unions, and state enterprises would completely derail the program. However, the Yeltsin government used tactical maneuvers to split the opposition and formed an alliance with the industrialists. By the autumn of 1992, high but relatively stable inflation (at about 25% monthly) had acquired respectability. The reformers were able to blame the failure to achieve stabilization on the industrialists, and the industrialists were able to claim credit for protecting their enterprises by reversing a tight monetary policy that otherwise could have closed many firms down.

After inflation of 700% for 1992 as a whole, through much of 1993 inflation held at monthly rates of about 25% (1,300% annually). In July, the central bank raised interest rates from 80 to 170%, still far below the rate of inflation. The IMF (1993b) warned that the country could transit to hyperinflation if massive fiscal subsidies were not ended and if large central bank credits were not brought under the budget.

In October 1993, growing conflict between the conservative Parliament, elected under Gorbachev, and the Yeltsin government culminated in the bloody closure of Parliament and the scheduling of an early election for its replacement, as well as a referendum on a new constitution. Yeltsin took the opportunity to implement a new round of reforms that sought to cut the fiscal deficit, raise the interest rate further, eliminate the remaining price controls, and eliminate export quotas. It remained unclear whether his administration could seize effective control of the central bank.

In the area of privatization, Yeltsin's new economic policy had sought massive and rapid results. The state owned 23,000 industrial enterprises. As of mid-1992, the government planned to privatize firms accounting for three-fourths of the capital of these enterprises by 1993 (Lipton and Sachs 1992). However, by late 1993, only 4,500 state enterprises had been privatized, accounting for only 20% of industrial workers (*Economist,* 2 October 1993). Moreover, managers and workers held 70% of the shares of the privatized firms, which worked in the direction of preserving jobs (arguably appropriate in the absence of a social safety net) but against cost-cutting rationalization involving lay-offs. Thus, the admonition of Tanzi (1991, p. 223) seems especially appropriate for Russia:

It is unlikely that all enterprises will be privatized. It is improbable that the public enterprises will become efficient enough in a relatively short time to turn a profit, given the changing economic situation. Thus, they will continue to need subsidies. Some subsidies may be directed toward enterprises that are restructuring.

This admonition, in turn, highlights the importance of some method for allocating support among state firms, such as the triage approach suggested above.

In drawing an overall assessment of the initial experience of economic transition in Russia, Lipton and Sachs, (1992) have emphasized that the collapse in production was not as bad as it seemed. They stress that the economy had been seriously biased toward heavy industry, especially in the military-industrial complex MIC, and away from services. Accordingly, much of the drop in GDP was in the production of unwanted tanks, guns, and other MIC products. Although there is some truth in this point (and the IMF itself warns that its data understate GDP by giving insufficient weight to new private and privatized activity), the actual output losses were surely enormous even with appropriate adjustments.

Thus, Lipton and Sachs place MIC output at 16% of industrial production before the reform (p. 218). This amount corresponds to about 10% of material-balances GDP.[4] On this basis, even if all MIC output was totally worthless, which it was not, and even if MIC output fell to zero, which it did not, there was still a real output loss of some 30% of material balances GDP elsewhere in the economy in order to reach the 40% decline from 1989 to 1993 estimated by the IMF. The two authors also argue that critics of the sharp decline in real wages also miss the point that wages had merely returned to their pre-1987 level from exaggerated and unsustainable levels after the Gorbachev reforms. Perhaps so, but an absence of major real wage decline seems inconsistent with the large fall in non-MIC output just suggested.

It seems clear that by 1993, as compared with 1991, life in Russia was easier for those who had money, especially dollars. The shortages and queues had disappeared. However, many social groups seem to have suffered unambiguous losses. Pensioners whose real income had fallen sharply from inflation and who had leisure time to stand in lines were one such group. Popular accounts suggest that teachers and scientists also found themselves in much worsened conditions. There had been an explosion of crime, organized and other. One suspects that Aleksandr Solzhenitsyn was not totally misled when he wrote about "the current nascent capitalism, fraught with unproductive, savage and repulsive forms of behavior, the plunder of the nation's wealth, the likes of which the West has not known" and a resulting "nostalgia for the 'equality in poverty' of the past" (*New York Times*, 28 November 1993).

Response from the West

There can be little doubt that the West has a historic opportunity to consolidate a political-economic system in the former Soviet Union and Eastern Europe that is much more compatible with Western ideas. The United States, Western Europe, and Japan should be prepared to devote considerable resources to this purpose, if only for reasons no more altruistic than the calculus of reduced probability of Russian belligerence, and hence lower requirements for future defense expenditures under scenarios of stability rather than economic chaos in the East. Western Europe has the additional interest of avoiding a wave of immigration by economic refugees from the East.

Sachs (1992b) has argued that the West should provide resources amounting to almost $30 billion annually to the former Soviet Union over the period 1992–95. For Russia, an initial $5 billion would be for currency stabilization. Then, $6 billion annually would be in general balance of payments support, and another $6 billion annually would go to food aid. Total assistance for the other FSU republics would be comparable. More realistically, the International Monetary Fund (1991b) has projected flows of $15 billion annually to the former USSR and a comparable amount for Eastern Europe.

In April 1992, the Group of seven industrial countries announced that support to the former Soviet Union could amount to $24 billion. However, the figure did not represent annual flows; rather it contained an aggregation of various programs in process, and it was unlikely to be fully delivered because of unmet conditions for economic policy performance. The program included $6 billion for a currency stabilization fund, but the fund was to be conditional on the establishment of exchange rate convertibility—not a promising prospect soon. There was to be $2½ billion in support through deferral of interest on bilateral debt, and $4½ billion in support from international financial institutions (IMF, World Bank, European Bank for Reconstruction and Development, EBRD). Another $11 billion was to be available in bilateral credits, mainly for exports.

One of the issues that has not been addressed adequately in the discussion of financial support to the former Soviet Union is whether Russia and the other republics can safely take on a large amount of new external debt on market terms. As discussed above, they have already found it necessary to secure debt reschedulings, and although Russia's debt/export ratio is not extremely high, it is questionable that major increases in its debt burden are advisable, especially when the internal transfer issue is taken into account. However, if debt on market-related terms is inappropriate, the implication is that either there will be little outside support or that it should be extended in the form of outright grants. Yet Russia is hardly a candidate comparable to Bangladesh or sub-Saharan Africa in the allocation of scarce international grant assistance funds, although poorer republics such as Kazakhstan might be.

In practice, the initial task of providing financial support to the transition toward a market economy in the former Soviet Union will fall to Western governments through their export and commodity credit agencies, as well as indirectly through such international agencies as the IMF, the World Bank, and the EBRD. Especially in the bilateral credits, there should be some room for blending lower interest loans (for example, commodity credit) with normal market-rate funds. Over the meduim term, when and if macroeconomic conditions stabilize, private direct investment and other private finance from abroad can play an important role. Major investment opportunities, such as rehabilitation of the oil sector, could mobilize external capital once macroeconomic conditions are more stable and legal institutions are more secure.

Eastern Europe

Institutional reform after the collapse of communism had begun earlier in several Eastern European countries, and Russian authorities as well as policy analysts internationally looked to these countries (especially Poland) for lessons that might apply to reform in the FSU.

A review of the experience of Eastern Europe reveals several patterns in the transition to market economies. First, market-oriented reform has been a recurrent theme in the Eastern European economies even in earlier decades. There have been previous attempts to decentralize decision making and to liberalize prices in at least Hungary and Poland. In general, these attempts were failures because Communist governments were not committed to thoroughgoing liberalization. Prices proved not to be very effective instruments for incentives in the absence of private ownership.

Second, in the more sweeping liberalizations of 1990–91, there was a pattern of initial inflationary shock, followed by subsequent price stabilization of varying degrees. However, the stabilization was accompanied by serious output declines. Production fell by 10% in Czechoslovakia, 20% in Poland, and 35% in Bulgaria.

Third, there was a major adverse impact on output in 1990–91 from the breakdown of intra-CMEA trade as the member countries shifted to hard currency payment. There was a large reduction in Eastern European exports to the market of the USSR for this reason. These trade effects translated into falling production. By 1992 rapidly growing exports to Western Europe were beginning to help compensate.[5] Nonetheless, a major need remains for further redirection of Eastern European exports to the markets of the West, especially Western Europe, in order to offset more fully the collapse of the CMEA market. For this purpose, in turn, it is important that protection in the European Community and other industrial countries be liberalized in such product areas as steel, textiles, agricultural goods, and coal that are important to Eastern European countries.

Fourth, there has been an ongoing debate on the strategy for privatization. The two alternative approaches are the big bang, a swift and comprehensive distribution of state firms to the population as in Poland and Czechoslovakia, and the British model of slower, more deliberate privatization that seeks to ensure the best price for the public as in Hungary. The central point is that, until privatization is carried out, the systems will lack the incentives provided by private ownership. A related pattern is the evidence that uncertainty about property rights can delay foreign investment. Moreover, with the breakdown in the command and control system but only partial privatization, managers of state firms begin to see themselves as answerable to no one. The result is an incentive to overpay workers so as to assure their cooperation while carrying out transactions that lead to personal gain.

Fifth, the Eastern European experience at the beginning of the 1990s most fundamentally reflected an utter rejection of decades of the command and control economy based on communist ideology. This rejection followed a historic decline in the growth performance of the system, from rates as high as 10% in the 1950s to 3% and lower in the 1980s. The easiest type of growth under the command economy, extensive growth through the accumulation of capital, tended to run out, and the more imaginative and consumption-oriented growth associated with technological progress seemed to have been difficult to mobilize in the absence of private incentives. Nor were attempts to simulate the market through sophisticated planning successful or even feasible in principle. By some estimates, there were as many as twenty-five million products to keep track of in the Soviet economy. Even with supercomputers, comprehensive replication of a smoothly functioning free market was infeasible with such complexity.

Poland

In many ways, Poland has served as the precursor and example for the process of transition being faced by the former Soviet Union. By 1993, there was mixed evidence as to whether the Polish example would prove to have been a happy one.

Polish authorities liberalized prices, and as promised, the shortages disappeared. They adopted classic stabilization measures that succeeded in halting hyperinflation. Prices rose more than twelvefold in 1989, but annual inflation was down to the range of 60–70% by 1990–91 and 45% by 1993. The measures included a large initial exchange rate devaluation, followed by an exchange rate held fixed to serve as a monetary anchor through 1990 and the first half of 1991 (followed by a crawling peg). The government eliminated the fiscal deficit and imposed wage controls. The trade balance moved sharply to surplus in 1990, before returning to moderate deficit.

The bad news was that real production fell by approximately 20% in the period 1989–91 and remained stagnant in 1992. By then there was increasing risk of a political backlash, pushing the country toward populism and blocking privatization. One of the architects of the reform plan, Harvard economist Jeffrey Sachs, argued that things were not as bad as they seemed. There had actually been a boom in the long-neglected services sector, the consumption of fruits and vegetables was increasing, and improved availability from elimination of shortages meant that the reported inflation overstated consumer hardship (as earlier inflation figures had failed to capture shortages or repressed inflation). In any event, Sachs argued, the father of Germany's postwar economic miracle, Ludwig Erhard, had also been blamed for creating unemployment rather than high living standards because "not until several years after the start of his reform did prosperity arrive" (Sachs 1992a, p. 40).

By 1993, there was a moderate upturn in the economy (see figure 6.1). Some in the financial press declared that the economy was in "un-recognisably better shape than four years ago, with industrial production rising, the private sector now accounting for over half of economic activity, and foreign investment making important inroads" (*Financial Times*, 21 September 1993). For their part, the Polish voters had a chance to make their own assessment in the elections of September 1993. The verdict was less than reassuring, as they placed in power two parties, the Democratic Left Alliance and the Polish Peasant Party, closely identified with the communists in the past. The vote was widely interpreted as a rejection of shock therapy and its seeming consequences of increasing disparity between rich and poor (*Washington Post*, 22 September 1993). Nonetheless, it was expected that the new government would not fundamentally reverse the course of the economic reforms, and some observers attributed the election loss mainly to infighting among the economic reform factions and such noneconomic matters as the role of the church.

In defense of Poland's economic strategy in 1990–93, its chief architect has argued that shock therapy involving sharp fiscal and monetary restraint and immediate price and trade liberalization was far superior to gradualism, because "gradual liberalization . . . would have resembled the previous failed attempts at economic reform . . . [and] would have precluded a radical elimination of shortages" (Balcerowicz 1994, p. 163). Nonetheless, he also acknowledges that:

The risk of this strategy was that the supply response of the public sector to the tough stabilization-liberalization package was likely to be worse than that of a largely private economy. (p. 162)

Overview

This risk of inadequate supply response turned out to be especially severe in Russia, perhaps in part because of institutional differences from other economies in transition (such as the greater breakdown in manageability of the macroeconomy from the center after the collapse of the USSR, and the longer historical reign of communism than in

Eastern Europe). Russian economic reformers tend to argue that the country's economic disarray by 1993 stemmed not from the application of shock therapy, but from the lack thereof. However, the dramatic collapse of output in the first quarter of 1992 suggests that the initial Yeltsin program was too austere, took inadequate account of the need to maintain production, and thus could have been expected to implode politically.

In sum, the massive decline in production in Eastern Europe and the former Soviet Union in the first four years after the collapse of the Berlin Wall makes it imperative that the next stage of the transition focus on the maintenance and recovery of production and macroeconomic stabilization. For this purpose, it seems likely that the economic strategy will need to move beyond simple shock therapy formulas. Much remains to be done in terms of intellectual innovation among Eastern and Western economists and in terms of the efforts by policymakers controlling the purse strings of industrial country support if the historic experiment of transition to the market economy in Eastern Europe and the former Soviet Union is to be assured of a successful outcome.

APPENDIX 6A: INTER-INDUSTRY ANALYSIS AND TRANSITION ECONOMICS

Figure 6.5 shows an input-output table describing the economy. In part A of the figure, each entry represents the value of the inputs provided by the sector listed by row on the far left into the sector listed by column in the center. Thus, steel provides 30 (e.g., billion rubles) of inputs into the machinery sector.[6] Total or gross production of the sector is shown as the last entry in each row. The difference between gross output and the sum of the sector's inputs into other sectors for intermediate use is what is left over for final demand, listed in the column next to gross output. Thus, the sum of intermediate uses of steel, reading across the row for steel, amounts to 60 units. Total steel output is 80 units, and so, 20 units of steel are available for the public to consume.[7]

In part B of figure 6.5, the information on intersectoral inputs is converted into input-output coefficients that state the required input from supplying sector (row) into using sector (column) as a fraction of gross output in the using sector. Thus, the coefficient for steel inputs into machinery is 0.38, or 30 units of intermediate steel inputs divided by 80 units of gross output in machinery. High input-output coefficients

Part A

Using industry:									Final demand	Gross output
Supplying industry:	1 Ag	2 St	3 Ch	4 Ma	5 Fd	6 Cl	7 Au	8 Sv	F	X
1. Agriculture	10	0	5	0	80	3	0	0	2	100
2. Steel	5	10	5	30	0	0	10	0	20	80
3. Chemicals	5	10	5	2	5	2	3	0	8	40
4. Machinery	10	20	5	10	5	5	5	2	18	80
5. Food	0	0	0	0	5	0	0	15	100	120
6. Clothing	0	0	0	0	0	0	0	10	90	100
7. Automobiles	3	0	0	0	0	0	2	5	30	30
8. Services	5	3	3	3	3	4	2	25	102	150
Value added	62	37	17	35	22	86	18	93	370	
Gross output	100	80	40	80	120	100	40	150		710

Part B

Input-output coefficients:

1. Agriculture	0.10	0	0.12	0	0.67	0.03	0	0
2. Steel	0.05	0.12	0.12	0.38	0	0	0.25	0
3. Chemicals	0.05	0.12	0.12	0.02	0.04	0.02	0.08	0
4. Machinery	0.10	0.25	0.12	0.12	0.04	0.05	0.12	0.01
5. Food	0	0	0	0	0.04	0	0	0.10
6. Clothing	0	0	0	0	0	0	0	0.07
7. Automobiles	0.03	0	0	0	0	0	0.05	0.03
8. Services	0.05	0.04	0.08	0.04	0.02	0.04	0.05	0.17

Part C

Input-output parameters:

1. Agriculture	a_{11}	a_{12}	a_{13}	a_{14}	a_{15}	a_{16}	a_{17}	a_{18}
2. Steel	a_{21}	a_{22}	a_{23}	a_{24}	a_{25}	a_{26}	a_{27}	a_{28}
3. Chemicals	a_{31}	a_{32}	a_{33}	a_{34}	a_{35}	a_{36}	a_{37}	a_{38}
4. Machinery	a_{41}	a_{42}	a_{43}	a_{44}	a_{45}	a_{46}	a_{47}	a_{48}
5. Food	a_{51}	a_{52}	a_{53}	a_{54}	a_{55}	a_{56}	a_{57}	a_{58}
6. Clothing	a_{61}	a_{62}	a_{63}	a_{64}	a_{65}	a_{66}	a_{67}	a_{68}
7. Automobiles	a_{71}	a_{72}	a_{73}	a_{74}	a_{75}	a_{76}	a_{77}	a_{78}
8. Services	a_{81}	a_{82}	a_{83}	a_{84}	a_{85}	a_{86}	a_{87}	a_{88}

Figure 6.5
An illustrative input-output table

represent high forward linkage from the supplying sector to the using sector, and high backward linkage from the using sector to the supplying sector. It may be seen that what may be called universal intermediary sectors (e.g., steel, chemicals, and machinery) tend to have high forward linkages. In contrast, sectors that are typically at the final consumer stage tend to have low forward linkages but high backward linkage. Thus, the food industry provides minimal intermediate inputs into other sectors but demands large intermediate inputs from the agricultural sector.

Part C of figure 6.5 repeats these coefficients in general notation rather than the specific values in the example. Each entry a_{ij} corresponds to the fractional value reported in part B of the figure, with i as the supplying sector and j as the using sector. Thus, a_{24} represents the inputs of sector two, steel, into sector four, machinery, expressed as a fraction of gross output in machinery.

The entire table of a_{ij} coefficients may be represented in matrix form by the notation $\underset{m \times m}{\mathbf{A}}$, where m is the number of sectors in the economy. Using matrix algebra, it may be shown that the vector $\underset{m \times 1}{\mathbf{X}}$ of gross outputs required to provide a target vector $\underset{m \times 1}{\mathbf{F}}$ of final consumption may be calculated as:

$$\underset{m \times 1}{\mathbf{X}} = \underset{m \times 1}{\mathbf{F}} \, [\underset{m \times 1}{\mathbf{I}} - \underset{m \times m}{\mathbf{A}}]^{-1}$$

where $\mathbf{I}$ is what is known as the identity matrix, with ones along the diagonal and zeroes elsewhere, and the exponent -1 refers to the inverse of the matrix in brackets.[8]

The details of matrix algebra and input-output analysis are not essential here; intuitively, the need to produce a greater amount of gross output to provide a given amount of net output available for consumption is not unlike recognizing that a larger amount of gross income will be needed if there is leakage from the household budget to pay taxes.[9] Instead, the purpose here is to use the input-output framework to help think about critical supply sectors.

During the transition, instead of adopting a big bang with all command and control disappearing overnight and with production being turned over to liberated prices to determine, the government could pay special attention to maintaining existing production in those sectors that provide crucial inputs into the rest of the economy. In the terminology of input-output analysis, these are sectors with forward linkages. Suppose that the steel sector has large inputs into the machinery sector (a_{24} is large). Then there would be a special effort to ensure that steel production did not fall. The reason is that, if steel output declines, a chain reaction of declining output in machinery ensues because of the bottleneck created by a lack of steel. In a smoothly functioning economy, export earnings can be used to purchase such bottleneck inputs from abroad. However, in conditions of extreme foreign exchange scarcity, if domestic output in the sectors with high forward linkages is not maintained, then the more likely outcome is simply a domino effect of declining production in the downstream products.[10]

Suggested Readings

Ericson (1991), Fischer and Gelb (1991), Fischer (1992), Berg and Sachs (1991), Lipton and Sachs (1992).

7　The Economic Future of Europe

Background

Change of historic proportions was sweeping not only Eastern Europe and the USSR at the beginning of the 1990s but also Western Europe. Ironically, while the historic forces were centrifugal in the East, where the Soviet empire was splintering into republics, they were centripetal in the West, where Europe was forming a more complete and probably larger economic union.

As recently as the mid-1980s, there had been great concern about "Eurosclerosis." In the European Community, unemployment had been persistently high at over 10%. Economic growth in the period 1983–87 was only 2.4% annually, compared with about 4% in the United States and Japan during the same period. The growth of real investment, which had averaged only 1.6% annually in 1973–82, fell to a negligible 0.1% annually in 1983–85.

In contrast, by the late 1980s, the mood had turned to "Europhoria" as expectations rose first in connection with the move toward complete trade liberalization in the single market of EC-92 and then from the added impulse of the move toward an European economic and monetary union. In its 1985 white paper, the EC Commission had called for full economic integration by 1992. This prospect stirred enthusiasm about the potential of the world's largest market, some 320 million consumers versus 250 million in the United States and 120 million in Japan. An investment boom emerged in response as investment rose at almost 5% annually in 1986–87 and nearly 9% annually in 1988–89. Economic growth rose to 3.7% annually in these two final years of the decade.

The move toward a more complete economic union took another quantum leap in December 1991, when EC members agreed at

Maastricht, the Netherlands, to establish a European Monetary Union (EMU), with the goal of a single common currency by 1999. However, by 1991 the economic boom had encountered an unexpected diversion as spillover from change in the East dampened this euphoria. West Germany seized the historic opportunity to reunite with East Germany but did so in a manner that chilled the economic climate for the rest of Europe. To counter the inflationary pressures of reunification, the Bundesbank raised interest rates sharply. Other European countries found it necessary to raise rates correspondingly, with a stifling effect on investment. By 1990, the EC's growth rate had slowed to less than 3% and investment growth to 4%, and by 1991, growth was down to 0.7% and investment expansion a weak 0.2%. Growth remained sluggish in 1992 at about 1% and fell to zero in 1993 (IMF 1993b).

By 1993, it remained unclear whether and by when Europe could recover from the temporary interruption caused by German reunification and thus restore economic growth. More fundamental issues for the longer term remained. How deep would the economic union be: would there be a single currency and a meaningfully unified monetary policy? How wide it would be: how many new member countries would join and would they include Eastern European states? These questions would have to be answered in an environment that may be described as living beside the volcano in view of the potential disruption from economic upheaval in the former Soviet Union. On the immediate horizon, there were also new questions raised by the European currency crises of the autumn of 1992 and August of 1993, as well as intra-EC disputes concerning agricultural liberalization in the Uruguay Round of GATT negotiations.

The Economics of Europe 1992: The Single Market

The European Commission's call for true integration in a single market by 1992 was a surprise to many economists outside of Europe who had thought the European Community already had free trade among members. However, the commission's recommendation required some 300 directives just to enumerate the measures to be taken to remove the remaining barriers. The implication was that, heretofore, the EC had gone only about half way to free trade within its common market.

The Barriers

The remaining barriers included the following:

• *Customs clearance.* Trucks had to stop at borders for inspection of cargo, and there were border tax adjustments for national differences in the value added tax rate.

• *Technical standards and regulations.* Firms considered the more than 100,000 different regulations among member states to be the most important barrier to full integration. To resolve this problem, the EC moved to the principle of mutual recognition, whereby products that met standards in one state automatically did so elsewhere in the Community. Correspondingly, there was to be a Communitywide board on standards.

• *Government procurement.* In their purchasing practices, member governments often excluded bids from firms in other EC countries.

• *Agriculture.* The practice of monetary compensation for different production costs was in effect a tariff on agricultural trade among members.

• *Production quotas.* In some sectors, such as steel and certain agricultural goods, there were quotas limiting production by country.

• *Transport regulations.* Air and road transportation faced differing regulations among member countries.

• *Border enforcement.* National quotas on imports of textiles, automobiles, and some other products meant that there had been border restrictions to prevent transshipment of such goods from member countries with more liberal imports to the more restrictive members.

• *Right of establishment.* In such areas as insurance and the professions, there were restrictions on the right of a firm or a person from one member country to establish activity in another.

Economic Effects

European economists emphasized five types of economic gains available through removal of the remaining barriers: traditional static efficiency gains from trade, reduction of inefficiency associated with oligopoly power, greater achievement of economies of scale,

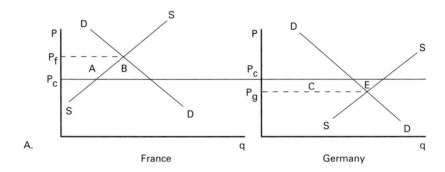

A.

France   Germany

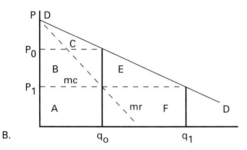

B.

Figure 7.1
Static efficiency and antimonopoly gains from the European single market

X-efficiency improvement from increased competitive stimulus, and macroeconomic gains associated with a reduction in prices.

Figure 7.1, panel A, illustrates the static welfare gains from eliminating barriers between members, such as France and Germany. Suppose that, in a given product, the equilibrium price in Germany is p_g, whereas in France production is less efficient and the price is p_f. Standards, border obstacles, and other barriers maintain the wedge, $p_f - p_g$. Then the single market eliminates these barriers and results in a common equilibrium price at p_c. Production increases in Germany, moving up the supply curve, SS, to where it intersects the p_c price line, and decreases in France, moving downward to the left along the French supply curve to the intersection with the p_c line. Conversely, the quantity consumed rises in France and declines in Germany.

Welfare gains may be measured by changes in consumer and producer surplus. Consumer surplus is the amount that consumers would have been prepared to pay if prices were higher, and producer surplus is the excess of firms' revenue above the amounts that would have been required to call forth production (see appendix 3A). These are inframarginal concepts because the marginal consumer is brought in just where his full willingness to pay is exhausted by the market price and because the marginal firm produces at a cost that leaves no profit. In figure 7.1(A), at any given market equilibrium, consumer surplus is the area under the demand curve, *DD*, and above the horizontal price line; producer surplus is the area under the horizontal price line and above the supply curve.

In France, full integration increases consumer surplus by the area A + B. However, of this gain, the area A is simply a transfer away from the French firms' producer surplus. Symmetrically, in Germany there is an increase of producer surplus amounting to areas C + E. Of this increase, the area C is merely a transfer away from German consumers to German producers. The net gains for the two countries thus amount to areas B + E. These are the classic welfare triangles of gains from free trade, and they represent the benefits from specializing according to comparative advantage (see appendix 3A). These triangles may be estimated by examining the size of the price changes $(p_f - p_c$ and $p_c - p_g)$ and the corresponding changes in output quantities. The quantity changes, in turn, will depend on the elasticities or degree of responsiveness of demand and supply to price changes.

As discussed in chapter 3 and appendix 3A, this process of more efficient allocation of production within the free trade area is the welfare-enhancing trade creation effect of integration. Moving to free trade within a common market can also cause trade diversion away from the rest of the world, with resulting welfare losses. Reviewing existing estimates, Hufbauer (1990, p. 23) concluded that increased exports from outside countries as a consequence of more rapid EC growth under the single market could exceed trade diversion by as much as threefold. Moreover, many of the EC-92 reforms in such areas as technical standards made the European market more transparent and thus potentially more open to outsiders as well as trade partners.

Panel B of figure 7.1 illustrates the second source of gains from barrier removal, a reduction of monopoly and oligopoly power. From society's standpoint, a monopoly firm produces too little and charges prices that are too high. From the firm's perspective, if it produces larger amounts, it will spoil its price and thereby reduce the high profits associated with holding back production. The monopoly firm differs from the competitive firm in that it is so large that it can influence the market price by its individual actions.

In figure 7.1(B), the monopoly firm, say, in Italy, maximizes profits where its marginal revenue curve, mr, intersects its marginal cost curve, mc, at output q_0. The marginal revenue curve lies below the demand curve, DD, facing the consumer. Thus, at output level q_0, the consumer pays price p_0 for one extra unit of the good. The firm also receives p_0 on the last unit, but it loses revenue on all of the previous units because of the price spoilage from driving down the price by making the extra unit available to the market. Deducting this lost revenue on all of the other units sold, marginal revenue is only p_1.

Now suppose the single market introduces competition from, for example, French and German firms in the Italian market. Now the former monopoly firm in Italy cannot get away with charging a price as high as p_0 because competitors will enter to take advantage of the high prices. The market equilibrium will now settle at the level of the competitive firms, where the demand curve DD intersects the supply curve or marginal cost curve mc. The new equilibrium output will be at q_1. Consumer surplus will have risen by areas B + E. The monopoly firm's producer surplus will have fallen by area B. The net gain from elimination of monopoly is thus area E.

Figure 7.2 illustrates the third type of gain from dropping trade barriers, increased achievement of economies of scale. The product has a declining marginal cost curve, mc, because of economies of scale. In isolation, France and Germany both have suboptimal plants that produce at a size where the marginal cost curve intersects the demand curves $D_f D_f$ and $D_g D_g$, at price p_0 (panel A). After full integration, the two plants are replaced by a much larger plant that has the same marginal cost curve but can sell to a market twice as large. In panel B, the demand curve $D_c D_c$ is the horizontal sum of national demand curves $D_f D_f$ and $D_g D_g$. At larger scale, marginal cost is much lower, so the supply curve reaches a zone of lower prices. The equilibrium price for the combined markets is thus lower at p_c, and production level q_c is considerably more than the original output sum $(q_0 = q_f + q_g)$.[1]

The welfare gains from greater economies of scale are shown as the increased consumer surplus in areas A + B + C. In this case, there is no offsetting loss of producer surplus. The reason is that previously production was at inefficient scale so that the consumer gains from larger scale come through an increase in overall efficiency rather than a reallocation of former producer surplus.[2]

The EC Commission estimated that, in over half of the industrial sectors, the single market would mean that there were twenty firms or

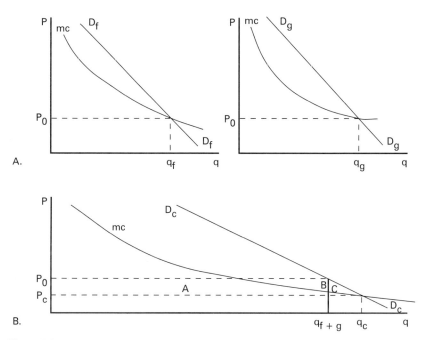

Figure 7.2
Gains from economies of scale in the single market

more of optimal size, whereas before each national market typically could accomodate only four firms of optimal size. The implication was a major potential for gains both in economies of scale and in reduced oligopoly power.

In 1988, the EC Commission published an economic analysis of the prospective gains from the move to the single market in the Ceccini Report (Emerson et al 1988). The study estimated that there would be ECU (European Currency Units) 9 billion annually in gains from removal of customs clearances at borders (one ECU was then worth about $1.20). Removal of technical standards regulations would amount to ECU 31 billion or about 3½% of the value added on the relevant products (reaching 5% for automobiles). Reduced oligopoly power would provide gains of ECU 20 billion in government procurement and another ECU 20 billion in financial services. In industry, the combined gains from reduced oligopoly power and increased economies of scale would amount to ECU 60 billion annually. Finally, X-efficiency gains from greater technical change spurred by increased competition would amount to ECU 50 billion annually. The total reached ECU 190 billion annually. Allowing for alternative assumptions, the microeconomic gains amounted to a range of 4½ to 6½% of GDP annually.

In addition, these microeconomic effects would permit an estimated 6% reduction in prices. This relief on inflationary pressure would permit a more expansionary monetary-fiscal policy, providing additional macroeconomic gains of some 2½% of GDP. Overall, the benefits would thus amount to at least 7% of GDP annually.

The Commission's estimates were much higher than those that had been estimated earlier for the original formation of the European Common Market in the 1960s. These latter had been typically placed in the range of 1 to 2% of GDP. Once again there was the irony that the completion of European free trade seemed to be more significant than its original implementation, for if the figures were taken literally, removal of the remaining barriers seemed to be even more important than the earlier move to more conventional free trade through elimination of tariffs. Part of the explanation was that the study for EC-92 incorporated large effects (economies of scale and antimonopoly) that had typically been omitted in the earlier calculations, which had tended to be only for static welfare gains. Another part of the explanation may have been that, in their enthusiasm, the Commission's economists may have overstated the prospective gains.[3]

The prospective gains seemed persuasive to investors, and in the late 1980s, there was a boom in investment, including foreign, in anticipation of the single market. By the time 1992 had actually arrived, however, investment had slowed, largely because of the influence of German reunification and high interest rates but perhaps also because the runup to the single market had been completed.

European Monetary Union

There has been a long-standing desire within Europe for stable exchange rates among key trading partners, in part because of their unusually high mutual trade (70% of Western Europe's trade is within the region) (GATT 1992). As the Bretton Woods international regime of fixed exchange rates was breaking down in 1971–73, the EC members adopted a snake of narrow margins of fluctuation among their currencies, as well as those of Norway and Sweden. The snake was to move within the tunnel of wider margins of fluctuation against the dollar. However, because domestic inflation rates differed, there were numerous exits from and reentries into the snake by France, Italy, the United Kingdom, and Denmark, and in the late 1970s it remained effective only for an inner core of low-inflation countries.

Nonetheless, the desire for exchange rate stability within Europe remained strong and eventually led to the exchange rate mechanism of fixed rates in the 1980s and the ambitious project for European Monetary Union in the 1990s. The following discussion reviews these successive institutional developments. First, however, it is appropriate to ask what economic theory has to say about the issue of a common currency.

Optimum Currency Areas

The principal theory of relevance to the issue of monetary union and a common currency is that of the optimum currency area. First stated by Mundell (1961), this theory holds that there is a certain domain of a single currency that is of optimal size. If a single currency is applied in too large an area, excessive unemployment is likely to develop in subregions of the area. These subregions will not have the instrument of exchange rate devaluation available to revive exports and activity. Thus, if New England enters into recession, it cannot achieve adjustment by devaluing a New England dollar against the U.S. dollar in pursuit of higher exports to the rest of the country. The question is then whether other adjustment mechanisms exist that nonetheless make the United States an optimum currency area rather than larger than optimum size.

The conditions for an optimum currency area will tend to be met more fully if there is either downward wage flexibility or labor mobility within the area. In the first case, subregions facing unemployment can adjust through reducing wages and prices, thereby becoming more competitive with the rest of the area. In the second case, unemployment in a subregion can be resolved by worker migrations to the rest of the region.

Subregional inflexibility in addressing unemployment through exchange rate depreciation is the cost of a single currency area. Its benefits arise from efficiency gains associated with the elimination of transactions costs of currency conversion and from the removal of uncertainty about the future exchange rate (de Grauwe 1992). A single currency can also reduce the scope for oligopolistic firms to price discriminate among different countries within a common market at the expense of consumers and overall efficiency. Exchange rate uncertainty can reduce the efficiency of the price mechanism in allocating resources. An additional benefit of a larger currency area is that it tends to make the currency a more useful store of value (McKinnon 1963).

De Grauwe (1992) notes that the monetarists tend to view the costs of a single currency area as low because they consider changes in the exchange rate ineffective as a means of adjustment (see chapter 2). In contrast, Keynesians tend to emphasize wage inflexibility and the importance of exchange rate flexibility for achieving full employment. For both schools, the size of trade with the partner area in a country's GDP is an important criterion. The larger this share, the more important the potential benefits of a single currency with the area.[4]

An important aspect of optimum currency area theory is its treatment of the role of economic diversity in the area's ability to respond to shocks. Mundell's original formulation assumed that the optimal area would be functionally uniform—for example, an area specializing in wheat production. In this way, when there was an exogenous shock in the demand for wheat, the area could appropriately respond uniformly through a change in its exchange rate against the rest of the world. In contrast, Kenen (1969) argued that a diversified economy is more suitable for a single currency area because the diversification would mean that employment opportunities in some sectors could offset employment losses in other sectors within the area without requiring a depreciation of an exchange rate among subregions.

As applied to the EMU, both the considerations of labor mobility (existing in principle within a common market) and high intra-area trade are present in the EC and so would tend to favor its definition as an optimum currency area. Moreover, use of the fixed exchange rate in the ERM was important in the 1980s as a form of anti-inflationary discipline for national fiscal and monetary policy; monetary discipline would be absolute under a single currency. This consideration is reminiscent of McKinnon's value of the currency argument.

However, there are at least two major problems with the EC and EMU as an optimal currency area. Both problems derive from the fact that the area is supranational. The first is that there is no system of major countercyclical fiscal transfers among nations within the EC. In contrast, the United States does have automatic stabilizers providing countercyclical interregional transfers in the form of unemployment insurance and federal income taxes. In Europe, fiscal revenue is almost wholly reserved to the country in question. The Community budget is small, and the EMU project foresees no mechanism for large countercyclical transfers among member countries.

The second problem is that the political units for fiscal policy in the EC are not to be coterminus with that for monetary policy, nor can they be unless the EMU changes into a European government. Again, in contrast, the United States has a fiscal area that coincides with the currency area: the federal government's spending and revenue.

De Grauwe (1992) provides an imaginative contrast between the adjustment processes of the state of Michigan and Belgium, two economies of similar size but one within a large currency area and the other not yet. Both states had severe unemployment in 1980–82. Michigan adjusted primarily through outmigration and fiscal transfers with minimal real exchange rate change through abnormally low wage increases. In contrast, Belgium depended heavily on real exchange rate depreciation to restore activity through improved competitiveness. Arguing, somewhat surprisingly, that, because "the mobility of labour between European countries is likely to remain limited" (p. 90), de Grauwe (1992) points out that the loss of the exchange rate instrument could impose a cost on some EMU member countries. However, he acknowledges that the fundamental drive for EMU may be political rather than economic.

In sum, important elements of the optimum currency area theory are consistent with the qualification of the EMU as such an area. Still, the absence of a single government coterminus with the single currency is a major reason to consider the EMU as considerably less appropriate for a common currency than the United States or Japan.

The Exchange Rate Mechanism

In 1979, in a context of increasing European concern about dollar instability and impelled by a political initiative by President Valery Giscard d'Estaing of France and Chancellor Helmut Schmidt of Germany, EC members adopted the European Monetary System (EMS).[5] The exchange rate mechanism (ERM) within this system provided for a regime of tight target zones for exchange rate parities as measured against the European Currency Unit, itself a basket of these currencies. Rates were to fluctuate no more than 2¼% around their central parity against the ECU. Whenever two currencies were at opposite extremes in the band, the two respective central banks were to intervene in support of the weaker currency.

At one extreme, an inner core of hard currency countries, Germany, the Netherlands, and Belgium, adhered to tight parities within the ERM. At the opposite extreme, the United Kingdom opted out and continued to allow the pound sterling to float. Italy and France were in intermediate positions as they joined the ERM but resorted to periodic devaluations within it. Spain and Portugal subsequently joined this intermediate group within the ERM.

Contrary to the predictions of many (especially U.S.) economists, the EMS enjoyed success during the next dozen years. France, Italy, and Spain found it especially useful as an anchor to inflationary expectations that enabled them to reduce inflation toward German levels. Importantly, economic authorities in these countries found the need to hold the fixed exchange rate provided a useful argument in diverting the chronic political pressures for higher domestic public spending. The drawback of the use of the ERM as an anti-inflationary vehicle was that by the mid-1980s, the ERM had increasingly become a regime of narrowly fixed exchange rates rather than one with substantial periodic realignments; and whereas this trend was convenient for limiting inflation, it involved growing risk for creeping overvaluation of the currencies of countries that nonetheless continued to experience relatively higher inflation.

In the United Kingdom, Prime Minister Margaret Thatcher had opposed entry into the ERM as an erosion of sovereignty. However, in the autumn of 1990, under her successor John Major the United Kingdom entered the ERM, largely in the hope that its dampening effect on inflationary expectations would permit a reduction in interest rates and an increase in investment and growth. The entry of the United Kingdom was eloquent testimony to the reputation for success that the ERM had acquired. This success was taken so much for granted that it came as a great shock when the fixed exchange rates temporarily broke down in the European currency crisis of September–October 1992.

The Move toward EMU

By the late 1980s, with the adoption of the commitment to the single market by 1992, it seemed obvious to many that the next step for the EC was a tighter monetary relationship. The market would not be wholly unified until there was a single currency.

The EC Commission's de Lors report of 1989 was the trigger for a major intensification of the move toward EMU. The report proposed that the Community move to monetary union in three phases. In the first, there would be the elimination of remaining controls on capital movements. This phase was in fact completed with the removal of controls in Italy and France by 1990. In the second phase, there would be a new European System of Central Banks. In the third phase, countries would adopt irrevocably fixed exchange rates. The transition from these firmly locked exchange rates to a single currency would then follow quickly and naturally.

Issues of Contention

In 1990 and 1991, there was intense debate within Europe over the question of European Monetary Union. The debate centered around several central issues. The positions that emerged formed the basis for the Maastricht Agreement of December 1991.

First, would the EMU be dominated by Germany? As it turned out, the other European countries essentially accepted this risk as tolerable. Their reasoning was that the Bundesbank already dominated the ERM, which was essentially a deutschmark zone. The institutionalization of a European System of Central Banks would at least provide an explicit role for the other countries. The French in particular anticipated that they would enjoy greater control over European monetary policy than under the existing Bundesbank-dominated arrangements of the ERM.

Second, would the EMU be under political control or central banker control? In France and Italy, for example, the tradition was that the director of the central bank served at the pleasure of the finance minister. In contrast, in Germany, there was a strong tradition of strict autonomy of the central bank. In the negotiations, the Germans successfully insisted that the model of an independent central bank be maintained for the EMU as a whole.

Third, would the United Kingdom would be a member of the monetary union? Sovereignty of the British pound sterling remained a major issue. In the negotiations, U.K. representatives suggested an alternative approach whereby member country currencies, including especially the pound, would be allowed to compete for preeminence in a transition to monetary union.

Fourth, would there be two tracks to the EMU, one for an inner group of countries with stable monetary conditions and the other for weaker economies? Germany, the Netherlands, and Belgium had long constituted a more solid hard money core of the snake and the EMS, and there were German fears in particular that the attempt to impose a single, all-inclusive monetary union by reaching the common denominator would so weaken monetary discipline that Germany's traditional anti-inflationary standards would be lost. On the other side of the debate, there was a strong political sense within German political (as opposed to monetary) circles that the whole objective of EMU transcended monetary and economic issues and had to be seen as part of the broader undertaking of political and economic union. Allowing two monetary tracks would split this political union and assign second-class status to second track members.

Fifth, would a major realignment of exchange rates be necessary before they were irrevocably locked into fixed rates for monetary union? International trade models (e.g., Cline 1989b) suggested that the British pound sterling and the Italian lira were substantially overvalued relative to the deutschemark and that the same was likely to be true for the Spanish peseta. Locking in the currencies at their existing rates could cause ongoing problems of external deficits for these countries, implying persistent need for German financing. Yet, the political embarrassment of devaluation and the preeminent view of the exchange rate as a monetary anchor against inflation had prevented any major realignments within the EMS since the late 1980s. The result was that some of the currencies had experienced large real appreciations, for example, the Italian lira, which had appreciated by some 30% since 1979.

The Maastricht Agreement

In December 1991, the members of the European Community agreed at Maastricht that they would achieve economic and monetary union by 1999 at the latest. The Maastricht Agreement established convergence criteria that would determine which countries were eligible for monetary union. There were five principal criteria:

• Inflation could be no more than 1½% above the average rate for the three lowest-inflation member countries.

• Long-term interest rates could be no more than 2% above the average for the three countries with the lowest long-term rates.

• The fiscal deficit could be no higher than 3% of GDP.

• Government debt could be no higher than 60% of GDP.

• The currency could not have undergone a major devaluation within the preceding two years and should have remained within its 2¼% margin of fluctuation within the ERM.

The agreement set an explicit timetable for the move to monetary union. The EMU was to be formed by 1997 if seven countries met the convergence criteria. The period for evaluation for this decision was to be 1996 and that deadline meant that fiscal adjustments had to take place in 1992–96. Moreover, the 1996 evaluation effectively ruled out any major exchange rate realignments after 1994.

If fewer than seven countries met the convergence criteria for the 1997 target date, then monetary union would take place only in 1999. At that date, whichever countries had met the convergence criteria would automatically become members of the union, even if there were fewer than seven that qualified.

The automatic entry by qualifying members meant that a country that performed well could not stay out of the union even if its authorities wanted to do so. This formulation was consciously designed to ensure that Germany did not get cold feet and refuse to join at the last minute. The only exception to automatic inclusion was for the United Kingdom, which negotiated the right to opt out of the union even if it met the convergence criteria.

The practical effect of the convergence criteria was to establish a de facto two-track structure for EMU. Countries that met the criteria would be admitted to the inner circle of full membership in monetary union, while countries that did not meet the criteria would remain in an antechamber of candidacy for admission pending their improved economic performance. European politicians insisted that this arrangement was not two-track because there was no formal delineation explicitly separating countries into the two respective groups and because the nations in the antechamber could always enter the inner circle by improving their economic performance. Economists, especially those outside Europe, interpreted the arrangement as a two-track system.

The Maastricht Agreement immediately initiated the European System of Central Banks, which was to begin its work with the development of procedures for unionwide monetary measures, such as coordinated open market operations, for implementation by 1997 or after. The terms of the agreement provided that sometime prior to the

establishment of EMU, the national governments were to grant independence to their respective central banks, along the lines of the German model. After transition to the EMU, the result would be
analogous to the U.S. Federal Reserve system with regional branches,
although in this case, the branches would correspond to national
members.

The agreement provided for incentives to improve fiscal performance. EMU members would be subject to penalties, including suspension of intra-EC regional development lending, if they did not
make progress toward fiscal targets.

Economic Implications

The medium-term implication of Maastricht was that, for the next several years, the European economy could be dominated by the attempt
of member countries to reach the convergence criteria. That task would
not be easy. Table 7.1 shows the performance of EC members against
these criteria in 1991. With inflation of 2.8% average for the three lowest-inflation members, the cutoff threshold was 4.3%. Greece, Italy,
Portugal, Spain, and the United Kingdom failed to meet this test. Indeed, for unified Germany by 1992–93 the inflation rate, at 4.8%, was
also above this threshold (IMF 1993a).

Because interest rates were high, this criterion was easier to meet.
Only Greece, Italy, Portugal, and Spain had long-term rates higher
than 2% above the average for the three lowest countries (8.5%).

In contrast, the deficit and debt targets were extremely ambitious.
Belgium, Greece, Italy, the Netherlands, and Portugal all exceeded
both the 3% of GDP deficit and the 60% of GDP government debt
thresholds.[6] In addition, Ireland failed the debt test; Germany and
Spain, the deficit test. Germany's situation meant that even the hard-
money country supposedly at the center of the system was temporarily
not qualified for EMU membership as judged by the inflation and
deficit criteria.

A crucial implication of this pattern of widespread divergence from
the membership criteria was that the period 1992–96 could be characterized by persistent fiscal contraction within Europe as countries
sought to reach the fiscal targets. As suggested in chapter 1, this prospect held potentially serious implications for economic slowdown.
Some reports indicated that unpublished estimates within the IMF calculated a reduction of 0.4 to 0.8% in average annual growth for the EC

Table 7.1
EMU convergence criteria for 1991

	Consumer prices *(percent change)*	Long-term interest rates on government securities *(in percent)*	General government budget balance *(percent of GDP)*	Ratio of public debt to GDP
Belgium	3.2	9.3	−6.3	129.4
Denmark	2.2	9.0	−1.0	66.7
Germany	3.5	8.5	−3.3	45.6
Greece	17.7	24.5	−17.0	96.4
France	3.1	9.2	−1.9	47.2
Ireland	2.5	9.7	−2.4	102.8
Italy	6.4	13.0	−10.2	101.2
Luxembourg	3.4	8.3	1.5	6.9
Netherlands	3.8	8.7	−3.6	70.4
Portugal	11.5	14.0	−6.7	64.7
Spain	5.9	12.8	−4.4	45.6
United Kingdom	5.9	9.9	−2.3	43.8
EMU criterion	4.3[a]	10.5[b]	−3.0	60.0

Source: International Monetary Fund, *World Economic Outlook*, May 1992, p. 53.
a. Average of 3 lowest, plus 1½%.
b. Average of 3 lowest, plus 2%.

over four years as the result of fiscal contraction to meet the Maastricht criteria. Although there would be benefits for private investment from lower interest rates as a result of fiscal adjustment, these effects would tend to occur later.

Over the longer term, European Monetary Union has other major implications. After EMU, member countries would no longer have independent monetary policies as the money supply would be set by the European System of Central Banks. The arrangement would also imply some loss of fiscal independence as fiscal policies could hardly diverge much if monetary policies were set at the union level. Moreover, the penalty system would exert pressure for fiscal conformity.

Non-European economists tended to ask how the adjustment process would work under these conditions. As noted, financial transfers among countries seemed destined to be relatively small, a few percentage points of GDP at most. Moreover, transfers within the system were likely to be heavily oriented toward the lower-income members, Spain,

Portugal, and Greece. Yet countercyclical transfers are important in facilitating adjustment of depressed regions within a large national economy such as that of the United States. Thus Texas receives unemployment transfers from the rest of the country when Texas is in depression.

Instead, it appeared likely that gold-standard adjustment would be the basic mechanism within EMU. Under the gold standard, a country with high prices and an external trade deficit will lose gold and thus suffer a reduction in its domestic money supply. The lower money supply causes domestic wages and prices to fall. At these lower prices, the country becomes competitive again, and its exports rise, its external deficit disappears, and it suffers no further loss of gold or domestic money supply. However, as international experience in the nineteenth and early twentieth century demonstrated, prices and wages are sticky downward. As a result, contraction in the money supply tends to cause recession and lower output rather than lower wages and a shift toward exports.

The broad implication seems to be both a medium-term and long-term deflationary bias in EMU. In the medium term, countries would pursue fiscal contraction to meet the convergence criteria. In the longer term, countries with external deficits would have little monetary or fiscal independence to adjust and would have to achieve adjustment primarily through monetary contraction along gold-standard lines—at considerable risk of recession. The solution to this potential problem implies a considerably deeper evolution toward political unity than seems to be contemplated. A single European government and parliament would be in a position to increase substantially the scope for cyclical transfer mechanisms among countries, or states in a United States of Europe. That structure, however, far outdistances even the most ambitious Maastricht goals.

Currency Crisis I: Autumn 1992

Europe suffered a rude jolt on the way to monetary union when a currency crisis broke out in the third quarter of 1992. By the end of the crisis, there had been large devaluations of key European currencies against the deutschemark and at least a temporary exit of two of them from the ERM.

The origins of the crisis lay in the growing misalignment of currencies within the ERM. The monetary anchor of fixed rates had slowed domestic inflation in countries such as Spain but not by enough to avoid creeping overvaluation. Thus, inflation in Spain fell from an average of 13% annually in 1981–84 to 9% in 1985–86 and 6% in 1987–91, but these rates were still far above the typical rates of 1½ to 2% for German inflation over these years.

More specifically, from 1988 until the second quarter of 1992, Germany's consumer price inflation was a cumulative 12%. The corresponding figure was 28% for the United Kingdom, 25% for Italy, 26% for Spain, and 49% for Portugal. To hold the real exchange rate constant would have required devaluations equal to the difference between these national inflation rates and the German rate. The closest any of these countries came to that outcome was in the United Kingdom, where the pound sterling depreciated against the DM by 9% over this period (as against the 14% that would have been required to compensate for the inflation differential). Portugal had a depreciation against the deutschemark of only 5%, compared with the 33% required for differential inflation.[7] In Spain, the peseta actually appreciated by 5% against the DM rather than depreciating by 12% as called for by differential inflation.

By 1992, it had become practically an article of faith within Europe that the exchange rates in the ERM could not be touched. The autumn crisis essentially reflected a resounding rejection of this thesis by the financial markets. Two developments forced the issue.

First, the deutschemark had strengthened against the dollar, from 1.66 DM/$ in 1991 on average to 1.46 by the end of August 1992. The result was that the countries with higher inflation became increasingly overvalued on a worldwide basis, not just against Germany. The 1992 rise of the DM, in turn, reflected the fact that the currency had been relatively weak in 1991, in part because of political uncertainty associated with events in the Soviet Union, but that by mid-1992 the market was responding in force to the dramatic difference between short-term interest rates in Germany (9%) and the United States (3%).

Second, tiny Denmark set off a serious bout of the Euronerves when, in mid-1992, its voters rejected the Maastricht Agreement. A similar referendum was scheduled soon for France, and the markets increasingly worried that a French "non" would destroy monetary union. Without monetary union, the rationale for and commitment to the existing fixed exchange rates would be undermined; hence, risks would rise for those who held Italian lire, pounds sterling, and Spanish pesetas rather than deutschemarks. Rising exchange rate risk began to swamp the modest interest rate differentials, and a speculative attack against the weaker European currencies was on.

The sophisticates added another causal factor. The terms of Maastricht set convergence evaluation at 1996 and abstention from major realignment during the two preceding years. Thus any seriously overvalued exchange rates would have to be depreciated by 1994 at the latest. There thus seemed to be an internal tension built into the agreement that would exert a rising pressure for realignment sometime in 1992–94, and this pressure could win out over the existing dogma of nonrealignment in the ERM.

As usually occurs in battles, the attack came first at the periphery, not at the center. Finland and Sweden had followed exchange rate policies that tied their currencies closely to the ECU but were not formal members of the ERM. Speculative pressure against the two currencies in September 1992 brought a 15% depreciation of the Finnish mark and a temporary increase in Swedish short-term interest rates to an unheard-of 500% annual rate to defend the krona.[8] These events brought crisis headlines and encouraged the attack to move on toward the weaker currencies of the ERM itself.

Germany and Italy then announced that Germany had agreed to reduce interest rates by 0.25%, and in return Italy had agreed to devalue the lira by 5%. The minimal German change was widely seen as inadequate to deal with the problem of recessionary spillover in Europe from high German interest rates, while a 5% Italian devaluation also looked meager. Within a short space of time, speculative attacks had forced both the United Kingdom and Italy to suspend their fixed rates within the ERM and float their currencies, and these attacks had also forced a realignment of the Spanish peseta and Portuguese escudo within the ERM. All of these currencies were soon down about 15% against the deutschemark. Through massive intervention, the Bundesbank drew the line at the French franc, which withstood the next attack in the speculative battle because it had much more underlying reason for holding strong in view of France's small external deficit. The failure of heavy intervention to defend the pound sterling and the Italian lira were excellent illustrations of the principle that intervention is unlikely to work if the rate being defended is seriously out of line with a fundamental equilibrium level (see chapter 2).

There were several major implications of the autumn 1992 crisis. First, the forced realignments and floats did not mean the underlying problems had been solved. Interest rates were still excessively high in Germany, and it was unclear that the realignments would provide much scope for lower interest rates in other European countries. Williamson (1992a) suggested a solution to this problem: the ERM should make the French franc the reference currency. The deutschemark would then be allowed to appreciate against the French franc and other European currencies. This jump in the DM would make it possible for a sizeable interest rate differential to exist between the DM on the one hand and the franc and other European currencies on the other.

The analysis is as follows. By the theory of interest-exchange rate parity, investors will be indifferent between holding two currencies only if their respective total rates of return are equal. The total rate of return equals the interest rate less any expected rate of depreciation of the currency. Now suppose the deutschemark rises 15% overnight against the franc. Suppose that authorities persuade the market that this rise is temporary and that, over a period of five years, the deutschemark will depreciate slowly back to its parity with the franc. Then the theory of interest-exchange rate parity explains how the markets would accept persistence of a 3% differential between German interest rates (9%) and French interest rates (6%).

The theory states that: $i_G - i_F = \dot{E}$, where i is the interest rate, subscripts G and F refer to Germany and France, and $\dot{E}$ is the rate of depreciation of the deustchemark against the franc (or, annual percentage rate increase in the number of DM per franc). This solution would not only provide the mechanism whereby an interest differential could be maintained between Germany and France, but it would also be consistent with the temporary needs of Germany for large resource availability to cope with the reconstruction of East Germany. That is, the temporary appreciation of the deustschemark would lead to an increase in imports and a decrease in exports, shifting resources toward domestic use for reconstruction.

Second, the autumn 1992 crisis revealed a rigid attitude on the part of Germany, along with that country's relative lack of consideration for the rest of Europe in German decision making. Thus, the negligible reduction in the German interest rate as part of the solution instead of a larger reduction coupled with a more substantial fiscal adjustment (moving the mix away from tight money and loose fiscal policy) provided a sobering example for the rest of Europe that German dominance of the monetary system could prove costly.

Third, the crisis showed that eventually the markets realign by force what the authorities are unwilling to correct by design. It would have been much better if European authorities had decided in advance to carry out these realignments, as indeed German officials had sought.

Fourth, the crisis revived talk of a two-speed Europe. There was even speculation that Germany and France might move to an early monetary union of their two currencies. In any event, the forced depreciation of the weaker currencies seemed to reinforce the expectation that they would remain in the antechamber rather than join the inner circle when union first arrived. At the same time, the validated diagnosis that the weaker currencies had been overvalued raised at least some possibility that the Maastricht terms would be renegotiated in order to provide for greater flexibility in dealing with this problem and thus a more explicit recognition of the two tracks (fast and slow) to monetary union.

By the fourth quarter of 1992, Europe had been badly shaken by the exchange rate crisis and the Danish rejection of Maastricht. Additionally, the French referendum had passed the accord by less than half of one percent majority, suggesting to some that Maastricht was on its last legs. Official Europe, however, soldiered ahead much as if nothing had happened, and after a solid favorable vote for Maastricht in Italy, the timetable toward EMU remained officially unaltered.

Currency Crisis II: August 1993

In early August 1993, the ERM experienced another crisis. In July, the financial markets mounted an attack on the French franc and other ERM currencies, excepting the deutschemark and the Dutch guilder. This time the reason for the attack was different from the autumn 1992 episode. By mid-1993, the other ERM currencies were not overvalued against the deutschemark. Instead, the problem was that the financial markets increasingly anticipated that France and other countries would be forced to reduce their domestic interest rates to combat severe unemployment, which had risen to 11½% in France. The expectation of a lower differential relative to the German interest rate meant expectation of devaluation relative to the deutschemark.

French inflation was lower than that in Germany, and France's external accounts were in balance so that, on the usual criteria, the franc was not overvalued. The new government of prime minister Balladur had forcefully stated its commitment to the *franc fort* policy as it sought to retain the important gains in anti-inflationary credibility achieved through the exchange rate anchor in the 1980s. However, German interest rates remained high as the discount rate fell from 8.3% at the end of 1992 to 7.3% by mid-1993. France had to hold interest rates comparably high or even higher because of a perceived risk premium. Yet with lower inflation than in Germany, France's real interest rates were substantially higher. With rising unemployment, the markets anticipated that, at some point, the French would have to reduce interest rates and abandon the *franc fort*.

The ERM central banks reportedly spent at least $40 billion to defend the exchange rates in the last week of July. In an emergency meeting, German authorities offered to revalue the deutschmark. This time French representatives reportedly agreed, but the Dutch and others refused. The compromise that emerged was a sharp widening of the bands around the central rates in the ERM, from ±2.25% to ±15%.

Despite the wide band, the franc depreciated only about 3% against the deutschemark. The French government did not immediately use its greater scope for reducing interest rates. Currency markets calmed, and the massive interventions ceased. By October, the ERM ministers were saying that there would not be an early return to the previous, narrow ERM margins. Nonetheless, financial officials were soon reaffirming that the EMU was back on track. Only the United Kingdom's John Major made public statements that the currency crisis and wide bands showed that the Maastricht timetable had been unrealistic. Major's former chancellor Norman Lamont went so far as to declare the "end of monetary union in Europe" (*Economist*, 7 August 1993).

Analytical Postmortems

The humbling of the vaunted ERM provided a laboratory result (or at least a Rorschach test) for economists' theories. It is useful to review the alternative interpretations.

Early in the ERM, British economist Alan Walters had argued that there was a fundamental inconsistency in the arrangement. He argued that, with fixed exchange rates, capital flows would equalize nominal interest rates. As a result, high inflation member countries would experience a reduction in real interest rates. Lower real interest rates would exert further expansionary pressure in these economies. This pressure would further aggravate inflation and overvaluation. Massive capital flows had indeed gone to Spain and other higher-inflation members of the ERM in the late 1980s, and overvaluations did indeed emerge.

After the September 1992 crisis, Portes (1993) responded to accusations by politicians that the economists had not warned them about such a crisis by citing numerous such warnings. Portes argued that the

ERM had sought three incompatible objectives: fixed exchange rates, capital mobility, and independent monetary policies. He stressed that the ERM was destined for trouble after capital controls were eliminated in 1990. He and others suggested that one solution would be to introduce the Tobin tax (named for U.S. economist James Tobin), which would place a small tax on all exchange transactions to discourage speculative capital flows. Portes emphasized that the crises did not mean a single currency was unworkable. On the contrary, he argued, the impossibility of exchange rate changes after rates were locked would mean speculators could not hope to profit from attacks.

In contrast, Williamson (1993) emphasized that it was not the elimination of capital controls that had led to the crisis but the increasing divergence of real exchange rates from equilibrium levels. To him, the central problem was the move to a much more rigid regime by 1987 without the periodic parity adjustments that had occurred before.

Thygesen (1994) argued that whereas in 1992 the ERM monetary authorities had erred by trying to defend misaligned exchange rates (especially that of the lira), in 1993, they had made the opposite error of failing to defend rates that were no longer out of line. Defending the continued relevance of EMU despite the currency crises of 1992–93, he argued that the ERM had been designed under the assumption that most shocks hitting Europe would be similar, or symmetrical, for all member countries (a Mundellian approach to the optimum currency area as functionally homogeneous) but that German reunification had been a historically unique asymmetrical shock falling only on one member. By implication, both the ERM and EMU might be more effective in the future than was the ERM in the early 1990s.

Other economists noted that if France had used fiscal stimulus to fight unemployment, there might not have been a run on the franc in 1993 because the markets would not have anticipated a reduction in French interest rates. They also noted that the times had changed from the heyday of the ERM in the mid-1980s, when inflation was the principal problem, to the early 1990s, when unemployment was the main problem. The implication was that the allure of the exchange rate anchor against inflation had diminished and that its burden as a straitjacket for interest rates had grown heavier.

One important analytical issue was whether German reunification had stimulated or depressed the other European economies. In 1990, the large shift of German resources to reunification had provided a strong boost to exports from European partner countries. However, by

1991 and later, these trade flows plateaued at their new levels so that there was little further growth stimulus from a further rise in trade balances against Germany. At the same time, high German interest rates spilled over to the rest of Europe (enforced by the ERM strait-jacket). High interest rates cause contractionary pressure across the entire economy, not just the trade sector. Moreover, the increase in interest rates needed within Germany to offset the expansionary pressure of reunification far exceeded the increase in interest rates needed in partner countries to offset expansionary pressure from increased exports to Germany. The reason was that the German expansionary pressure as a fraction of GDP was much greater than the induced trade-expansionary pressure as a fraction of GDP of partner countries.[9]

In sum, as the dust was settling on the second European currency crisis, there was growing consensus that rates as rigidly set as in the ERM after 1987 were inherently unstable. Additionally, there was some debate about whether the principal reason for this instability was incompatibility with capital mobility or misalignment from equilibrium levels. The optimists pointed out that even a band of 30% was narrower than the fluctuations of European currencies against the dollar in the 1980s and that the wider band could facilitate the eventual reentry into locked EMU parities.

Depth and Breadth of Union

Despite the currency crises of 1992 and 1993, by late 1993, the political hurdles to Maastricht had all been cleared, and the treaty entered into force. Voters in Denmark had passed a slightly amended version in the spring of 1993, the U.K. parliament approved the treaty in the summer, and the German courts confirmed the treaty's constitutionality in the fall. After predictable turf controversy, the member countries designated Frankfurt as the location for the European Monetary Institution, precursor to an eventual European Central Bank. The EC formally became the European Union.

The implications were broader than monetary union. The Maastricht Agreement had included a Common Social Policy, signed by eleven members (but not the United Kingdom). The policy provided for development of a common minimum wage, social security benefits, and worker conditions. The agreement also provided for a common policy on foreign affairs, with a special coordinating secretariat. There was also to be a common defense policy, with revival of the Western

European Union as a defense entity theoretically capable of mounting a European military operation. However, the credibility of common foreign and defense policy suffered seriously from the EC's inability to take effective action on the Croatian and then Bosnian crises.

The Maastricht Agreement provided scope for national diversity as well as political-economic unity by adopting the principle of subsidiarity. Like states' rights in the U.S. constitution, subsidiarity provided that whatever responsibilities were not explicitly assigned to the economic and political union were to reside with the national states. When the Maastricht Agreement began to run into trouble with ratification by European publics, authorities quickly highlighted the importance of the subsidiarity principle to reassure voters that their national identities would remain.

The future of Europe with economic and political union seemed likely to be much wider geographically as well as deeper functionally. By Maastricht, European leaders were emphasizing that the original Common Market had provided that any European nation was eligible. The EC joined with the European Free Trade Association (EFTA) nations to form the European Economic Area, embracing three of the four freedoms, trade in goods, trade in services, and capital flows (the fourth, labor mobility, remained the reserve of the EC). By 1993 Austria, Sweden, Finland, and Norway were in negotiations with the EC for membership (in Switzerland, the voters had cooled official enthusiasm by rejecting even the European Economic Area). It is likely that the EU will grant membership relatively rapidly to these four countries.

In contrast, although leaders in Eastern Europe have begun to speak about seeking membership as well, it is unlikely that the EU will extend admission to those countries before the late 1990s, and even then, membership is more likely to be limited to Czechoslovakia, Hungary, and Poland. The differences in labor force composition, wage levels, and economic structure make the Eastern European countries prospectively more difficult for the EU to absorb than the more similar applicant countries of Western Europe.

Global Economic Implications

The move toward European economic and monetary union has implications for the international monetary system beyond arrangements within Europe. One implication is that there could be a large shift in the demand for dollar reserve holdings. With a monetary union, there should be less need for individual countries to hold foreign exchange reserves as there will be reserves pooling. Because a large share of reserves is held in dollars, the implication is that after monetary union, there could be an excess of such reserves. There could be downward pressure on the dollar as a result and a reappearance of the dollar overhang debate from the 1960s when Europe had built up excess holdings of dollars in support of the fixed rates under the Bretton Woods regime.

In the area of international trade, implications from European economic unity are perhaps even greater. There had already been a major impact of EC-92, the move to the single market. Thus, the elimination of internal barriers has necessitated more explicit voluntary export restraint (VER) agreements with the Japanese on automobile exports to Europe. Previously there had been two groups within Europe: countries with restrictive national quotas (France, Italy, United Kingdom) and countries with more open imports of Japanese automobiles (although Germany had moderate VERs as well). In 1991, Japan and the EC reached a managed-trade agreement indicating a timetable for market shares over the next few years.

The issue of EU expansion to include other countries also poses questions for world trade. The members of the European Free Trade Association (EFTA), such as Sweden and Switzerland, typically have had agricultural sectors even more protected than the EU. Their incorporation into the EU might thus arguably liberalize world agricultural trade. Moreover, these countries have economic structures sufficiently similar to those of existing EU members that their incorporation is unlikely to cause severe pressure for protection to accommodate adjustment difficulties. In contrast, an eventual absorption of Poland, Czechoslovakia, and Hungary seems much more likely to pose such pressures and thereby raise the risk of a tightening of EU protection against goods from outsiders.

More generally, a central question for world trade is whether Europe's move toward economic and political union means a transition to a protected "fortress Europe." European leaders are tireless in repeating that the answer is no, that Europe will not increase barriers against other countries just because it is eliminating intra-European barriers. Nevertheless, some adjustment pressures seem inevitable, with correspondingly increased pressures for protection. Moreover, even without increased barriers to the outside world, closer European integration will impose trade diversion away from exports by third countries to the EU. The classic question in this process is whether there will be sufficient stimulus to EC growth as a consequence of widening and deepening that the markets for third countries will grow by enough in volume to offset this trade diversion (see chapter 3).

The Uruguay Round of trade negotiations provided an important early test on these questions. The ability of the EU, especially France, to reach a compromise agreement with the United States on agriculture in late 1993, thereby paving the way for a tentative Uruguay Round agreement by the December 15 deadline for U.S. fast-track authority, augured favorably for an open-door rather than fortress Europe.

Europe's future evolution depends importantly on the outcome of historic changes in the former Soviet Union. The European Community, with or without expansion, is in a position of living beside the volcano, never knowing when it may erupt. There is great concern in Europe about a potential innundation of immigrants from a stricken Russian economy, and already a wave of anti-immigrant violence in Germany has been an ugly reminder of events half a century earlier. Investment flows to Europe, as well as the strength of the deutschemark, are likely to be inversely related to the level of political instability in Russia, the Ukraine, and other republics of the former U.S.S.R. Awareness of this fact is a major reason that Europe can be expected to lead in assisting Russia and the other republics to carry out their transition from communism to capitalism.

Overview

The political tectonic plates were shifting in Europe as the 1990s began. Under these circumstances, the move toward European Monetary Union had much broader implications than just a fine-tuning of, or even reconstructive surgery on, the existing exchange rate mechanism. In the second half of the twentieth century, a large, powerful United States had played a major positive role in the international economic and political system. There are grounds for hoping that in the first half of the twenty-first century, an even larger European political economy based on the same democratic principles could similarly contribute to international growth and political stability.

The short-run challenges to be overcome in this process include prospective recessionary pressures from convergence as well as the unique pressures from German reunification. The ultimate outcome will probably depend more fundamentally, however, on the ability of European nations to set aside differences on matters ranging from agricultural protection to the choice between price stability and growth. This ability in turn will depend on whether the centrifugal forces evident in such places as the former Yugoslavia, the former Soviet Union, and even Ireland dominate or are dominated by the centripetal forces leading to a more unified Europe.

Suggested Readings

Emerson (1988), de Grauwe and Gros (1991), IMF (1992), Portes (1993).

8

Environment and the Global Economy

Trade and the Environment

Growing Trade Issues

At the beginning of the 1990s, even as the United States and Mexico neared agreement about becoming free trade partners, they found themselves in conflict over two sea animals: tuna and dolphins. U.S. authorities sought to restrict imports of tuna from Mexico because the Mexican fleet did not meet U.S. standards for nets with dolphin-escape features. A GATT panel ruled that the U.S. restrictions were illegal because dolphins trapped in international waters were extraterritorial to the United States, and thus the United States had no claim to an interest in their well-being. The decision graphically illustrated the potential for conflict between existing trade law and environmental concerns. One of the chief environmental problems is precisely that of private depredation of global commons, such as the oceans and atmosphere, which by definition are extraterritorial to every country.

Other instances of the rising interconnection between trade and the environment are numerous. One area concerns species preservation. The 1975 Convention on International Trade in Endangered Species (CITES) was a formal recognition that the environment could transcend freedom to trade. An international embargo on trade in ivory from elephants was a major example. Similarly, there were rising restrictions on trade in the furs of leg-trapped animals.

The question of environmental pollution was central in the U.S.-Mexico negotiations on the North American Free Trade Agreement. U.S. environmental and labor groups were concerned that lax Mexican regulations would induce a flight of factories and jobs to Mexico. They also maintained that something must be done to clean up severe pollution along the U.S.-Mexico border as part of the NAFTA agreement.

A wholly new area of potential environmental-trade conflict is emerging with the rise in attention to two issues of global pollution: the problems of stratospheric ozone depletion and global warming. The Montreal Protocol of 1987 committed signatories to reduce emissions of chlorofluorocarbons (CFCs), which strip ozone from the upper atmosphere and thereby increase exposure of humans, plants, and animals to harmful ultraviolet-B radiation.[1]

The protocol contains provisions for restrictions on trade in CFCs and products containing them against noncooperating countries. However, there is no provision in GATT that explicitly allows such restrictions, and it seems likely that an attempt to implement such measures would be declared GATT-illegal, just as in the case of the U.S. tuna embargo on Mexico. The otherwise all-encompassing Uruguay Round of GATT negotiations contains no section on environmental issues, and although many argue that a subsequent round of negotiations should turn its attention to the environment, for the time being, international trade and environmental policies are on separate, and potentially conflicting, tracks.

Toward Principles of Environmental Trade Policy

In striking the appropriate balance between legitimate concern for the environment and the economic benefits of free trade, several principles would seem appropriate. These principles, and perhaps others, will have to be considered in any reform of existing trade rules to take account of environmental objectives.

Economic Growth and Efficiency Are Environmentally Friendly

Some environmental groups seem to oppose international trade on the general grounds that it promotes economic growth, which they see as destructive to the environment. However, it would be a fundamental mistake to pursue environmental goals through suppression of economic growth and trade.

Free trade makes production more efficient. It thus makes it possible to achieve a given standard of living with less exhaustion of resources, including natural. Moreover, there is a well-documented relationship between pollution and economic growth that shows pollution at first rising but then declining in absolute terms. Thus, sulfur dioxide concentrations tend to rise as per capita income increases from $300 to

$1,200, but then, they fall to much lower levels as per capita income rises to higher levels (World Bank 1992, p. 41). A clean environment tends to be an income elastic good, for which demand rises more than proportionately with income.

These patterns suggest that it is primarily in the poorest countries where higher production may be linked to higher pollution. Even in these countries, higher per capita income may reduce certain types of environmental damage. For example, the stripping of forests for firewood will tend to decline as employment opportunities increase and the opportunity cost of people's time for simple wood-gathering rises. More fundamentally, however, the same concern for ethical considerations that motivates environmental objectives would surely find it unacceptable to recommend that the poorest populations of the world somehow be kept near subsistence levels to avoid any adverse environmental effects.

Do Not Penalize LDC Exports on Pollution-Haven Grounds

A common view is that developing countries have lax environmental standards and attract polluting industries, thereby eliminating jobs in industrial countries with tough standards. There are three reasons why this concern does not justify trade intervention. First, after the tragedy and costly liablity of the Union Carbide plant explosion in Bhopal, India, most multinational firms now apply world-class environmental technologies in their international investments. Second, as revealed in the U.S. debate on NAFTA, the additional production costs imposed by U.S. environmental standards are only a small fraction of total cost so that, even if a multinational firm could completely escape these costs by locating plants in developing countries, the savings would tend to be swamped by other additional costs, such as macroeconomic instability, transportation, and the risk of expropriation. Third, as for local pollution, it is the host country's right to make the decision about the tradeoff between increased employment and output on the one hand and pollution on the other.

Free Trade Is Not Sacrosanct

At the same time, there is no basis for asserting that free trade must always dominate any environmental concerns. There is ample precedent for the use of trade sanctions, typically outright embargos, to achieve political objectives. The most recent episodes include international embargos on most trade with Iraq during and after the Gulf War and with Serbia because of its aggression in the former Yugoslavia.

When environmental external diseconomies are omitted from private sector cost calculations, a price distortion is present. It is well established in economic theory that the application of the usual efficiency criteria, including free trade, can make matters worse rather than better in the presence of a price distortion. For example, trade in cocaine is illegal, yet if we ignored its social external diseconomies, we would falsely conclude that it should be traded freely for efficiency's sake.

International trade is the principal interface among nations. If persuasion fails on vital environmental issues, there may be no other recourse than a trade sanction to achieve a change in the country's policy, at least none short of military action.

Other Instruments Are More Efficient
In principle, measures other than trade restrictions will usually be more efficient to curb adverse environmental effects of production and trade. If a *maquiladora* plant along the U.S.-Mexico border is polluting the Rio Grande, it will be more efficient if Mexico subsidizes the cost of cleanup than if the United States prohibits imports of the good. However, this can be a counsel of perfection that is difficult to apply as developing countries typically face serious fiscal constraints. As a result, trade measures may be necessary as a second-best remedy.

Self-Determination in Local-Reversible Pollution
In the example just given, the importing nation has a direct stake because the polluting nation causes environmental damage for the importing nation. More often, however, the damage is local and does not directly affect the environment of the importing country.

It is important to distinguish between two types of environmental damage: local reversible and global irreversible. The simplest example of local-reversible pollution would be the visual pollution of a garish and tasteless billboard. It affects only those in the immediate vicinity, and it can be torn down in the future. More important cases of local-reversible pollution include river pollution. The Potomac River is cleaner today than twenty years ago, and at its dirtiest its pollution primarily affected only the residents of Washington, D.C. Its pollution was local and reversible. Urban smog is another example of local-reversible pollution.

Each country should retain the right (i.e., self-determination) to set its own standards for local-reversible pollution. The people of Los Angeles, California, are richer than the people of São Paulo, Brazil.

Although both cities have a serious problem with smog, the residents of Los Angeles may well be prepared to accept more costly output trade-offs to reduce smog (e.g., electric-car fleet requirements). If so, California has no legitimate standing to insist on identical standards for São Paulo because those standards are a matter for Brazilians to decide.

In short, self-determination should govern decisions on local-reversible pollution. The case of local irreversible pollution is somewhat more difficult. If the construction of a dam in India will innundate a beautiful canyon, there is a trace of validity to the notion that the international community has a legitimate stake; German tourists will no longer be able to view the canyon. However, this trace is slight. The underlying decision in local-irreversible pollution is essentially between generations within the country. The Indian authorities will have to judge whether future generations of Indians will condemn them for having destroyed a natural treasure that belongs to India.

Transborder Decisions for Transborder Pollution
When the environmental damage directly affects other nations, those nations have a legitimate claim to a voice in the decision on whether to permit continued pollution. The affected nations correspondingly have potential grounds for imposing trade sanctions to retaliate against the country causing this pollution, if other means of persuasion fail. Acid rain is an important example of transborder pollution. Particulates from high smoke stacks in the United Kingom drift with westerly winds toward the Netherlands and Denmark. The European Community has dealt relatively well with the crossborder external diseconomies of acid rain by establishing the principle that all parties have a voice rather than just the originating country. The same issue is present in Mexican border-industry pollution of the Rio Grande.

The new global pollution problems are extreme examples of the need for multicountry participation in the environmental decision. Both stratospheric ozone depletion and global warming are in the category of global-irreversible pollution. CFCs released today affect the ozone layer for decades, while the time horizon for reversing increases in atmospheric carbon dioxide (the greenhouse effect) is two to three centuries. Both problems are inherently global. Thus the extent of sea-level rise in Bangladesh or drought in middle America will depend in part on the amount of coal burned in China.

It is in the global-irreversible pollution that the strongest case exists for international action on the environment. Precisely for this reason, the Montreal Protocol is an example of the proper policy approach: the development of an international agreement. It may well be that trade penalties will be required for the effective implementation of such agreements, although such penalties should not be the first resort.

Internalize Environmental External Diseconomies
Environmental problems arise primarily because the expenses of production do not incorporate an adequate, if any at all, cost to cover the social damage.[2] The best solution to the problem of conflict between free trade and environmental goals is to combine free trade with "full cost pricing" that builds the environmental costs into the calculations of the producers. Thus, for the problem of global warming, the most efficient remedy is a tax on carbon (or its equivalent in other greenhouse gases) set at a uniform rate internationally. A carbon tax that reflects future greenhouse damage will induce producers to rely less on fossil fuels. This approach will lead to more efficient allocation of resources than such alternatives as, for example, an embargo on coal trade.

The chief difficulties in making this principle operational include the free-rider problem, whereby some nations seek to avoid the extra costs implied by the measure (for example, of shifting from coal to solar energy), and the problem of properly measuring the external diseconomy. There is little agreement among economists on just how much damage global warming would do or even on how to choose the discount rate to evaluate this damage over time. As for the free-rider problem, it is precisely to address this problem that the issue of possible trade penalties arises.

Multilateral Action, Not Unilateral
Legitimate invocation of trade restraints in pursuit of environmental objectives is thus likely to arise primarily, if not only, in cases of transborder pollution, especially global-irreversible pollution. Even in such cases, however, any trade action taken should be on a multilateral basis rather than unilaterally. Action by a single country seriously risks imposition of its unique standards on other countries, whereas multilateral action ensures that the environmental goals are widely shared.

The proper format for such action requires, first, the existence of an international agreement on the environmental problem in question. Second, there is a need to reform the GATT to provide explicit provision for trade measures taken in implementation of such international agreements, of which the Montreal Protocol is an important example.

Joint Action in Defense of Global Commons
Such problems as species extinction, ozone depletion, and global warming require joint action by nations.[3] As noted above, in the absence of successful mobilization of joint action, the result is widespread free-rider behavior that undermines the overall effort.

Measured Response versus Ethical Absolutes
In international environmental issues as in those at home, it is essential for public policy to take a balanced approach rather than one of extremes, even if the extremes are argued by some to be warranted on ethical grounds. In general, the benefits of an environmental intervention, such as a tax, must warrant the costs. The benefits are typically the avoidance of social damage, while the costs are increased production costs required by using alternative methods, such as noncarbon energy. In this calculus, it is essential that appropriate allowance be made for the public or social values in estimating the benefits of abatement. The cost in human lives lost to increased urban air pollution is one example of such a social value.

In the United States, the environmental movement has been moving toward the benefit-cost approach as a means of becoming more effective. Whereas in the past, there was a dominant abhorrence of any license to pollute, recent U.S. legislation and implementation have adopted such mechanisms as tradable permits for pollution so as to allow the market to identify the most efficient response to the targets for declining pollution. More broadly, a flexible sense of proportion in comparing costs and benefits, as opposed to rigid prohibitions, seems the most likely way to achieve environmental preservation and improvement. Otherwise, the risk is that the abatement effort will be discarded altogether as simply unrealistic.

Economics of the Greenhouse Effect

The problem of global warming poses a unique and enormous challenge for international policy, and it has major implications for long-term economic growth. Its solution requires unprecedented international economic cooperation. To complicate matters further, this solution requires judgments on difficult scientific issues, involves decisions that have consequences lasting centuries instead of a few years, and calls for a reexamination of fundamental elements of economic theory. The discussion that follows presents a benefit-cost analysis of international action on the greenhouse problem.[4] This issue is of crucial importance in its own right, but it also serves as a major example for methodology in international decision-making.

Background

As represented by the Intergovernmental Panel on Climate Change (IPCC 1990), the majority scientific view is that, in the absence of policy intervention, the greenhouse effect will cause significant global warming by the middle of the next century. At Rio de Janeiro in June 1992, most nations agreed to a framework Climate Convention on global warming. In effect, the convention called for industrial as well as formerly socialist nations to reduce emissions of carbon dioxide and other greenhouse gases back to 1990 levels by the year 2000. Although the United States under the Bush administration insisted on ambiguous wording, the new Clinton administration explicitly embraced this goal in 1993. However, 1990-level emissions are still too high to limit global warming substantially. Further, the developing countries made no commitment, although they too were to present action programs on limiting emissions growth, and the Rio convention was tacit about emission levels beyond the year 2000.

Economists have entered the global warming debate primarily by estimating models of the cost of abatement (e.g., Manne and Richels 1992; Jorgenson and Wilcoxen 1990). Nordhaus (1991, 1994) has gone further and examined the optimal degree of abatement by considering benefits of damage avoidance as well. He finds that only modest action is warranted. My own analysis (Cline 1992a) suggests instead that social benefit-cost ratios are favorable for an aggressive program of international abatement. The difference between these two studies stems in part from differing approaches to the estimation of damages over extremely long horizons and from alternative methods for discounting.

Scientific Framework and Very Long-Term Warming

Carbon dioxide and other trace gases (methane, chlorofluorocarbides, nitrous oxide, and ozone) are transparent to incoming shortwave solar radiation but opaque to outgoing longwave (infrared) radiation from the earth. The natural levels of these gases raise the earth's average temperature from -18°C to +15°C. Climatologists have applied large general circulation models (GCMs) to estimate that a doubling of the carbon-dioxide equivalent above preindustrial concentrations would increase global mean temperatures by a best-guess estimate of 2.5°C ($= \Lambda$, the climate sensitivity parameter), with bounds of 1.5 and 4.5°C.

Most analyses have focused on this rather artificial benchmark. Yet, the doubling of the carbon-dioxide equivalent is expected to arrive as soon as the year 2025 under business as usual, with corresponding warming already committed by that date actually arriving by perhaps 2050 after allowance for ocean thermal lag. Because global warming is cumulative and irreversible, a much longer horizon should be considered. The IPCC itself calculates that under business as usual, the commitment to warming would reach 5.7°C by the year 2100 (central estimate). However, further warming would be likely to continue through at least the year 2300 when deep ocean mixing could begin to reverse partially the increase in atmospheric concentrations (Sundquist 1990).

In view of economic growth and fossil fuel reserves, especially massive coal resources available at relatively low cost, global emissions could increase from six billion tons of carbon (GtC) today to twenty by the year 2100 and over fifty GtC by late in the twenty-third century. By then, atmospheric concentrations of carbon alone could multiply eightfold. Global temperatures would rise by a central estimate of 10°C for $\Lambda = 2.5$ and by 18°C for the upper-bound $\Lambda = 4.5$, based on the standard logarithmic formula for radiative forcing of carbon dioxide and incorporating the influence of other trace gases (Cline 1992a). Warming of 10°C would take the earth back to temperatures of the Cretaceous period some 100 million years ago. Thus global warming in the very long term is far higher than the 2° to 3°C range usually considered, simply because the process does not stop at the conventional $2xCO_2$ benchmark.

Recent calculations with the GCM based at Princeton University provide confirmation of this view of high very long-term warming. Manabe and Stouffer (1993) estimate that, under business as usual, atmospheric concentrations of carbon dioxide would quadruple by the year 2130, and that global warming would reach 7½°C. Their results imply that my central estimate of 10°C over 300 years could be on the conservative side.

Technological Change

Any attempt to compare the costs and benefits of greenhouse abatement must face the question of technological change. Even over the four decades until a doubling of carbon dioxide concentrations, technical change is likely to be large, while over a three-century horizon, it should generate possibilities unimagined today. Some change in technologies can be reasonably predicted, such as gradually rising agricultural yields and the arrival of probable new technologies in energy production, and they are included in the estimates discussed below. However, the bulk of technological change cannot be predicted.

A simple but powerful assumption makes it possible to proceed with benefit-cost analysis without making specific assumptions about these unpredictable technical changes. The assumption is that these changes will be equally distributed on the two sides of the benefit-cost calculus. The benefit of reducing global warming damage through abatement of emissions might be lowered if a miracle variety of wheat were developed that could grow in the Sahara desert. However, a breakthrough in nuclear fusion could similarly reduce the cost of carbon dioxide abatement by making it much cheaper to produce electricity without burning coal. Thus, unpredictable technological change should reduce both the benefits and the costs of abatement, in principle leaving the benefit-cost ratio unchanged from what is estimated on a basis of the more predictable trends.

Most of the analyses to date (including that here) do not formally incorporate endogenous technological change that occurs as the response of policy, yet there is good reason to believe that technological change responds to price signals. If so, then a policy that sends such signals, for example, imposing carbon taxes is likely to result in more rapid development of new technology for carbon-avoiding energy. The incorporation of induced technical change would tend to raise the estimated benefit-cost ratio for carbon abatement by reducing the estimated cost of lowering carbon emissions.

Economic Damage

In a benefit-cost analysis of global warming policy, it is the potential avoidance of greenhouse damage that is the benefit of carbon dioxide abatement. The first step in the analysis is to estimate the severity of greenhouse damage if no action is taken.

Attempts to measure damage from global warming have produced surprisingly similar estimates, perhaps misleadingly so. Nordhaus (1991) suggested that a central estimate for damage from benchmark $2xCO_2$ warming was 1% of GDP for the United States, and he set 2% as an upper bound. More detailed analysis in Cline (1992a) also identified 1% of GDP as a conservative estimate for this amount of warming but also suggested the central range could be as high as 2% of GDP, with an upper bound reaching 4% of GDP. Titus (1992) arrived at a central estimate of 2½% of GDP for U.S. damage, largely because of high damage estimates for forest loss and increased water pollution resulting from lesser stream flow. Fankhauser (1992) concluded that damages from benchmark warming would amount to some 1½% of GDP for the OECD countries but could be significantly higher for developing countries.

Rightly or wrongly, the range of estimates for the impact of a doubling of carbon dioxide (the usual benchmark) transforms the global warming issue from one of survival of civilization into one of substantial but not fatal loss. Thus, by comparison, the oil price shock of 1973–74 imposed losses on the order of 1½% of GDP for the United States and some 3% of GDP for more import-dependent Japan (IMF 1991a). The direct economic damages of benchmark $2xCO_2$ warming might thus be seen as somewhere on the order of a permanent OPEC oil shock. In contrast, damages for much higher warming over a longer time scale could reach as high as 20% of GDP or more. Losses on this scale would be tantamount to a permanent Great Depression.

If the lower end of the range of damage estimates is applied, if attention is focused primarily on benchmark carbon dioxide doubling, and if relatively high discount rates are used, calculations tend to show that it is not efficient on solely economic grounds to reduce carbon emissions enough to avoid the bulk of global warming (Nordhaus 1991). Under such approaches, action on the greenhouse problem must instead be justified, if at all, on the judgment that the prospective ecological damages are of greater value to society than is captured in the quantitative estimates of damage. However, if appropriate attention is paid to the much higher warming and more severe damages over the very long term, if careful thought is given to the appropriate way to apply discounting to such an unusual problem, and if attention is given to risk, even an analysis on strictly economic grounds can lead to the conclusion that aggressive abatement action is warranted, as found in Cline (1992a).

This latter study estimated that, scaled to the current size of the U.S. economy, agricultural losses from heat stress and drought associated with benchmark (2.5°C) warming would amount to some $18 billion annually. Warming accelerates plant life cycle, reducing mass accumulation. Global warming increases both evaporation and precipitation. However, higher precipitation would tend to be concentrated in the highest latitudes. Midcontinental areas, such as the U.S. corn belt, are thus expected to experience greatly increased drought as a result. Carbon fertilization effects of higher carbon dioxide are sometimes believed to neutralize damages to agriculture, but such calculations tend to forget that increases in other trace gases mean atmospheric carbon dioxide is considerably less than double when carbon equivalent doubles. Similarly, farm adaptation is often cited as an offset, but at least one careful study suggests that about two-thirds of these losses would occur even with favorable adaptation assumptions.

Further, annual losses from sea-level rise would amount to an estimated $7 billion. Increased electricity requirements for air conditioning would amount to some $12 billion annually, with an offset of only about one-tenth for reduced heating costs, largely because of the much greater inefficiency of electric power in view of transmission losses. Lesser runoff in water basins would cause costs of some $7 billion annually from curtailed water supply. Increased urban pollution (tropospheric ozone) associated with warmer weather would impose an annual cost on the order of $4 billion. Increased incidence of mortality from heat stress would amount to some $6 billion in annual losses with life conservatively valued at lifetime earnings (risk pooling would suggest higher valuation). The lumber value of forest loss would be over $3 billion annually as the poleward perimeters of forests could not migrate fast enough to compensate for tree death on the equatorward perimeters. Ski industry losses would be some $1½ billion annually, and there is little basis for expecting offsets in other leisure industries since higher precipitation along coastal areas could reduce beach and camping activity.

Other tangible damages would arise from increased hurricane and forest fire damage and net infrastructure costs from increased immigration. As this enumeration indicates, it is misleading to argue that damages would be small in economies where the share of agriculture and other outdoor sectors is small. Several major effects are not limited to such sectors, and even agricultural effects must take account of loss of consumer surplus (the value of food to consumers above what they have to pay for it) and so can be understated by consideration of agri-culture's present share in GDP.

Overall, a conservative estimate for damages from 2.5°C warming at present U.S. economic scale would be close to $60 billion, or 1% of GNP. Intangible losses, particularly species loss but also human dis-amenity, could raise the total considerably higher. Avoiding green-house damages would provide a corresponding benefit from abatement measures, primarily the reduction of fossil fuel burning. Such measures would probably have large spillover benefits as well because they would reduce air pollution. The United States currently spends some $60 billion annually to combat air pollution, and a size-able portion of this expense could be avoided as a side effect of re-duced burning of fossil fuels. In all, the benefits of greenhouse abatement could easily reach 2% of GDP or more for 2.5°C warming. For other countries, especially island nations, losses could be much higher.[5]

The damages would be much higher with very long-term warming. Even a linear damage function would mean losses four times as high for 10°C warming instead of 2.5°C. However, damage is likely to be nonlinear. Consider sea-level rise. In the initial range, the Antarctic does not contribute to sea-level rise because temperature is in a low range where increased melting is more than offset by increased snow carried by air with more moisture. On the scale of 10°C warming, the Antarctic would become a major source of sea-level rise, especially if the West Antarctic ice shelf disintegrated. Similarly, for agriculture, heat stress could be expected to impose nonlinear damage. Cline (1992a) applied a central estimate of nonlinearity at an exponent of 1.3 and various authors have suggested that the damage function could be quadratic or even cubic.[6] With the more moderate exponent (1.3), and with the conservative estimate for benchmark damage (1% of GDP for 2xCO$_2$), overall damages reach 6% of GDP for 10°C very-long-term warming. In higher damage cases involving greater nonlinearity of damage (e.g., quadratic) or upperbound climate sensitivity ($\Lambda = 4.5°C$), damages could reach 20% of GDP or more.

Abatement Costs

Much more work has been done on the side of carbon abatement costs than on damages from global warming. Several energy-economic-car-bon models provide simulations of the economic cost of constraining

carbon emissions. Some have more detail on alternative energy technologies (Manne and Richels 1990; Edmonds and Barns 1990), others emphasize economic sectoral detail (Jorgenson and Wilcoxen 1990), and
still others stress international trading (Burniaux and Martin 1991).

These models may be interpreted in the following neoclassical
framework. Output responds to the energy input in accordance with a
production elasticity (responsiveness) revealed by the share of energy
in the economy, about 8%.[7] On this basis, the elasticity of output with
respect to energy is on the order of 0.08. Energy availability responds
to the carbon cutback according to another elasticity, this one reflecting
the scope for substitution to nonfossil fuels (nuclear, solar, and biomass) and intrafossil fuel substitution (lower emission gas for higher
emission coal).[8] The range of simulation results suggests that the overall elasticity of energy availability with respect to carbon is about 0.5,
that is, it is possible to eliminate 1% of carbon emissions with a reduction of only 0.5% in energy use. On this basis, a 50% cutback in carbon
requires a 25% reduction in energy. If the output elasticity of 0.08 is in
turn applied, the result is a GDP loss of 2% (25% x 0.08). As it turns
out, this is the range of economic impact that most of the models identify for carbon emissions cutbacks from baseline by 50% circa 2025–
2050.

From the various model results, it is possible to estimate an abatement cost function relating cost as a percent of GDP to the percentage
cutback in emissions from their business as usual baseline. The model
estimates indicate that, the more distant the date, the lower this cost for
a specified percent emissions cutback because of the widening range of
technological alternatives.[9]

There is another body of literature that suggests some initial cutback
can be obtained for free. The engineering tradition cites several areas,
such as switching to compact fluorescent lights, where energy needs
may be reduced at zero or even negative cost. Market imperfections,
such as utility pricing rules that do not reward energy saved, may
contribute to this situation. So do information costs for numerous
households facing complicated decisions about heating and cooling
systems for potential savings that may be modest relative to time input. Studies by the U.S. National Academy of Science (1991) and others
suggest that it may be possible to cut carbon emissions by some 10 to
40% at zero or very low cost.

Abatement costs can be further cut through forestry measures.
Whereas the marginal cost (and tax) required to cut industrial carbon

emissions is on the order of $100 to $250 per ton from the simulation models described above, afforestation, or reduced deforestation, can provide the same cutback at a marginal cost of only about $10 to $20 per ton of carbon. However, there are feasible limits for an afforestation area. Moreover, afforestation absorbs carbon only during the growing period of some thirty years, while a steady-state forest provides no further contribution because the carbon sequestered in new trees is offset by that released by those that die.

Finally, carbon permit trading across nations can reduce global abatement costs by as much as one-half (Burniaux and Martin 1991) by shifting the cutbacks to the areas where they have the smallest impact on output. A classic example is that carbon reductions for, say, the Netherlands can be more economically accomplished indirectly through assisting, for example, Poland to reduce its high emissions levels than by cutting already low emissions at home still further.

Discounting

Policy analysis over a 300-year horizon depends crucially on the time discount rate, especially when there is a significant lag between abatement costs and the later benefits of avoided global warming. Present practice varies widely. The U.S. Office of Management and Budget discounts at 10% real, while the Congressional Budget Office does so at the real long-term government bond rate, or 2%. For intergenerational issues, there is a case for applying a zero discount rate (Mishan 1975, p. 209). Environmental degradation may oppress the future generation even if it is richer (Sen 1982, pp. 347–9).

State-of-the-art discount theory has been formulated by Kenneth Arrow, David Bradford, Martin Feldstein, and Mordechai Kurz (ABFK) (see for example Gramlich 1990, p. 102). It has long been recognized that there is a problem in identifying the discount rate for public policy purposes because corporate taxes and other influences introduce a substantial wedge between the rate of return on capital (perhaps 8%) and the lower rates households are prepared to accept on saving (e.g., real treasury bill rates of 1% or less). For a time, many suggested the use of weighted discount rates, with the weights based on the proportions in which the resources for the project were drawn from investment and consumption. ABFK refined this approach by showing that all effects involving investment should be expanded by a shadow price on capital (for example, where one unit of capital is worth two units of consumption). These consumption equivalents should be added to direct consumption effects. The resulting time stream of overall consumption equivalents should be discounted at the social rate of time preference (SRTP).

Resources withdrawn to reduce carbon emissions would come out of the general economy and thus would be drawn in about the proportions 20% from investment and 80% from consumption. A plausible shadow price for capital is about two, considering rates of return and equipment life. The key question is then the proper value for the SRTP.

There is general agreement about the concept, although not the value, of the social rate of time preference. It equals the sum of two components. One is for pure time preference for earlier rather than later consumption even when no future rise in per capita consumption is expected. The second is for utilitybased discounting that discounts only because incomes are expected to be higher in the future so that the marginal utility of extra consumption will be lower. Thus, SRTP $= \pi_m + \pi_u$, where subscript m stands for myopia and thus pure time preference and where u stands for utility-based discounting.[10] Grasshoppers have a high rate of pure time preference; ants have a low rate. There is a strong tradition in the economics literature that suggests that the myopic component should be set at zero (Ramsey 1928). That view is especially compelling when intergenerational comparisons are made, considering that future generations cannot take part in today's decisions.

The other component of the social rate of time preference, the utility-based discount rate, π_u, will depend on how fast per capita income is rising. If g is the growth rate of per capita income and consumption, the most commonly used (logarithmic) utility function will set utility-based discounting also at this growth rate ($\pi_u = g$). More generally, the utility-based discount rate equals some constant Θ times the per capita growth rate, where Θ tells how rapidly marginal utility drops off as consumption rises. Technically, Θ is the elasticity of marginal utility. In the logarithmic utility function, this parameter equals unity. Fellner (1967) and Scott (1989) have independently suggested that the parameter is higher, at 1.5. This means that if per capita income rises by 10%, the marginal utility of consumption falls by 15%.

The overall result is that the discount rate applied in Cline (1992a) is relatively low. The social rate of time preference is set at 1.5%, comprised of $\pi_m = 0$ and $\pi_u = \Theta g = [1.5][1]$, under the assumption that per capita income will grow at only 1% over the extremely long horizon being considered ($g = 1\%$). After incorporating the effect of shadow pricing capital, the effective overall discount rate is approximately 2%.

If instead a discount rate of 8 to 10% were applied, the result would be a serious discrimination against future generations. It would be extremely difficult to argue that the SRTP is as high as 8%. At this rate, over 200 years, the discount factor reaches 4.8 million to one. Surely few would argue that society would have been better off over the past two centuries if today's average citizen could have been compelled to give up $4.8 million just to make her bicentennial ancestor better off by one dollar (at constant prices). (Indeed, there is information in the fact that this act would have been impossible because today's average citizen does not have $4.8 million to give back.) Even an SRTP of 1.5% means that this trade-off is $20 to $1, already steep.

A second possibility is that 8 to 10% should be used as the discount rate because this is the rate of return on capital. This approach is sometimes argued by conservative economists but is not in the mainstream of the social discounting literature. There is simply no reason to believe that all resources for greenhouse abatement would come out of investment.[11]

The capital opportunity cost approach would further imply that society would be better off to set aside money in what might be called the Fund for Future Greenhouse Victims. The money would be invested at 8%, and the future income could compensate the future generation for global warming damage. One problem with this approach is that it is highly doubtful that real rates of return of 8% will be maintained over the next two to three centuries. A second problem is the intertemporal transfer problem: we cannot identify producer goods that yield a steady chain of producer goods that at the end of two centuries deliver consumer goods of relevance to the population at that time. A third problem is that we are not sure the damage estimates for global warming really capture the change in the relative price between goods and environment. How many video cassette recorders will the future generations really consider an adequate compensation for 10°C or more of global warming? A fourth problem is that it is not enough to talk about the possibility of such a fund; tax revenue would actually have to be collected to implement it.

Benefit-Cost Synthesis

The analysis in Cline (1992a) went on to examine a global policy of
cutting carbon emissions back to four GtC annually and holding them
at that level over three centuries. This ceiling is approximately equivalent to the IPCC's accelerated policies scenario, the most ambitious policy response that the panel considers. All costs are scaled up by 20%
to cover parallel action on other greenhouse gases. Benefits are set at
80% of greenhouse damages under the assumption that 20% cannot be
avoided. Benefits are expanded to include 30% of carbon tax revenue
on the grounds that this revenue would reduce the excess burden
(dead-weight loss) of the existing tax revenue that it would replace.
For the first thirty years, much of the emissions cutback is accomplished by forestry measures at low cost and by a 20% free cutback
from a move to the best-practices frontier. However, by the year 2100,
carbon cutbacks in the rest of the economy are on the order of 80%
from baseline. Even so, total abatement costs peak at about 3½% of
GDP by about 2040 and plateau thereafter at 2½% (a floor imposed;
otherwise the time variable for technological change in the cost function would push costs even lower, raising the benefit-cost ratio for
abatement).

Figure 8.1 shows the time profile of the benefit-cost comparison. The
costs of abatement come early, while the benefits of damage avoided
come late. This feature makes the choice of the time discount rate critical. Moreover, the benefits in the high-damage case can be very large.
This consideration makes it important to incorporate risk aversion into
the analysis.

With the central values $\Lambda = 2.5$, benchmark 2xCO_2 damage of 1% of
GDP, SRTP = 1.5%, and nonlinearity exponent = 1.3, benefits of damage avoidance do not quite cover costs. The ratio of the present discounted value of benefits to that of costs is approximately 0.75.
However, if policymakers are risk averse and apply a weight of 0.5 to
the central outcome, 0.375 to high-end damage, and only 0.125 to low-
end damage, the weighted present value of benefits exceeds that of
abatement costs with a benefit-cost ratio of about 1.3.

Those who consider an SRTP of 1.5% too low may still find aggressive abatement attractive if they consider even a modest possibility of
catastrophe, which would sharply raise the estimate of damages and
therefore increase the benefits of abatement. Importantly, the new estimates of Manabe and Stouffer (1993) suggest that one of the possible

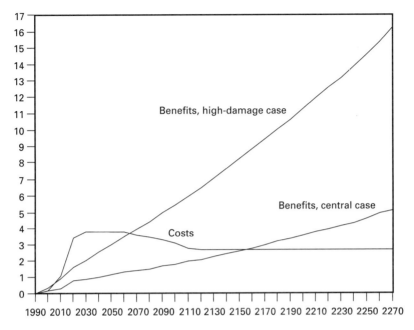

Figure 8.1
The costs and benefits of aggressive abatement of greenhouse warming, 1990–2270
(% of GNP)

catastrophes that scientists have discussed should actually be considered part of the base case. The authors' GCM shows that, with a quadrupling of carbon dioxide concentrations over 140 years and 7.5°C warming, the ocean conveyor belt shuts down. This ocean mechanism involves the sinking of cold water near Greenland into the deep ocean and a resulting counterflow in the Gulf Stream, which keeps Northern Europe from being an eastern version of Alaska.[12]

Policy Implications

In sum, the analysis in Cline (1992a) indicated that, under risk aversion, it makes sense on economic grounds to undertake aggressive abatement to curtail sharply the greenhouse effect. An important alternative study by Nordhaus (1994) finds to the contrary that the optimal path for carbon emissions is only about 10 to 15% below the business as usual path, a far milder abatement recommendation than setting a ceiling of four GtC, which is one-third below even today's emissions. Under the Nordhaus optimal path, the great bulk of future global warming would be allowed to occur. However, it may be shown that running Nordhaus's dynamic optimization model with the rate of pure time preference set to zero, as is appropriate under the argument here, rather than 3%, the rate used by Nordhaus, generates extremely deep optimal cutbacks that are comparable to the aggressive abatement program discussed here (Cline 1992b).

If policymakers do decide to act aggressively on the greenhouse problem, they could face formidable free-rider problems in mobilizing efforts around the world. Nonetheless, these problems may not be insurmountable. Just ten countries account for nearly three-fourths of global emissions, facilitating joint action. Moreover, moral suasion should make free riding difficult at least among the industrial countries. Eventually, the developing countries would have to be brought into a program of emissions limitations as well, especially China, with its massive coal reserves. For this purpose, the true key to overcoming free riding will probably be compelling scientific evidence on prospective greenhouse damage, including to developing countries. Few political leaders are likely to want to be recorded by history as being responsible for major damage to future generations within their own country.

Because of the crucial role of scientific confirmation, the policy response should be staged in two separate phases. In the first decade, there should be moderate measures, primarily designed to send a signal to the market that future emissions could be severely restricted. During this period, there should be intensive scientific work, such as the earth satellite experiments currently planned for late in the 1990s to sharpen measurements on the role of clouds.[13] In a second phase, contingent on further scientific confirmation of the severity of the problem, policy measures would be greatly intensified.

In the first phase, an obvious step is to remove subsidies to carbon emissions (e.g., German coal subsidies, as well as subsidized electricity in China and other developing countries). An optimal strategy will probably include emphasis on low-cost forestry measures for at least the first decade as scientific consensus is strengthened. It would be advisable to put machinery in place for a carbon tax regime, with mild rates at first, such as $5 per ton, rising by perhaps $5 yearly, but with scope for intensification upon scientific confirmation.

It will be important for developing countries to participate eventually because, by the end of the next century, they are expected to account for at least half of global emissions, and their share would continue to rise. For this purpose, some portion of carbon tax revenue would appropriately be channeled to developing countries in order to support a technological shift toward a carbon-lean economy and reduced deforestation. Over the longer term, it may be necessary to come to grips with some form of international carbon quotas, along with tradable permits. Allocation of such quotas would presumably have to incorporate elements of realism (e.g., existing GNP and carbon emissions shares) and equity (e.g., baseperiod population). By early in the twenty-first century, it could also prove necessary to supplement positive incentives with negative reinforcement in the form of trade sanctions, as provided for in the case of CFCs under the Montreal Protocol.

Conclusion

The greenhouse problem is a dramatic illustration of the incursion of environmental problems into the more traditional and familiar realms of international economic policy. Confirmation of the severity of the problem could eventually lead to protocols to the Climate Convention involving stiff international commitments in order to restrain emissions. Under such arrangements, it could be appropriate to include possible trade measures as means of enforcement. In the more ambiguous phase, when no such firm international agreement exists, it would be inappropriate for any individual country to adopt trade penalties in the name of the greenhouse effect.

More generally, the challenge in the coming decades will be to achieve a balanced incorporation of environmental issues into the international economic rules of the game. This process will require a considerable degree of open-mindedness on the parts of both environmentalists and economists. Moreover, it will require more than the usual amount of informed political leadership to overcome resistance by affected interest groups when economic measures must be taken to deal with international environmental issues. In this policy area, the additional dimensions of scientific uncertainty, the difficulty of evaluating ecological effects, and the problems of international free riding are superimposed on the full array of the more familiar difficulties associated with effective management of the world's trade and monetary affairs.

Suggested Readings

Cline (1992a), Esty (1994).

Epilogue

Although most of the underlying forces that drive the international economy and policies affecting it are persistent over periods of years or even decades, the course of political and short-term macroeconomic developments is mercurial and can soon leave the details of a specific analysis dated. Much has happened since the completion of the manuscript for this book in October of 1993. This epilogue makes no attempt to provide a full updating on specifics, because that in its turn would soon be bypassed by events. However, the salient recent trends warrant comment and interpretation of their implications for the central diagnoses and prognoses of this study.

The global economic outlook presented in chapter 1 is one of concern about slow growth in the industrial countries, combined with the suggestion that world inflation could become somewhat more of a problem once growth does return to more normal levels. By early 1994 it was evident that the U.S. economy had grown at an exceptionally strong rate in the final quarter of 1993 (about 7% at an annual rate). Evidently the stimulus of lower real interest rates was proving stronger, and the contractionary influence of fiscal adjustment less severe, than had earlier seemed likely.

The International Monetary Fund was reportedly upgrading its estimate of U.S. growth for 1994 to 3.8% (*Wall Street Journal*, 7 April 1994). With the high growth rate of the fourth quarter of 1993 having broken the inertia of relatively sluggish recovery-phase growth, the concern expressed in chapter 1 about the contractionary effect of fiscal adjustment during 1994–97 may be overstated. The Council of Economic Advisers (CEA 1994, p. 92) has predicted average U.S. growth of 2.75% annually in 1994–97. The Congressional Budget Office (CBO 1994, p. xiv) has predicted the same average rate, though with a slightly lower rate the first year (2.9% instead of the CEA's 3.0%).

At the same time, growth performance continued to be below expectations in Japan and Europe. The result was that the outlook for industrial country growth in 1994 remained about the same overall, but was composed of a higher U.S. component and lower contributions from Europe and especially Japan. The divergence raised the question of how long the United States could decouple its growth rate from those of the other industrial countries.

The suggestion in chapter 1 that inflation might not be as distant as had generally been assumed was beginning to be borne out by early 1994, at least in terms of expectations revealed by the nervous reaction of the U.S. bond market to stronger growth. After the Federal Reserve raised short-term interest rates slightly, long-term treasury bond rates rose from 6% to 7% in early 1994, contributing to an abrupt downward correction in the U.S. stock market. Commodity prices were also on the rise, although oil prices continued to decline.

The central policy needs broadly remain the same: Europe needs lower interest rates, and Germany, a shift in policy mix toward tighter fiscal and less tight monetary policy. Japan may require still further fiscal stimulus. In the United States, the need is to stick to the budget correction path begun a year ago under the Clinton administration. A major challenge will be to ensure that ambitious plans for national health coverage do not derail this correction.

The principal implications of recent events for the analysis of chapter 2 on external adjustment are that slower than expected growth in Japan, combined with faster than expected growth in the United States, will mean greater persistence of the Japanese trade surplus, and a more substantial rise in the U.S. trade deficit, than previously seemed likely. These trends in turn aggravate U.S.-Japan trade tension.

On the broader trade policy front of Uruguay Round negotiations, a historic breakthrough was reached when, on the eve of the December 15 U.S. legislative deadline, U.S. and EC negotiators reached agreement, permitting formal signature of the round's agreements by April 15 of 1994. The EC gave up slightly more than it wanted to in agriculture, while the United States yielded on some positions such as that demanding removal of European quotas on US motion pictures and television time. The final result on textiles and apparel called for a historic phaseout of quotas over ten years. For the first time there was agreement to replace agricultural quotas (such as Japan's rice restrictions) with tariffs subject to subsequent reduction. Results were mixed on antidumping provisions, in which GATT adopted U.S. practices rather than vice versa, arguably with a potential for increased process protection.

The Uruguay Round created a General Agreement on Trade in Services (GATS), with subagreements in which countries were to list sectors they were willing to liberalize. Liberalization commitments were extensive in such activities as advertising, construction, insurance, accounting, and land transport. They were more disappointing in audiovisual services, banking and securities, telecommunications, and maritime services. U.S. and EC negotiators resolved conflicts in these areas in part by agreeing that further negotiations on services would continue through mid-1996, and at the same time U.S. authorities retained the right to apply unfair trade law.

The Uruguay Round negotiators creatively resolved the tension between MFN and conditional-MFN principles by requiring that any member of the new World Trade Organization also join the GATS and the corresponding umbrella agreements on intellectual property and investment practices. The WTO represents a major step beyond the existing machinery of the GATT, with important new machinery for dispute settlement and review of country trade practices.

Perhaps most fundamentally, however, successful conclusion of the Uruguay Round meant that the trading world was headed into an era of continued liberalization. Collapse of the round would have meant a high likelihood of backsliding into protection, and an increased incentive for trading arrangements such as the NAFTA and the European Union to move in the direction of exclusive blocs. That outcome would have been costly to world production and efficiency.

By April of 1994, an unsuspected obstacle to ratification of the Uruguay Round by the U.S. Congress had arisen: budget rules required that Congress come up with revenue to replace the tariff collections that would be sacrificed as the result of lower tariffs, estimated at some $14 billion over five years. In the longer scheme of things, however, this issue was likely to prove minor, in part because the administration had every right on grounds of economic theory to claim that the extra revenue from increased activity and from welfare benefits of liberalization would more than make up for the loss of revenue collected directly through tariffs (and thus had good grounds for seeking a waiver to the budget rule).

In the critical trade policy area of U.S.-Japan conflict (chapter 5), in February of 1994 discussions reached an impasse in which Japanese

negotiators refused to accept the quantitative indicators of trade opening demanded by U.S. representatives. The Japanese refusal is salu-
tary. There is substantial risk that otherwise U.S.-Japanese trade, and
then perhaps trade more widely, could go the direction of proliferating
market-share arrangements like that in semiconductors. This would be
an unhealthy direction for market capitalism at the turn of the century.
It will be far better if negotiators can again turn to the explicit practices
considered to be in obstruction of trade, and take direct measures to
remove them, rather than assign arbitrary market shares based on a
general discontent with the outcome of the market. Proper policy
should emphasize the use of antitrust instruments where the un-
fairness of the practice is judged to be monopolistic behavior by private firms. By March of 1994 the Clinton administration had invoked
Super 301 procedures to deal with the Japan trade problem. If this
process is implemented in a way that focuses on specific barriers (as in
the case of the Bush administration's Super 301), the results could be
much more positive than a generalized turn toward quantitative trade
targets. Operationally, resort to Super 301 probably delays the actual
imposition of any trade sanctions for a period of at least a year, to
allow for negotiated response to complaints on unfair practices.

On international debt (chapter 5), by April of 1994 Brazil had finally
reached agreement with the banks on debt reduction, thereby effectively closing the book on the debt crisis of the 1980s (certainly for all
of the major countries originally involved). Brazil's domestic inflation
was still too high for IMF approval, but the government had passed
important fiscal legislation and was on the verge of a monetary reform.
Moreover, Brazil's dollar reserves were so high that it had been able to
purchase U.S. Treasury zero-coupon bonds for use in collateralizing
Brady bonds even without the help of the U.S. Treasury. A new chapter on the debt problem was opening, however: the one on how well
the capital market resurgence of the early 1990s holds up in the face
of tightening conditions in U.S. credit markets. The best bet is that
developing countries that adhere to good fiscal, trade, and exchange
rate policies will continue to have access to foreign capital, albeit at the
higher going international interest rates.

The most tumultuous change in the past six months has been in
Russia. Parliamentary elections in late 1993 revealed profound dis-
countent, most visibly in the success of extreme nationalist Vladimir
Zhirinovsky and his sizable faction in Parliament. By early 1994, the

Yeltsin government had replaced radical economic reformers Yegor Gaidar and Boris Fyodorov with managers Viktor Chernomyrdin and Alexander Shokin. Some (such as Afanasyev 1994), declared that "Russian reform is dead." Western politicians worried that they and the International Monetary Fund had been too stringent in setting past conditions for Russian economic policy, and Strobe Talbott remarked that the policy of shock therapy had been too much shock and not enough therapy. Enraged, the reformers responded that there had not been a shock program, and that Western financial support had been too little and too late. They warned that Russia was headed toward hyperinflation.

The new team adopted a program of fiscal and monetary tightening, although whether its targets could be met was questionable. In March of 1994 the IMF finally agreed to give its support in a $1.5 billion loan. The new authorities also pushed ahead in privatizing agricultural land. The deputy prime minister punned that Shokin therapy consisted of more balance between low inflation and selective support to the major branches of industry.

An optimistic interpretation might be that the changes in early 1994 represent a move toward a coherent "triage" approach similar to that outlined in chapter 6. The pessismistic, and more common, interpretation would be that the new government is dominated by lobbies instead of sound policy and could easily see the economy collapse into hyperinflation.

Finally, in Europe (chapter 7) the European Community became the European Union as the Maastricht Treaty took effect in late 1993. The EU held further negotiations with Austria, Finland, Norway, and Sweden over membership, dealing with such issues as Norwegian fishing rights and setting the stage for entry by the four countries by the beginning of 1995. Expansion brought the need to shift from the old system of single-member veto right to a weighted voting mechanism, which in turn raised disputes by some members (United Kingdom and Spain) that felt their voting share was inadequate. In short, the homework was being done for the next stages of the European agenda discussed in chapter 7. The principal thematic shift was that increasingly the emphasis was on the problem of chronic unemployment in Europe, with proposals by some (especially in France) that future trade policies address the "social dumping" of cheap imports from countries with low-cost labor.

These changing currents left the broad flow of international economic policy issues largely the same as described in the previous chapters of this volume. It is the author's hope that the insights and analytical approaches set forth in this book will continue to shed light on international economic policy despite the inevitable changes in actors and circumstances that the coming years will witness.

WRC
Washington, D.C.
9 April 1994

Notes

Prologue

1. Cline (1984, p. 45) explicitly predicted a decline in the value of the dollar and was right in direction and broad magnitude, although not timing.

Chapter 1

1. Payment to the factor equals its marginal product times the amount of the factor. Dividing this payment by GDP gives the factor share. We thus have: $S_f = [MP_f \times F]/Q$, where S is the factor's share in the economy, MP is marginal product, subscript f identifies the factor in question, F is its absolute amount, and Q is national production. The elasticity is the percentage change in output for a percentage change in the factor input. It can be shown to equal the ratio of the marginal product to the average product. We may thus rewrite the right-hand side as: $MP_f/[Q/F]$, where the denominator may be seen to be the average product per unit of the factor in question. The right-hand side is thus the elasticity of output with respect to the factor, and the factor share is the proper weight to apply in the sources of growth equation.

2. The model is developed in Cline (1993b). It estimates G-4 inflation in year t as:

$$\dot{p}_t = 1.8\% + 0.77\,\dot{p}_{t-1} + 0.85 G_{t-1} - 0.4 i*_{t-1} + 0.17 \dot{\pi}_t + 0.007\,\dot{c}_t,$$

where $t - 1$ indicates the previous year, G is the gap between actual and trend growth rate in industrial countries, $i*$ is real LIBOR, $\dot{\pi}$ is oil price inflation, and $\dot{c}$ is commodity price inflation (IMF index of nonfuel commodities). The degree of explanation is: (adjusted) $\bar{R}^2 = 0.92$.

3. Otherwise there are serious problems of separating out which direction the causation runs (the simultaneity problem).

4. The model reported in a previous note applies a constrained estimate of the coefficients for GDP gap and real LIBOR. Unconstrained estimation places a greater weight on oil price increases but achieves little increase in the statistical fit.

5. Output declined by 1.4% in 1982 and a cumulative 3.1% in 1974–75, versus 0.7% in 1991 (CEA 1993, p. 351).

6. In 1989, the value of residential capital and nonresidential buildings was $6 trillion (Commerce 1993, pp. 182, 302).

7. Note however that the data exclude nonwage compensation. Rising health care costs in particular meant that total compensation rose faster than wages.

8. Suppose that the goal is just to stabilize government debt as a fraction of GDP, or at about 0.5. Define k as the permissible fiscal deficit as a fraction of GDP. If the debt/GDP ratio is to hold constant, the growth rate of debt should equal that of GDP: $g_D = g_Y$. The growth rate of debt is the deficit divided by last year's debt, or approximately: $g_D = [kY]/D = [kY]/[0.5Y] = 2k$. The growth rate of nominal GDP is the real growth rate, g_{Y*}, plus inflation, $\dot{p}$. Suppose the GDP deflator (price index) is rising at 2% annually (about the rate expected if consumer prices rise at 3%). Then, with real potential growth at $g_{Y*} = 2.5\%$, nominal growth is 4.5% ($g_Y = .025 + .02 = .045$). With $g_D \le g_Y$, we have: $2k \le .045$, and $k \le .0225$. The deficit can be no more than about 2% of GDP.

9. The quantity theory of money holds that: $PQ = MV$, where P is the average price level, Q is the quantity of transactions, M is the money supply, and V is the velocity of money (the average number of times it turns over to finance transactions during the course of a year). By this theory, expansion of the money supply induces inflation: $\uparrow M[V] \to \uparrow P[Q]$.

Chapter 2

1. In Cline (1985), I suggested that a hard landing for the dollar and thus the U.S. economy seemed less likely than a gradual, stair-step decline in the currency. The argument set forth in this article was that, at each successively lower plateau of the dollar, there would be some investors that would consider the U.S. currency to have become a bargain investment.

2. From 1978–79 to 1984–86, federal revenue fell by about ½% of GDP (to about 18%), whereas federal spending rose by 2½% of GDP (to about 23%). (CEA 1992, p. 385).

3. Note that, in many countries, for example those of Latin America, a fiscal deficit leads to an external deficit through another causal chain. Without a strong central bank to exercise monetary discipline, the fiscal deficit translates into the printing of money and higher inflation. With a fixed exchange rate or one that lags behind inflation, the result is a real appreciation of the currency (fewer real pesos per real dollar, for instance). As a consequence, such a country's exports become uncompetitive, causing a trade balance deterioration that brings in a larger net amount of foreign goods and services to cover the resource gap caused by the fiscal deficit in the first place.

4. Thus, in the developing country case outlined in the previous note, there is also a real appreciation of the exchange rate. However, unlike the U.S. experience, the developing country's appreciation tends to occur not by a nominal change in which there are, for example, more deutschemarks per peso, than before but through the failure of the peso-deutschemark exchange rate to move fast enough to keep up with the excess of the developing country's inflation over German inflation.

5. Rational expectations, in contrast, are formed by firms, households, or investors who have a consient model of the market implicitly in mind and who look ahead to make a prognosis of what the market price will have to be to clear future demand and supply.

6. The 1986 reform did kill real estate tax shelters, thereby ending the boom in commercial real estate and setting the stage for the collapse of that market and the difficulties of the U.S. savings and loan banks.

7. From the national income identity shown in equation (2.5), it might be thought that there would be a one-for-one relationship between the fiscal deficit and the trade deficit and that the equation implies that a rise of S_g by \$1 billion reduces [M-X] by \$1 billion. However, Helliwell (1991) has surveyed model results for industrial countries in the 1980s and found that, in that period, the 50-percent rule of thumb applied. Thus, whereas the budget and external problems have often been called the problem of the twin deficits, Helliwell concludes that they are merely siblings.

A further important technical point is that the close relationship between the fiscal and external deficits holds only for conditions of full employment. When the economy falls into unemployment, its trade balance tends to rise because of a drop in import demand, but its fiscal balance tends to fall because of lower revenue and higher unemployment and other automatic stabilizer spending. Under these conditions there is a negative relationship between the change in the two deficits.

8. The apparent disappearance of the U.S. deficit in 1991 is misleading because there were unusual receipts of about \$50 billion that year from the Gulf War contributions.

9. In a famous article, Houthakker and Magee (1969) calculated that the income elasticity of demand was higher for U.S. imports than for U.S. exports. This finding meant that, if growth were similar at home and abroad, the U.S. trade balance would tend to deteriorate because the growth rate of imports would exceed that of exports. However, this phenomenon has long remained a fact without a theory. There is no inherent reason for the income elasticity of U.S. imports to exceed that of its exports. It seems likely that the statistical estimates are instead picking up the effects of outward shifting export supply curves for newly industrializing countries and Japan. If the available price indexes fail to capture rising quality and falling prices of such supply, a rise in U.S. imports will falsely be attributed to rising domestic income rather than to falling effective price.

10. In addition, though not in my model, there had reportedly been high imports of French paintings and other unusual assets at the height of the bubble economy.

11. Public disputes between U.S. and German authorities on the direction of the dollar-DM rate in the autumn of 1987 helped precipitate the sharp drop in world stock prices in October of that year.

Chapter 3

1. Consider figure 3.6 in Appendix 3A. The Stolper-Samuelson theorem predicts that free trade will make the price line (PP) between capital (or skilled labor) and unskilled labor flatter in the United States because lower price for unskilled labor and higher price for skilled labor and capital means a flatter price line that equates less capital with more unskilled labor. As a result, the tangency points of the isoquants for both the two products with the new factor price line will shift to the right, toward factor combinations using more unskilled labor and less capital (or skilled labor) in each product. The essential force is that, if the United States shifts toward greater specialization in capital and skilled-labor-intensive products, it will not have enough of these factors to keep producing at the old factor ratios and will need to use less capital and skilled labor combined with more unskilled labor in each activity. The falling relative price of unskilled labor will provide the price signal to bring about this change in factor ratios.

2. Different product groupings can give different results in answering the question of whether relative import prices of labor-intensive goods are falling. In addition, the test

of falling skilled/unskilled factor ratios is for a static world where the supply of both is unchanged, whereas skills upgrading has caused the relative supply of skilled workers to rise.

3. Note that this is the Cobb-Douglas production function.

4. This section is from Cline (1978), pp. 483–84; 526.

5. At any given quantity, the demand curve shows the price consumers would be willing to pay. As there will always be some consumers ready to pay a higher price if scarcity were greater (i.e., at a point upward to the left on the demand curve), those consumers enjoy a windfall gain of consumer surplus when the market clears at a lower unit price and higher quantity.

6. The least efficient producer has supply cost equal to the price at market equilibrium, but the inframarginal producers (those who would have been at the margin at a point further down to the left along the supply curve) have lower unit cost. The excess of price over unit cost (i.e., over the supply curve) for these more efficient producers is the producers' surplus.

Chapter 4

1. Parts of this section draw on Cline (1993c and 1993d).

2. Oil imports are excluded because they are driven by OPEC price shocks and domestic energy conservation rather than by the real exchange rate.

3. Note, moreover, that this analysis is not distorted by high growth in Japan and low growth in Europe. While Japan had its bubble economy and high growth in this period, Europe had its EC '92 boom.

4. See chapter 2 for a discussion of the dangers of much larger external imbalances.

5. The measure of intra-industry trade is: $[\sum(X_i + M_i) - (|X_i - M_i|)]/[X + M]$, where X is exports, M imports, i is the product sector in question, and the unsubscripted variables are totals. This measure varies from zero for no intra-industry trade to unity for a trade structure in which imports always exactly equal exports in each product category. While the index for an individual European country, such as the U.K. stands at 88, for the EC as a group the index is only 73. The corresponding figure is 70 for the United States and 49 for Japan. The increase has been more rapid for Japan, up from only 32 in 1981 (versus 59 for the EC and 58 for the United States in that year).

6. However, both results, which used the same data set, had the curious conclusion that the presence of oligopoly power increased imports. Yet, the mechanism whereby the *keiretsu* are supposed to repress imports is essentially oligopolistic behavior. If one considers the sign on market concentration to be wrong, then the right sign on the *keiretsu* variable in the same equations is suspect.

7. Saxonhouse (1993, p. 27) cites several survey studies showing this same result.

8. In 1992, Compaq computers announced plans to market a personal computer in Japan for $1,000. The project held promise as a case study of whether a high-volume, low-price strategy could work for a foreign firm in the Japanese market.

9. Recent estimates by Sazanami et al. (as reported in Bergsten and Noland 1993, p. 184) do find several sectors where domestic prices are much higher than international prices at the border. These data are from input-output statistics and do not distinguish between Japanese and foreign brand products in the domestic market. The Sazanami results indicate unusually high protection only for about one-tenth of the 500 product categories examined. Moreover, most of these high-protection sectors are ones that are familiar from the anecdotal literature: seventeen food product categories with a median tariff-equivalent of 240%, including rice at 737%; gasoline, caustic soda, and soda ash, median of 230%; and footwear, 52%. There are potential problems with the estimates because of quality differences, as the authors acknowledge with respect to their high estimate for radios and television (443%), which simply reflects the fact that imports consist of lower-quality East Asian products.

10. The same report criticized the Japanese government for frequently reaching bilateral deals. However, these deals are typically in response to a protectionist threat from a major trading partner.

11. U.S. firms with plants in Mexico had wanted a more restrictive 70% requirement, while Japanese firms, more dependent on parts from Japan, had sought 50%.

12. As summarized in CBO (1993a), the most extreme study estimated that NAFTA would eliminate 500,000 U.S. jobs. This calculation required the assumption that any increase in investment in Mexico would come directly at the expense of a corresponding reduction in investment (and jobs) in the United States. The CBO authors noted that even the 500,000 job estimate was modest when compared with a total of some twenty million job displacements in the U.S. economy in the 1980s.

13. Actually the Leamer study did not make a specific calculation about NAFTA. Instead, it calculated how much unskilled labor had lost from trade in the past, under alternative assumptions, and then simply postulated that NAFTA would have a similar effect by ruling out future U.S. protection to forestall further such erosion.

14. By Hinojosa-Ojeda and Sherman Robinson, as cited in CBO (1993b), pp. 89, 93. This model found that NAFTA would reduce the wages of U.S. rural and unskilled urban workers by 1.3% and 1.7%, respectively, while increasing wages of skilled urban and white-collar workers by 0.1% (CBO 1993a, p. 17). The reason was primarily that there would be a temporary rise in immigration resulting from displacement of Mexican agricultural workers.

Chapter 5

1. Debt-equity swap programs were important in 1987–88 but thereafter fell out of fashion as debtor governments and international agencies became concerned with the inflationary consequences of increasing the domestic money supply to pay banks in local currency. Where fiscal budgets and inflation were under control, as in Chile, this was less of a problem. Elsewhere, governments eventually tended to limit debt-equity swaps to purchases of privatized state enterprises, where the cash would go back to the government rather than adding to the public's money holdings.

2. As shown in Cline (1994), the core problem with falling inflation was that interest rates did not fall as fast so that the real interest rate and real burden of the debt rose.

Chapter 6

1. By the quantity theory of money, $\uparrow M[V] \rightarrow \uparrow P[Q]$, where M is money supply, V velocity, P the price level, and Q output.

2. In principle the central bank could have followed compensating monetary policies that would have permitted these credits to be extended without causing a large rise in the money supply. Western central banks can sell government obligations in the market to soak up money in "open market operations," thereby "sterilizing" the monetary effects of action in specific areas such as credit to state firms. As the credibility of ruble bonds was minimal in the context of high inflation and institutional uncertainty, however, the Russian central bank was in no position to carry out open-market sterilization operations in 1992.

3. In practice, the outbreak of high inflation tends to make the unified price settle closer to the original free or black market price in nominal terms even though the rate is well below that price in real terms. That, for example, was the outcome in the Venezuelan case in 1989.

4. In the formerly socialist countries, national accounts typically included only the goods industries and largely excluded services.

5. From 1989 to 1992, exports from Poland, the former Czechoslovakia, Hungary, and Bulgaria to Western Europe more than doubled (OECD 1994).

6. Note that there may be inputs from the sector into itself, namely all of the entries along the diagonal. Thus, the upper left entry refers to agricultural goods used as inputs into agricultural production, such as hay for livestock.

7. Note that the final entry in each column is once again the gross output of the sector. This time, however, the difference between gross output and the vertical sum of the intermediate input entries is what the sector produces as value added. Thus, the column for steel shows a vertical sum of 43 for inputs from other sectors. Subtracting from 80 gross output, there is value added of 37 in the steel sector.

8. The inverse is analogous to the reciprocal of a single-dimensioned variable.

9. The analogy would be $X = F/(1 - a)$ where X is gross household income, F is household final consumption, and a is the fraction of gross income that must be paid in taxes.

10. Specifically, consider production in the machinery sector, sector 4. The amount of machinery that can be produced is the minimum of four alternative values that can be supported by the amounts of required inputs: $X_4 = \text{Min } [X_{14} / a_{14}, X_{24} / a_{24}, X_{34} / a_{34},$ and $X_{54} / a_{54}]$, where X_{i4} is the absolute amount of input from sector i available for use in sector four's production.

Chapter 7

1. The discussion here assumes marginal cost pricing and thus government regulation if the economies of scale lead to monopoly.

2. Note that producer surplus does not exist in the case of economies of scale. The reason is that with a declining marginal cost curve, the supply curve is declining rather

than rising. There is thus never any initial phase where the supply curve lies below the market-clearing price.

3. Peck (1989) estimated that the gains are more likely to be in the range of 1.5 to 2% of GDP. However, Baldwin (1989) argues that investment effects and economywide economies of scale could provide benefits not counted in the Ceccini report.

4. De Grauwe suggests that in the European case, a common currency could be more important to Ireland, Belgium, and the Netherlands, where exports to EC partners are in the range of 40 to 50% of GDP, than to Portugal, Germany, Denmark, France, and Greece (12 to 20%) or Spain, Italy, and the United Kingdom (7 to 10%) (p. 84).

5. One motive for forming the EMS seems to have been Germany's concern that without a broader grouping to disperse capital flows, weakness of the U.S. dollar would translate into an excessively strong deutschemark and loss of German competitiveness (Gros and Thygesen 1992, p. 42).

6. Most economists considered the 60% target unoperational. A country can quickly reduce its fiscal deficit, which is a residual between current revenue and taxes—two annual flows. It cannot quickly reduce its outstanding debt, which is a stock that is the result of years of accumulation of annual deficits and which moves only slowly with changes in these flows.

7. The required depreciation, d, is calculated from: $1 + d = (1 + i_k) / (1 + i_g)$, where i is cumulative inflation, g refers to Germany, and k refers to country k.

8. Within two months, the Swedish government yielded to a 15% depreciation.

9. Thus, the resource cost of reunification was at least 3% of German GDP annually. In contrast, the increase in the French trade balance with Germany from 1989 to 1991 amounted to only one-half of one percent of French GDP.

Chapter 8

1. Ultraviolet-B radiation can increase the incidence of skin cancer, reduce immunities in humans and other animals, and cause crop damage.

2. Even where such charges are levied, some will perceive the environmental problem as inadequately resolved, implying that their own personal valuation of the damage in question is higher than that attributed by the public at large.

3. Dolphins are not yet an endangered species. However, if most nations consider this mammal to have special status because of its superior intelligence, the dolphin may be viewed as an important international resource worth protecting along with other resources of the global commons.

4. For the full analysis, see Cline (1992a).

5. Developing countries tend to be located closer to the equator where warming would be lesser. However, their economies tend to be more rigid and more exposed to hurricanes and agricultural damage.

6. Nonlinearity in the damage function is of the form: $d_1 = [w_1 / w_2]^n d_o$, where d is damage as a percent of GDP, w is warming (degrees centigrade), and n is the degree of damage response ($1 = $ linear, $> 1 = $ nonlinear).

7. The proposition that the elasticity (percent change in output for a 1% change in the factor input) equals the factor's share in production stems from the theory that a factor is paid its marginal product. In the Cobb-Douglas production function (appendix 3A), $Q = K^a L^b E^c$, where Q is output, K is capital, L is labor, and E is energy. The marginal product of energy is the derivative, or $\partial Q / \partial E = cK^a L^b E^{c-1} = c[Q/E]$. Total payment to the factor is: $[\partial Q / \partial E]E = c[Q/E]E = cQ$. The production function's parameter c is thus simply energy's share in GDP. It may be shown that, in such a production function, this parameter is also the elasticity of output with respect to the factor (energy). The simplest demonstration stems from the relationship that the elasticity equals the marginal product divided by the average product, or $[\partial Q / \partial E]/[Q/E]$. In the present case, this ratio is: $c[Q/E]/[Q/E] = c$.

8. Biomass is particularly important. In the growing phase, it removes from the atmosphere carbon that is then reemitted upon burning, thereby providing a closed cycle.

9. The Manne and Richels (1992) model in particular includes an advanced, noncarbon backstop technology that becomes available after some decades.

10. Pure time preference is myopic because it implies that the consumer cannot clearly envision the future deprivation that will be required in payment for the current increase in pleasure.

11. See the debate in Birdsall and Steer (1993) and Cline (1993a).

12. That a shutting down of the Gulf Stream could cause vast disruption seems plausible. One potentially catastrophic consequence could be that the fraction of carbon dioxide emissions absorbed back into the ocean rather than remaining in the atmosphere would drop sharply, thereby accelerating the greenhouse effect. Otherwise, any catastrophes might have more to do with disturbance of marine life and with more widely distributed climatic effects rather than a severe cooling of Northern Europe. By the time global temperatures had increased by 7½°C (even more at the high latitudes), this area could welcome the removal of incremental warming from the Gulf Stream. Thus, today the temperature difference between Juneau, Alaska, and Stockholm, Sweden, both at about the same latitude, is about 3½°C (January-July averages). On this basis, cooling of Northern Europe from a shutdown in the Gulf Stream could be less than half of the warming of the region from 4xCO$_2$.

13. Varying calibration of the extent of cloud feedback amplifying the direct warming effect of more carbon dioxide has been shown to be the principal cause of the wide range of estimates for the amount of warming expected, that is, a climate sensitivity parameter Λ ranging from 1.5°C to 4.5°C.

References

ACTPN, 1989. Advisory Committee for Trade Policy and Negotiations, *Analysis of the U.S.-Japan Trade Problem* (Washington, D.C.: February).

Afanasyev, Yuri N., 1994. "Russian Reform is Dead," *Foreign Affairs*, vol. 73, no. 2, March/April, pp. 21–27.

Anderson, Kym, 1992. "Economic Growth, Environmental Issues, and Trade" (Geneva: GATT, mimeographed, July).

Ardeni, P. G., and B. Wright, 1992. "The Prebisch-Singer Hypothesis: A Reappraisal Independent of Stationarity Hypotheses," *Economic Journal*, vol. 102, no. 413, July, pp. 803–12.

Balassa, Bela, ed., 1975. *European Economic Integration* (Amsterdam: North Holland Publishing Company).

Balassa, Bela, and Marcus Noland, 1988. *Japan in the World Economy* (Washington, D.C.: Institute for International Economics).

Balcerowicz, Leszec, 1994. "Poland," in John Williamson, ed., *The Political Economy of Policy Reform* (Washington, D.C.: Institute for International Economics).

Baldwin, Richard E., 1989. "The Growth Effects of 1992," *Economic Policy*, no. 15, October, pp. 248–81.

Berg, Andrew, and Jeffrey Sachs, 1992. "Structural Adjustment and International Trade in Eastern Europe: The Case of Poland," *Economic Policy*, no. 14, April, pp. 118–173.

Bergsten, 1991. C. Fred Bergsten, ed., *International Adjustment and Financing: The Lessons of 1985–1991* (Washington, D.C.: Institute for International Economics).

Bergsten, C. Fred, and William R. Cline, 1982. *Trade Policy in the 1980s* (Washington, D.C.: Institute for International Economics, Policy Analyses in International Economics No. 3, November).

Bergsten, C. Fred, and William R. Cline, 1985. *The United States-Japan Economic Problem* (Washington, D.C.: Institute for International Economics, Policy Analyses in International Economics No. 13, October).

Bergsten, C. Fred, and Marcus Noland, 1993. *Reconcilable Differences? United States-Japan Economic Conflict* (Washington, D.C.: Institute for International Economics, June).

Bhagwati, Jagdish, 1992. "Regionalism and Multilateralism," *World Economy*, vol. 15, No. 5, September, pp. 535–55.

Birdsall, Nancy, and Andrew Steer, 1993. "Act Now on Global Warming—But Don't Cook the Books," *Finance and Development*, vol. 30, no. 1, March, pp. 6–8.

Bound, John, and George Johnson, 1992. "Changes in the Structure of Wages in the 1980s: An Evaluation of Alternative Explanations," *American Economic Review*, vol. 82, no. 3, June, pp. 371–92.

Brander, James A., and Barbara J. Spencer, 1985. "Export Subsidies and International Market Share Rivalry," *Journal of International Economics*, vol. 18, pp. 83–100.

Branson, William H., and James P. Love, 1987. "The Real Exchange Rate and Employment in U.S. Manufacturing: State and Regional Results," NBER Working paper No. 2345 (Cambridge, Mass.: National Bureau of Economic Research).

Burniaux, J.M., and J.P. Martin, 1991. "The Costs of Policies to Reduce Global Emissions of CO_2: Initial Simulation Results with GREEN," (Paris: OECD Economics and Statistics Department, Working Paper).

Catte, P., G. Galli, and S. Rebecchini, 1992. "Exchange Markets Can Be Managed!" *International Economic Insights*, vol. 3, no. 5, September/October, pp. 17–21.

CBO, 1993b. Congressional Budget Office, *Estimating the Effects of NAFTA: An Assessment of the Economic Models and Other Empirical Studies* (Washington, D.C.: CBO, June).

CBO, 1993a. Congressional Budget Office, *The Budgetary and Economic Analysis of the North American Free Trade Agreement* (Washington, D.C.: CBO, July).

CBO, 1994. Congressional Budget Office, *The Economic and Budget Outlook: Fiscal years 1995–1999* (Washington, D.C.: CBO, January).

CEA, 1992; 1993; 1994. Council of Economic Advisers, *Economic Report of the President* (Washington, D.C.: CEA, February).

Cline, William R., 1978. "Benefits and Costs of Economic Integration: Methodology and Statistics," in William R. Cline and Enrique Delgado, eds., *Economic Integration in Central America* (Washington, D.C.: Brookings Institution, pp. 483–529).

Cline, William R., 1983a. *International Debt and the Stability of the World Economy* (Washington, D.C.: Institute for International Economics, Policy Analyses in International Economics No. 4, September).

Cline, William R., ed., 1983b. *Trade Policy in the 1980s* (Washington, D.C.: Institute for International Economics).

Cline, William R., 1984. *International Debt: Systemic Risk and Policy Response* (Washington, D.C.: Institute for International Economics).

Cline, William R., 1985. "Changing Stresses on the World Economy," *World Economy*, vol. 8, no. 2, June, pp. 135–52.

Cline, William R., 1987. *Mobilizing Bank Lending to Debtor Countries* (Washington, D.C.: Institute for International Economics, Policy Analyses in International Economics No. 18, June).

Cline William R., 1988. "International Debt: Progress and Strategy," *Finance and Development*, vol. 25, no. 2, June, pp. 9–11.

Cline, William R., 1989a. "The Baker Plan and Brady Reformulation: An Evaluation," in Ishrat Diwan and Ishac Diwan, eds., *Dealing with the Debt Crisis* (Washington, D.C.: World Bank, pp. 176–92).

Cline, William R., 1989b. *United States External Adjustment and the World Economy* (Washington, D.C.: Institute for International Economics).

Cline, William R., 1990a. "From Baker to Brady: Managing International Debt," in Richard O'Brien and Ingrid Iversen, eds., *Finance and the International Economy 3: The AMEX Bank Review Prize Essays* (Oxford: Oxford University Press, pp. 84–101).

Cline, William R., 1990b. *The Future of World Trade in Textiles and Apparel* (Washington, D.C.: Institute for International Economics, revised edition).

Cline, William R., 1990c. "Japan's Trade Policy" (Washington, D.C.: Institute for International Economics, mimeographed, May).

Cline, William R., 1991a. "Japan: Return of the Megasurplus?" *International Economic Insights*, vol. 2, no. 6, November/December, p. 42.

Cline, William R., 1991b. *Mexico: Economic Reform and Development Strategy* (Tokyo: Export-Import Bank of Japan, *Exim Review*, Fall, special issues).

Cline, William R., 1991c. "U.S. External Adjustment: Progress, Prognosis, and Interpretation," in Bergsten (1991), pp. 15–55.

Cline, William R., 1993e. *The Economics of Global Warming* (Washington, D.C.: Institute for International Economics).

Cline, William R., 1992b. "Optimal Carbon Emissions over Time: Experiments with the Nordhaus DICE Model" (Washington, D.C.: Institute for International Economics, mimeographed, August).

Cline, William R., 1993a. "Give Greenhouse Abatement a Fair Chance," *Finance and Development*, vol. 30, no. 1, March, pp. 3–5.

Cline, William R., 1993b. "Is World Inflation Returning?" (Washington, D.C.: Institute for International Economics, mimeographed).

Cline, William R., 1993c. "Japan's Current Account Surplus" (Washington, D.C.: Institute for International Economics, mimeographed, July).

Cline, William R., 1993d. "Macroeconomics and the U.S.-Japan Trade Imbalance," *International Economic Insights*, vol. 4, no. 4, July/August, pp. 5–8.

Cline, William R., 1993e. "A Note on U.S. Labor Productivity" (Washington, D.C.: Institute for International Economics, mimeographed).

Cline, William R., 1994. *International Debt Reexamined* (Washington, D.C.: Institute for International Economics, forthcoming).

Commerce, 1993. *Fixed Reproducible Tangible Wealth in the United States, 1925–89* (Washington, D.C.: U.S. Department of Commerce, January).

de Grauwe, Paul, 1992. *The Economics of Monetary Integration* (Oxford: Oxford University Press).

de Grauwe, Paul, and Daniel Gros, 1991. "Convergence and Divergence in the Community's Economy on the Eve of Economic and Monetary Union," in Peter Ludlow, ed., *Setting European Community Priorities 1991–92* (London: Brassey's, pp. 9–37).

Destler, I. M., 1992. *American Trade Politics* (Washington, D.C.: Institute for International Economics, second edition, June).

Dixit, A., and J. Stiglitz, 1977. "Monopolistic Competition and Optimum Product Diversity," *American Economic Review*, vol. 67, pp. 297–308.

Dominguez, Katherine M., and Jeffrey A. Frankel, 1993. *Does Foreign Exchange Intervention Work?* (Washington, D.C.: Institute for International Economics, September).

Edmonds, Jae, and David W. Barns, 1990. "Factors Affecting the Long-Term Cost of Global Fossil Fuel CO_2 Emissions Reductions" (Washington, D.C.: Pacific Northwest Laboratory, mimeographed, December).

Emerson, Michael, et al., 1988. *The Economics of 1992*, (Oxford: Oxford University Press).

Ericson, Richard E., 1991. "The Classical Soviet-Type Economy: Nature of the System and Implications for Reform," *Journal of Economic Perspectives*, vol. 5, no. 4, Fall, pp. 11–27.

Esty, Daniel C., 1994. *Greening the GATT: Trade, Environment, and the Future* (Washington, D.C.: Institute for International Economics).

Fankhauser, Samuel, 1992. "Global Warming Damage Costs: Some Monetary Estimates" (London: Centre for Social and Economic Research on the Global Environment, mimeographed, August).

Fellner, William, 1967. "Operational Utility: The Theoretical Background and a Measurement," in *Ten Economic Studies in the Tradition of Irving Fisher* (New York: John Wiley & Sons, pp. 39–74).

Fischer, Stanley, 1992. "Stabilization and Economic Reform in Russia," *Brookings Papers on Economic Activity*, 1992: 1, pp. 77–126.

Fischer, Stanley, and Alan Gelb, 1991. "The Process of Socialist Economic Transition," *Journal of Economic Perspectives*, vol. 5, no. 4, Fall, pp. 91–105.

Flamm, Kenneth, 1990. "Semiconductors," in Gary C. Hufbauer, ed., *Europe 1992: An American Perspective* (Washington, D.C.: Brookings International, pp. 225–91).

GATT, 1992. General Agreement on Tariffs and Trade, *International Trade 1990–91* (Geneva: GATT).

Gramlich, Edward M., 1990. *A Guide to Benefit-Cost Analysis* (Englewood Cliffs, New Jersey: Prentice Hall, 2d ed.).

Gros, Daniel, and Niels Thygesen, 1992. *European Monetary Integration* (London: Longman).

Grossman, Gene, 1986. "Strategic Export Promotion: A Critique," in Paul R. Krugman, ed., *Strategic Trade Policy and the New International Economics* (Cambridge, Mass.: MIT Press, pp. 47–68).

Helliwell, John F., 1991. "The Fiscal Deficit and the External Deficit: Siblings but not Twins," in Rudolph G. Penner, ed., *The great Fiscal Experiment* (Washington, D.C.: Urban Institute, pp. 23–58).

Houthakker, Hendrick S., and Stephen P. Magee, 1969. "Income and Price Elasticities in World Trade," *Review of Economics and Statistics*, vol. 51, no. 2, May.

Hufbauer, Gary C., 1990. "An Overview," in Gary C. Hufbauer, ed., *Europe 1992: An American Perspective* (Washington, D.C.: Brookings Institution, pp. 1–64).

Hufbauer, Gary C., and Jeffrey J. Schott, 1992. *North American Free Trade: Issues and Recommendations* (Washington, D.C.: Institute for International Economics).

Hufbauer, Gary C., and Jeffrey J. Schott, 1993. *NAFTA: An Assessment* (Washington, D.C.: Institute for International Economics, revised edition, October).

IMF, 1991a. International Monetary Fund, *International Financial Statistics Yearbook* (Washington, D.C.: International Monetary Fund).

IMF, 1991b. *World Economic Outlook* (Washington, D.C.: International Monetary Fund, October).

IMF, 1992. "The Maastricht Agreement on Economic and Monetary Union," *World Economic Outlook*, May, pp. 52–55.

IMF, 1993a. International Monetary Fund, *International Financial Statistics* (Washington, D.C.: International Monetary Fund, September).

IMF, 1993b. International Monetary Fund, *World Economic Outlook* (Washington, D.C.: International Monetary Fund, October).

IPCC, 1990. Intergovernmental Panel on Climate Change, *Scientific Assessment of Climate Change: Report Prepared for IPCC by Working Group I* (New York: WMO and UNEP, June).

Jorgenson, Dale W., and Peter J. Wilcoxen, 1990. "The Cost of Controlling U.S. Carbon Dioxide Emissions," (Cambridge, Mass.: Harvard University, September).

Kenen, Peter B., 1969. "The Theory of Optimum Currency Areas: An Eclectic View," in R. A. Mundell and A. K. Swoboda, eds., *Monetary Problems of the International Economy* (Chicago: University of Chicago Press, pp. 41–60).

Krugman, Paul R., 1980. "Scale Economies, Product Differentiation, and the Pattern of Trade," *American Economic Review*, vol. 70, pp. 950–59.

Krugman, Paul R., 1989. "Market-Based Debt-Reduction Schemes," in Jacob A. Frenkel, Michael P. Dooley, and Peter Wickham, eds., *Analytical Issues In Debt* (Washington, D.C.: International Monetary Fund, pp. 258–78).

Krugman, Paul R., 1991. *Has the Adjustment Process Worked?* (Washington, D.C.: Institute for International Economics).

Krugman, Paul R., 1992. "Does the New Trade Theory Require a New Trade Policy?" *World Economy*, vol. 15, no. 4, July, pp. 423–41.

Lawrence, Robert Z., 1987. "Imports in Japan: Closed Markets or Minds?" *Brookings Papers on Economic Activity*, no. 2, pp. 517–54.

Lawrence, Robert Z., 1991. "Efficient or Exclusionist: The Import Behavior of Japanese Corporate Groups," *Brookings Papers on Economic Activity*, 1991: 1, pp. 311–41.

Lawrence, Robert Z., 1993. "Japan's Different Trade Regime: An Analysis with Particular Reference to Keiretsu," *Journal of Economic Perspectives*, vol. 7, no. 3, summer, pp. 3–19.

Lawrence, Robert Z., and Matthew J. Slaughter, 1993. "Trade and U.S. Wages: Great Sucking Sound or Small Hiccup?" (Cambridge, Mass.: Harvard University, Faculty Research Working paper no. R93–16, June).

Leamer, Edward, 1988. "Cross-Section Estimation of the Effects of Trade Barriers," in Robert E. Baldwin, ed., *Trade Policy Issues and Empirical Analysis* (Chicago: University of Chicago Press, pp. 147–200).

Leamer, Edward, 1991. "Wage Effects of a U.S. Mexican Free Trade Agreement," (Los Angeles: University of California, mimeographed).

Lipton, David, and Jeffrey D. Sachs, 1992. "Prospects for Russia's Economic Reforms," *Brookings Papers on Economic Activity*, 1992: 2, pp. 213–83.

McKinnon, Ronald I., 1963. "Optimum Currency Areas," *American Economic Review*, vol. 53, no. 4, September.

McKinnon, Ronald I., 1993. "Gradual versus Rapid Liberalization in Socialist Economies: Financial Policies and Macroeconomic Stability in China and Russia Compared" (Washington, D.C.: World Bank, Annual Conference on Development Economics, May 3–4).

Manabe, Syukuru, and Ronald J. Stouffer, 1993. "Century-scale Effects of Increased Atmospheric CO_2 on the Ocean-Atmosphere System," *Nature*, vol. 360, 10 December, pp. 573–76.

Manne, Alan S., and Richard G. Richels, 1992. *Buying Greenhouse Insurance: The Economic Costs of CO_2 Emission Limits* (Cambridge, Mass.: MIT Press).

Marris, Stephen N., 1984. *Deficits and the Dollar* (Washington, D.C.: Institute for International Economics, Policy Analyses in International Economics No. 14, December).

Mau, Vladimir, 1994. "Russia," in John Williamson, ed., *The Political Economy of Policy Reform* (Washington, D.C.: Institute for International Economics, January, pp. 432–38).

Mishan, E. J., 1975. *Cost Benefit Analysis: An Informal Introduction* (London: Allen & Unwin).

Mundell, Robert A., 1961. "A Theory of Optimum Currency Areas," *American Economic Review*, vol. 51, no. 4, September, pp. 657–65.

National Academy of Sciences, 1991. *Policy Implications of Greenhouse Warming* (Washington, D.C.: National Academy Press).

Noland, Marcus, 1992. "Public Policy, Private Preferences, and Japanese Trade Patterns," (Washington, D.C.: Institute for International Economics, mimeographed).

Nordhaus, William, 1991. "To Slow or Not to Slow: The Economics of the Greenhouse Effect," *The Economic Journal*, vol. 101, no. 6, pp. 920–937.

Nordhaus, William, 1994. *Managing the Global Commons: the Economics of Climate Change* (Cambridge, Mass.: MIT Press, forthcoming).

OECD, 1993. Organization for Economic Cooperation and Development, *OECD Economic Outlook*, no. 53, June.

OECD, 1994. Organization for Economic Cooperation and Development, *Monthly Statistics of Foreign Trade* (Paris: OECD, March).

Peck, Merton J., 1989. "Industrial Organization and the Gains from Europe 1992," *Brookings Papers on Economic Activity*, 1989:2, pp. 277–300.

Petri, Peter, 1991. "Japanese Trade in Transition: Hypotheses and Recent Evidence," in

Paul R. Krugman, ed., 1992. *Trade with Japan: Has the Door Opened Wider?* (Chicago: University of Chicago Press, pp. 51–84).

Portes, Richard, 1993. "EMS and EMU After the Fall," *World Economy*, vol. 16, no. 1, January, pp. 1–15.

Prestowitz, Clyde V., Jr., 1988. *Trading Places: How We Allowed Japan to Take the Lead* (New York: Basic Books).

Ramsey, F. P., 1928. "A Mathematical Theory of Saving," *Economic Journal*, vol. 138, no. 152, pp. 543–59.

Rogoff, Kenneth, 1992. "Dealing with Developing Country Debt in the 1990s," *World Economy*, vol. 15, no. 4, July, pp. 475–86.

Sachs, Jeffrey, 1989. "Making the Brady Plan Work," *Foreign Affairs*, no. 68, summer, pp. 87–104.

Sachs, Jeffrey, 1992a. "Building a Market Economy in Poland," *Scientific American*, March, pp. 34–40.

Sachs, Jeffrey, 1992b. "Helping Russia: Goodwill Is Not Enough," *Economist*, 3 January, pp. 101–04.

Saxonhouse, Gary R., 1983. "The Micro- and Macroeconomics of Foreign Sales to Japan," in Cline, ed. (1983a), pp. 259–304.

Saxonhouse, Gary R., 1993. "What Does Japanese Trade Structure Tell us about Japanese Trade Policy?" *Journal of Economic Perspectives*, vol. 7, no. 3, summer, pp. 21–43.

Schott, Jeffrey J., 1990. *The Global Trade Negotiations: What Can Be Achieved?* (Washington, D.C.: Institute for International Economics, September).

Schott, Jeffrey J., 1994. *The Uruguay Round: An Assessment* (Washington, D.C.: Institute for International Economics, Policy Analyses in International Economics No. 39, forthcoming).

Scott, Maurice F., 1989. *A New View of Economic Growth* (Oxford: Clarendon Press).

Sen, Amartya K., 1982. "Approaches to the Choice of Discount Rates for Social Benefit-Cost Analysis," in Robert Lind et al., eds. *Discounting for Time and Risk in Energy Policy* (Washington, D.C.: Resources for the Future, pp. 325–53).

Solow, Robert, 1956. "A Contribution to the Theory of Economic Growth," *Quarterly Journal of Economics*, vol. 70, no. 1, pp. 65–94.

Srinivasan, T. N., and Koichi Hamada, 1990. "The U.S.-Japan Trade problem" (New Haven: Yale University, mimeographed).

Sundquist, Eric T., 1990. "Long-term Aspects of Future Atmospheric CO_2 and Sea-Level Changes," in Roger R. Revelle et al., *Sea-Level Change* (Washington, D.C.: National Research Council, National Academy Press), pp. 193–207.

Tanzi, Vito, 1991. "Fiscal Issues in Economies in Transition," in Vitorrio Corbo, Fabrizio Coricelli, and Jan Bossak, eds., *Reforming central and Eastern European Economies: Initial Results and Challenges* (Washington, D.C.: World Bank).

Thygesen, Niels, 1994. "Monetary Arrangements," in C. Randall Henning, Eduard

Hochreiter, and Gary Clyde Hufbauer, eds., *Reviving the European Union* (Washington, D.C.: Institute for International Economics, April, pp. 43–66).

Titus, Jim, 1992. "The Cost of Climate Change to the United States," in S. K. Majumdar et al., eds., *Global climate Change: Implications, Challenges, and Mitigation Measures* (Pennsylvania Academy of Science).

Tyson, Laura D'Andrea, 1992. *Who's Bashing Whom? Trade Conflict in High-Technology Industries* (Washington, D.C.: Institute for International Economics, November).

Uimonen, Peter, and John Whalley, 1992. "Trade and Environment" (Washington, D.C.: Institute for International Economics, mimeographed, July).

Van Wijnbergen, Sweder, 1991. "The Mexican Debt Deal," *Economic Policy*, April, pp. 13–56.

Viner, Jacob, 1950. *The Customs Union Issue* (New York: Carnegie Endowment).

Williamson, John, 1983. *The Exchange Rate System* (Washington, D.C.: Institute for International Economics, Policy Analyses in International Economics No. 5, September).

Williamson, John, 1988. *Voluntary Approaches to Debt Relief* (Washington, D.C.: Institute for International Economics, Policy Analyses in International Economics No. 25, September).

Williamson, John, 1992a. "How to Reform the ERM," *International Economic Insights*, vol. 3, no. 6, November/December, pp. 37–39.

Williamson, John, 1992b. *Trade and Payments after Soviet Disintegration* (Washington, D.C.: Institute for International Economics, Policy Analyses in International Economics No. 37, June).

Williamson, John, 1993. "EMS and EMU after the Fall: A Comment," *World Economy*, vol. 16, no. 3, May, pp. 377–79.

World Bank, 1992. *World Development Report 1992* (Washington, D.C.: World Bank).

World Bank, 1993. *World Debt Tables 1993–94*, vol. 1, Analysis and Summary Tables (Washington, D.C.: World Bank).

Yoshitomi, Masaru, 1991. "Surprises and Lessons from Japanese External Adjustment in 1985–91," in Bergsten (1991), pp. 123–44.

Index